THE SEAS

PATRON

Dato' Seri Dr Mahathir Mohamad

SPONSORS

The *Encyclopedia of Malaysia* was made possible thanks to the generous and enlightened support of the following organizations:

DRB-HICOM GROUP

MAHKOTA TECHNOLOGIES SDN BHD

MALAYAN UNITED INDUSTRIES BERHAD

MALAYSIA NATIONAL
INSURANCE BERHAD

MINISTRY OF EDUCATION MALAYSIA

PERNAS INTERNATIONAL
HOLDINGS BERHAD

PETRONAS BERHAD

RENONG BERHAD

STAR PUBLICATIONS
(MALAYSIA) BERHAD

SUNGEIWAY GROUP

TENAGA NASIONAL BERHAD

UNITED OVERSEAS BANK GROUP

YAYASAN ALBUKHARY

YTL CORPORATION BERHAD

© **Editions Didier Millet, 2001**
Published by Archipelago Press *an imprint of* Editions Didier Millet Pte Ltd
121, Telok Ayer Street, #03-01, Singapore 068590
Tel: 65-6324 9260 Fax: 65-6324 9261 E-mail: edm@edmbooks.com.sg

Kuala Lumpur Office:
25, Jalan Pudu Lama, 50200 Kuala Lumpur, Malaysia
Tel: 03-2031 3805 Fax: 03-2031 6298 E-mail: edmbooks@edmbooks.com.my

Websites: www.edmbooks.com • www.encyclopedia.com.my

First published 2001
Reprinted 2003, 2007

Colour separation by Overseas Colourscan Sdn Bhd (236702-T)
Printed by Tien Wah Press (Pte) Limited
ISBN 978-981-3018-45-7

ACKNOWLEDGMENT

The Encyclopedia of Malaysia was first conceived by Editions Didier Millet and Datin Paduka Marina Mahathir. The Editorial Advisory Board, made up of distinguished figures drawn from academic and public life, was constituted in March 1994. The project was publicly announced in October that year, and eight months later the first sponsors were in place. By 1996, the structure of the content was agreed; later that year the appointment of Volume Editors and the commissioning of authors were substantially complete, and materials for the work were beginning to flow in. By early 2001, seven volumes were completed for publication, and the remaining eight volumes fully commissioned and well under way.

The Publishers are grateful to the following for their contribution during the preparation of the first seven volumes:
Dato' Seri Anwar Ibrahim,
who acted as Chairman of the Editorial Advisory Board;
and the following members of the Board:
Tan Sri Dato' Dr Ahmad Mustaffa Babjee
Prof. Dato' Dr Asmah Haji Omar
Puan Azah Aziz
Dr Peter M. Kedit
Dato' Dr T. Marimuthu
Tan Sri Dato' Dr Noordin Sopiee
Tan Sri Datuk Augustine S. H. Ong
Ms Patricia Regis
the late Tan Sri Zain Azraai
Datuk Datin Paduka Zakiah Hanum bt Abdul Hamid

SERIES EDITORIAL TEAM

PUBLISHER
Didier Millet

GENERAL MANAGER
Charles Orwin

PROJECT COORDINATOR
Marina Mahathir

EDITORIAL DIRECTOR
Timothy Auger

PROJECT MANAGER
Noor Azlina Yunus

EDITORIAL CONSULTANT
Peter Schoppert

EDITORS
Dianne Buerger
Alice Chee
Chuah Guat Eng
Elaine Ee
Irene Khng
Jacinth Lee-Chan
Nolly Lim
Kay Lyons
Premilla Mohanlall
Wendy (Khadijah) Moore
Alysoun Owen
Amita Sarwal
Tan Hwee Koon
Philip Tatham
Sumitra Visvanathan

DESIGN DIRECTOR
Tan Seok Lui

DESIGNERS
Ahmad Puad bin Aziz
Lee Woon Hong
Theivanai A/P Nadaraju
Felicia Wong
Yong Yoke Lian

PRODUCTION MANAGER
Sin Kam Cheong

VOLUME EDITORIAL TEAM

EDITORS
Alice Chee
Dianne Buerger

CONSULTANT EDITOR
Vivien Stone

DESIGNERS
Ahmad Puad bin Aziz
Yong Yoke Lian

ILLUSTRATORS
Anuar bin Abdul Rahim
Chai Kah Yune
Chu Min Foo
Lee Sin Bee
Sui Chen Choi
Tan Hong Yew
Yeap Kok Chien

CONTRIBUTORS

Prof. Ir. Dr Abdul Aziz Ibrahim
Universiti Industri Selangor

Dr Almah Awaluddin
Maritime Institute of Malaysia

Assoc. Prof. Dr Chan Eng Heng
Kolej Universiti Terengganu,
Universiti Putra Malaysia

Dr Chan Hung Tuck
Forest Research Institute of Malaysia

Peter Chang
Marine Environmental Consultant

Chee Phaik Ean
Fisheries Research Institute, Penang

Assoc. Prof. Chong Ving Ching
Universiti Malaya

Choo Poh Sze
Fisheries Research Institute, Penang

Dr Chua Thia-Eng
International Maritime Organization,
Manila

Albert Chuan Gambang
Fisheries Research Institute, Sarawak

Prof. Dr Gong Wooi Khoon
Universiti Sains Malaysia

Dr B. A. Hamzah
Maritime Consultancy Enterprise

Kevin W. P. Hiew
Department of Fisheries Malaysia

Prof. Dr H. M. Ibrahim
Universiti Putra Malaysia, Serdang

Ibrahim Saleh
Department of Fisheries Malaysia

Dr Japar Sidik Bujang
Universiti Putra Malaysia, Serdang

Kamaludin bin Hassan
Jabatan Mineral dan Geosains Malaysia

Kanda Kumar
Telekom Malaysia Station Pantai
Radiomaritime Services

Prof. Dr Lai Hoi Chaw
Universiti Sains Malaysia (retired)

Prof. Dr Law Ah Theem
Kolej Universiti Terengganu,
Universiti Putra Malaysia

Prof. Dr Lee Chong Yan
Universiti Sains Malaysia

Prof. Dr Lee Kam Hing
Universiti Malaya (retired)

Ir. Dr Lee Say Chong
National Hydraulic Research Institute
of Malaysia

Prof. Dr Leong Tak Seng
Consultant

Liew Hock Chark
Kolej Universiti Terengganu,
Universiti Putra Malaysia

Dr Lim Boo Liat
Consultant, Department of Wildlife
and National Parks, Kuala Lumpur

Dr Lim Joo Tick
Malaysian Meteorological Service

Kristine Low Choi Chin
PETRONAS

Assoc. Prof. Dr Mohd Lokman Husain
Kolej Universiti Terengganu,
Universiti Putra Malaysia

First Admiral Mohd Rasip bin Hassan
Royal Malaysian Navy

Assoc. Prof. Dr Noor Azhar Mohd Shazili
Kolej Universiti Terengganu,
Universiti Putra Malaysia

Prof. Dr Ong Jin Eong
Universiti Sains Malaysia

Gregory Ong Leng Gin

Prof. Dr Phang Siew Moi
Universiti Malaya

Hajah Rosnani bt Ibarahim
Department of Environment Malaysia

Saifullah A. Jaaman
Universiti Malaysia Sabah

Assoc. Prof. Dr Sakri bin Ibrahim
Kolej Universiti Terengganu,
Universiti Putra Malaysia

Prof. Dr Sam Teng Wah
Universiti Sains Malaysia

Samsudin bin Basir
Fisheries Research Institute, Penang

Dr A. Sasekumar
Universiti Malaya (retired)

Prof. P. M. Sivalingam
Universiti Sains Malaysia (retired)

Subramaniam Moten
Malaysian Meteorological Service

Aileen Tan Shau Hwai
Universiti Sains Malaysia

Teh Tiong Sa
Nanyang Technological University,
Singapore

Dr H. D. Tjia
PETRONAS Research and Scientific Services

Prof. Dr Wazir Jahan Karim
Universiti Sains Malaysia

Prof. Dr Wong Tat Meng
Open University of Hong Kong

Dr Zelina Zaiton Ibrahim
National Hydraulic Research Institute
of Malaysia

Prof. Dr Zubir bin Haji Din
Universiti Sains Malaysia

Assoc. Prof. Dr Zulfigar bin
Haji Yasin
Universiti Sains Malaysia

THE ENCYCLOPEDIA OF
MALAYSIA

Volume 6

THE SEAS

Volume Editors
Prof. Dr Ong Jin Eong and Prof. Dr Gong Wooi Khoon
Universiti Sains Malaysia

ARCHIPELAGO PRESS

Contents

Mapping Malaysia

From any map of Malaysia it is immediately obvious the importance the seas assume in the economy and society of the country. Strategically located at the centre of Southeast Asia and brimming with resources and biodiversity, Malaysia's seas and coastlines offer a variety of landscapes and ecosystems, each with their unique attributes. Coral reefs are found in the South China and Sulawesi seas, oil and gas in the basins of the Sunda Shelf, mangroves along the coasts of Sabah and Sarawak, while rich marine life and seafood abound all around this maritime nation.

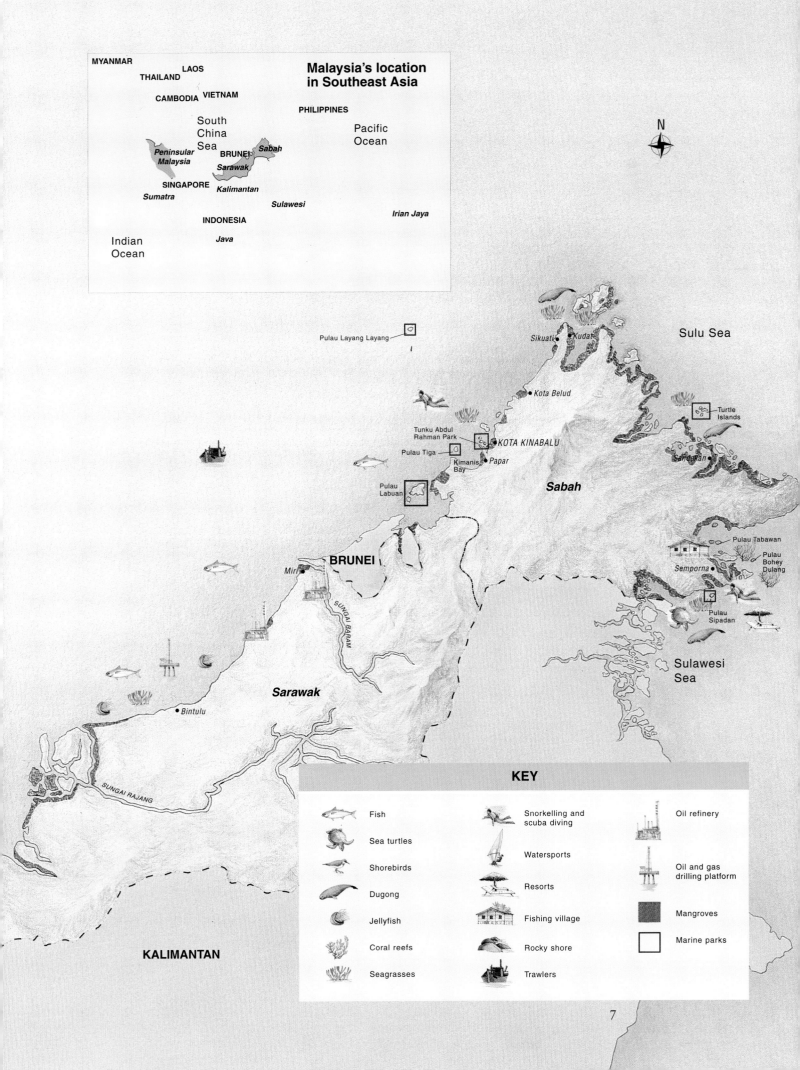

Malaysia's location in Southeast Asia

MYANMAR
LAOS
THAILAND
CAMBODIA VIETNAM
PHILIPPINES
South China Sea
Pacific Ocean
Peninsular Malaysia
BRUNEI
Sabah
Sarawak
SINGAPORE
Kalimantan
Sumatra
Sulawesi
Irian Jaya
INDONESIA
Java
Indian Ocean

N

Pulau Layang Layang

Sikuati
Kudat
Sulu Sea

Kota Belud

Turtle Islands

Tunku Abdul Rahman Park
KOTA KINABALU
Pulau Tiga
Kimanis Bay
Papar
Sandakan

Pulau Labuan

Sabah

Pulau Tabawan
Pulau Bohey Dulang
Semporna

BRUNEI
Miri

SUNGAI BARAM

Pulau Sipadan

Sarawak

Sulawesi Sea

• Bintulu

SUNGAI RAJANG

KALIMANTAN

KEY

Fish		Snorkelling and scuba diving		Oil refinery	
Sea turtles		Watersports		Oil and gas drilling platform	
Shorebirds		Resorts		Mangroves	
Dugong		Fishing village		Marine parks	
Jellyfish		Rocky shore			
Coral reefs		Trawlers			
Seagrasses					

Introduction

Porcupine fish.

Malaysia's coastline—stretching along the Malay Peninsula, Sabah and Sarawak—bounds much of the southern part of the South China Sea, which is one of the world's most fascinating and productive seas. The country today has a 200-nautical-mile Exclusive Economic Zone (EEZ) making Malaysia's seas larger than its land territory. Thus, Malaysia is very much a maritime nation with a long history strongly shaped by its geographical position and make-up. From the myriad species which inhabit the waters and coastal habitats to the rich economic resources, Malaysia's seas are an ecosystem to be treasured and sustained.

A traditional Malay fishing boat on the east coast of Peninsular Malaysia with an intricately carved mast guard (*bangau*).

History of Malaysian seas

Many seas surround Malaysia. The South China Sea lies off the east coast of Peninsular Malaysia and to the west of Sabah and Sarawak; the Sulu Sea lies to the north of Sabah and the Sulawesi Sea to the east; while the Andaman Sea is to be found northwest of the Peninsula. The narrow straits of Melaka and Johor run west and south of the Peninsula.

In the distant past, much of what is now sea was land. Peninsular Malaysia, Borneo (Sabah, Sarawak, Brunei and the Indonesian province of Kalimantan), Sumatra, Java and their surrounding seas made up a region called Sundaland. The entire area was above sea level during the last glacial period when waters were 150 metres below their present level. About 12,000 years ago, at the start of the present inter-glacial period, global temperatures began to increase causing the sea level to rise rapidly. Geologically speaking, the Malaysian seas are young; they are also very shallow.

For centuries these easily navigated waters have been at the heart of, first, Southeast Asian and then later world maritime trade. This trade brought waves of traders and travellers from China, India and further afield including Arabia and Europe, all of which have influenced the cultures and traditions that developed throughout the country.

CENTRE: The lion fish (*Pterois volitans*), found off Pulau Sipadan in Sabah, has venomous spines. It is a sedentary bottom feeder, waiting motionless among the corals for its prey.

A chromolithograph from *The Royal Natural History*, Richard Lydekker (ed.), Vol. VI, London, 1896, illustrates the variety of sea anemones found in tropical seas, such as those around Malaysia.

Landscapes of the sea and coast

The coastal and underwater landscapes Malaysia has to offer are some of the region's most stunning—from palm-fringed beaches to colourful fringing reefs and magnificent mangrove-lined estuaries. Each of these important habitats has its own unique set of permanent inhabitants and temporary visitors. This can be seen in the mangroves which nurture the young of commercially important prawn species and which offer rich overwintering grounds for migrant bird species. The golden strands of beach found around Malaysia's coastline offer many opportunities for tourism and recreational activities and, if sympathetically developed, can retain both their natural aesthetics and their environmental functions.

Biological treasure trove

Malaysian waters are at the heart of one of the world's most biodiverse regions. The seas and the coastlines surrounding Malaysia support thousands of species of plants and animals. These range from the smallest planktonic life—invisible to the human eye—to large mammals such as whales and the endangered dugong. This web of life is interconnected by the constantly

moving waters of their habitat, the food chain and a complex variety of survival adaptations, all of which mean that many species are dependent upon those around them, and the well-being of their environment, for their existence.

Purse seiners, named after their large nets called purse seines, are used to catch anchovies. Schools of fish become enclosed in the nets when the bottoms are drawn shut by means of a line.

Rich marine resources

As the seas have always been considered common property, one consequence is what is termed the 'tragedy of the commons', where everybody exploits them but few look after their welfare. With the Exclusive Economic Zone as encompassed in the United Nations Convention on the Law of the Sea (UNCLOS), countries are encouraged to look after the seas, especially since these are rich, sustainable marine resources. Apart from the supply of an endless variety of fish and seafood, the seas also harbour other resources, including oil and gas. In the last few decades, these finds have made a great contribution to the development of the whole country. They also provide Malaysia's greatest tourist attractions—glorious tropical beaches and coral reefs—and it is thought that their marine life may be the source of many potentially valuable pharmaceuticals.

All the marine and coastal ecosystems along Malaysia's long coastline are important. Unfortunately, they have tended to be valued on appearance. The most spectacular, the coral reefs, are regarded as the most valuable, whereas muddy mangroves are commonly deemed of little value. Coastal land reclamation schemes have destroyed many stretches of mangrove which are highly productive nursery areas for marine life and offer protection to the coast from rough monsoon waters. Today, the tide is thankfully turning as Malaysia has started to realize the importance of mangroves along with the other elements making up the marine environment. This recognition is evidenced in the Matang mangrove conservation project.

Top: Sea horses, which are used locally for medicinal purposes, are sold in a market in Sabah.

Bottom: Cockles are big business, particularly in Johor—Malaysia's biggest producer.

Sustaining the seas

The importance of adopting a sustainable approach to utilizing the resources of the sea is slowly being realized. Growing pressures on the seas have been a feature of the oceanic environment worldwide in recent decades. These pressures take many forms, including pollution from land-based activities—such as runoff from agricultural chemicals, industrial waste, sewage and excess sediments from deforested landscapes—and oil spills, urban and recreational developments along the coast and overfishing. All these take their toll on the natural ecosystems and many species, especially sea mammals. Some fish are now endangered. The long-tailed shad or *terubuk* (*Tenualosa toli*) came close to extinction and, with the drastic decrease in landings on Malaysian beaches, it it now clear that the leatherback turtle (*Dermochelys coriacea*) is headed for extinction within the next few years. In the light of such developments, efforts to sustain the seas take on a new urgency.

Conservation strategies, anti-pollution measures, the implemention of global agreements regarding this most international of environments, and education initiatives, need to be strengthened to ensure that the gift that is the Malaysian seas can continue to play its role in the global environment and remain an endless source of natural resources.

The pyjama nudibranch (*Chromodoris quadricolor*) is found on the reefs off Pulau Redang.

History of the Malaysian seas

Strategically located and richly endowed, the seas around Malaysia have long shaped its development. Linking the Indian and Pacific oceans, and having the sheltered coast of the Strait of Melaka providing the necessary stopping points in the days of sail, were great natural advantages. Since prehistoric times, these waters have acted as a major sea crossing, and later they were at the heart of an early international trading system. Down the centuries, products for the world's markets have passed through Malaysian waters. This has brought traders and travellers, and influenced early state formation and culture.

The beginning of maritime trade

Evidence for the rise of maritime trade networks by the latter half of the 1st century BCE is based on the discovery of Dongson bronze drums on both the west and east coasts of Peninsular Malaysia. Named after the cultural centre of North Vietnam where they originated, the drums were transported along the maritime trade route via the South China Sea. Although the function of the drums is not certain, they have common decorative motifs comprising concentric bands around a central sun or star.

Ancient trade

Archaeological artefacts, including Dongson drums, have been found in the Malay Peninsula and in northwest Borneo, attesting to growing regional trade which started some 4,000 years ago. Cowrie shells, the rare black coral (*akar bahar*) and sea slugs (*teripang*) were early trade goods. Malay traders are documented in southern China from the 3rd century BCE. They purchased cinnamon there which, according to Roman accounts, was exported to the West. Malays are also believed to have reached Madagascar at this time.

The turn of the first millennium

The kingdom of Srivijaya, based in eastern Sumatra and with its capital at Palembang, established the first maritime empire along the Strait of Melaka in the 8th century CE, subduing neighbouring ports and exerting economic influence as far as the Kra Isthmus. By 1000 CE, Arab and Indian traders had arrived in Malaysia, developing what was to become the fabled spice trade. Cloves and nutmeg, transported from the

This early photograph shows Chinese junks discharging cargo near the south end of Weld Quay in Penang around 1900. Bullock carts and push carts were used to transport cargo to and from the harbour.

eastern Malay Archipelago, were shipped to the Red Sea and on to Mediterranean ports. Pepper, sandalwood and camphor joined the list of highly prized products. In return, huge quantities of brightly coloured cloth—cottons and silks—from India were imported. The ports in the region prospered and grew.

The rise and fall of Melaka

Towards the end of the 14th century, commercial and political power shifted to Melaka. A prince from Palembang (Sumatra) founded the city and what was to became the greatest Malay maritime empire. Its rulers subdued the Orang Laut (sea people), once feared as pirates, to help maintain security and order in the Strait. With a population of 100,000, Melaka was the largest Malay city in the Peninsula. The seas around Malaysia were not only a transport hub but a cultural crossroad too. Buddhist pilgrims and Christian merchants passed through, and Indian trading ships brought Hindu preachers. There are archaeological remains showing Hindu–Buddhist influences in Kuala Kedah and Sabah. In the 15th century, Islam took hold—reaching Malaysia via Indian and Arab Muslim traders. Pasai, to the north of the Peninsula, became Muslim and shortly after the rulers of Melaka embraced the faith. Islam offered a common maritime code throughout the Muslim trading world.

The lure of spices and the reputed wealth of Melaka inspired early Europeans explorations. Vasco Da Gama rounded the Cape of Good Hope in

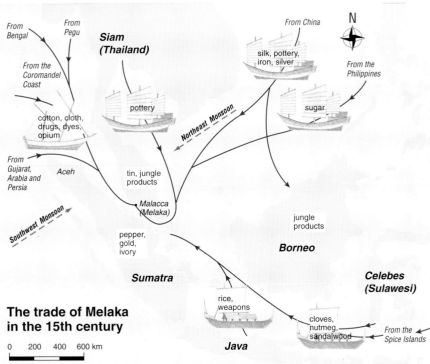

The trade of Melaka in the 15th century

0 200 400 600 km

From Bengal
From Pegu
Siam (Thailand)
From China
silk, pottery, iron, silver
From the Philippines
From the Coromandel Coast
pottery
Northeast Monsoon
sugar
cotton, cloth, drugs, dyes, opium
From Gujarat, Arabia and Persia
Aceh
tin, jungle products
Malacca (Melaka)
jungle products
Borneo
Southwest Monsoon
pepper, gold, ivory
Sumatra
Celebes (Sulawesi)
rice, weapons
cloves, nutmeg, sandalwood
From the Spice Islands
Java

1498, and a decade later the Portuguese reached Melaka. In 1511, the Portuguese captured Melaka, and this marked the entry of successive European maritime powers into the Strait's region.

Colonial powers

The Portuguese found it increasingly difficult to control the Strait of Melaka. New centres of power emerged. Descendants of the former Melaka ruler set up a kingdom in Johor to the south, while Aceh flourished as a rival emporium in northern Sumatra. For more than a century, they and Melaka contested for supremacy in the Strait. A new entrepôt also emerged along the northwest Borneo coast. Extending over today's Sabah, Sarawak, and the Sulu islands, the Sultanate of Brunei attracted Chinese ships sailing across the South China Sea in search of forest and sea produce.

In 1641, the Dutch seized Melaka. Seeking to control the Strait's trade, they required all ships to

Ceramics, textiles and beads were among the trade items imported through early Malaysian entrepôts.

obtain passes from Melaka. Dutch interest later shifted to Batavia, to the east, but Melaka remained useful, if only to prevent other powers from using it. Indeed, the British East India Company was also active in the Strait of Melaka. Private English traders carried out a profitable business exchanging cloth and opium for local tin and pepper. The Strait was also important as a passage through to China. Kuala Terengganu, on the east coast, was used by English traders en route to China. The East India Company preferred a strong base in the Strait. In 1786, the English established a presence in Penang, then in 1795 took possession of Melaka. In 1819, Stamford Raffles established a trading post in Singapore.

Remarkably during these times, the Malay maritime tradition—skilled boat builders and experienced seafarers—survived. Malay traders, the Acehnese and the Bugis from the Celebes, remained active in the Strait of Melaka. Plying the coastal waters, they connected with the international commercial network based in Penang and Singapore. The Bugis were powerful in Johor–Riau in the early 18th century and established the ruling dynasty in Selangor.

The modern era

Penang and Singapore spurred modern economic development in the interior. Tin was mined and commercial cultivation of new crops, such as coffee, tapioca, rubber and oil palm, was introduced in the late 19th and early 20th centuries. The two major ports were connected to smaller ones—Port Weld, Port Swettenham, Port Dickson, Kuantan, Teluk Anson and Labuan—which grew in importance.

In recent times, Pulau Pangkor, Kuala Kurau and Kuala Terengganu have supported large-scale fishing industries, and, within the last 40 years, oil and natural gas have been exploited.

Since 1973, following the declaration of Malaysia's 12-nautical-mile territorial waters and 200-nautical-mile Exclusive Economic Zone, the seas around Malaysia have assumed even more economic and strategic importance. The growth of huge container port facilities, for example at Port Klang, has also become a key industry. There are prospects of further fishing, mineral, and oil resources. And with the march of globalization, the trade and naval routes passing through Malaysian waters will continue to command even greater significance.

The seas around Malaysia acted as a crossroad of cultures. The head of a granite Nandi, the sacred Hindu bull deity, found in the Bujang Valley of Kedah (above top), and a greenstone Buddha head, discovered at Sungai Mas (below), are evidence of early contact by visitors and traders.

The island of Labuan, once a resting place for fishermen, has a fine harbour and free port status, and has become an important ship building centre.

Port Klang, once a small coastal port, is now Malaysia's largest and most important container port on the Southeast Asian maritime network.

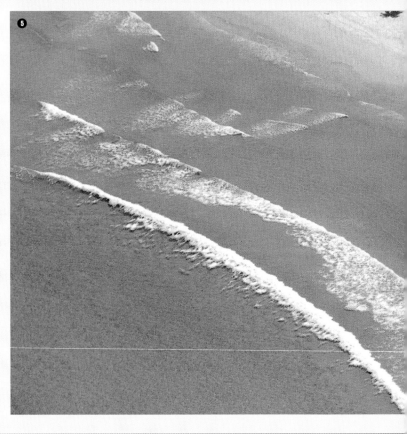

1. Villages in Kelantan on the east coast of Peninsular Malaysia are frequently flooded during the northeast monsoon.

2. Salt from the sea provides both food and a means of livelihood. At the Sulabayau salt factory in Sabah, raw salt is collected before being taken to the factory for refining.

3. Long jetties, such as this one at Pulau Pinang, Redang, are built out into the sea to allow boats to come in at low tide.

4. The sea around Pulau Sulug in the Tunku Abdul Rahman State Park in Sabah displays different shades of blue because of the different rates of absorption of light of different wavelengths in the water.

5. An aerial view of the beach at Pulau Perhentian Besar, off Terengganu on the east coast of Peninsular Malaysia, washed by large waves. Larger waves than usual form during the northeast monsoon at the end of the year.

PHYSICS AND CHEMISTRY OF THE SEAS

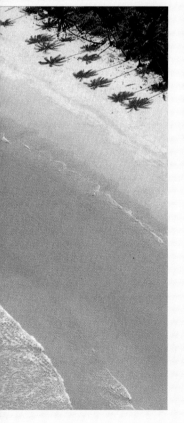

Water, a unique compound without which there can be no life, is the main component of the seas. To understand and appreciate the myriad processes taking place in the seas, it is important to understand the physical and chemical properties of sea water, including those occurring at the global scale.

This green seaweed (*Caulerpa racemosa*), or 'sea grapes', is found in shallow waters because it requires red light to develop, which only penetrates the surface waters.

From space, the earth looks blue because it has more ocean than land. About 80 per cent of the earth's water is sea water, containing salts. It is from this combination of water, salts and simple organic molecules that life on earth originated. The salinity of the water in the Strait of Melaka is lower than that of other seas because it is diluted by large amounts of fresh water from rivers. Salinity levels have a bearing on the type of organisms present. Besides salts, sea water also contains sediments. These determine light penetration, and, again, the range of living organisms found. Both the amount of sediment and type of organisms present affect the colour waters appear. Coastal waters, such as those around the west coast of Malaysia, are often a dirty brownish green because of the presence of much sediment and plankton. Conversely, those to the east, in the South China Sea, are much clearer because they harbour much less sediment.

The gravitational pull of the sun and the moon creates tides, and because of the size, shape and shallow nature of the seas, Malaysia's tides are among the most complex in the world. The sun causes differential heating of the atmosphere, resulting in winds which, in turn, create waves. Differential heating of the oceans globally, combined with the earth's rotation, result in currents which keep sea water circulating, and also strongly influence the climate of the nearby landmasses. The monsoon winds are a good example of this action, and as Malaysia lies within the monsoon regime, seasonal characteristics in terms of waves, currents, sea surface temperatures and sea level variations are greatly affected. The northeast and southwest monsoons have had, and continue to exert, a major influence on the economy and culture of the country. The forces of the waves and currents help shape Malaysia's coastline and, in turn, the variety of habitats found along its shorelines—from strands of fine, golden sand to muddy, mangrove-lined estuaries.

Water moves around, or cycles, flowing as currents, evaporating from seas, and condensing as mist, cloud and rain. It moves with it both dissolved and small particles. Water also aids in the cycling of other materials like carbon and nitrogen. Disturbances of these biogeochemical cycles result in disruptive global changes.

El Niño is an excellent example of atmosphere–ocean interaction. Although this phenomenon has long been known to Peruvian sardine fishermen, it has only recently become familiar to Malaysians. El Niño is now known to affect much of the tropics, bringing coastal flooding and reduced fish stocks to the southeast Pacific, but drought to Southeast Asia, particularly Sabah and Sarawak.

Salts in the sea

Salts in the sea come from various sources, including the recycling of organisms and from being washed into the seas by rivers carrying sediments. In Malaysia, deforestation over the past two decades has resulted in greater amount of sediments, and thus minerals, being deposited in the seas. On average, sea water contains 96.5 per cent pure water and 3.5 per cent salts. However, the addition of rain or river water affects salinity in specific locations. Minerals play a vital role in the biological and chemical processes of all living organisms in the sea.

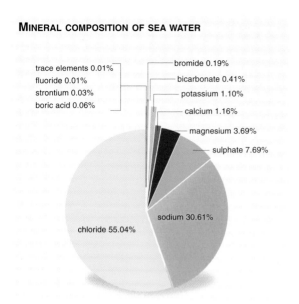

MINERAL COMPOSITION OF SEA WATER

trace elements 0.01%
fluoride 0.01%
strontium 0.03%
boric acid 0.06%
bromide 0.19%
bicarbonate 0.41%
potassium 1.10%
calcium 1.16%
magnesium 3.69%
sulphate 7.69%
sodium 30.61%
chloride 55.04%

Eleven major constituents account for more than 99 per cent of the dissolved minerals usually found in sea water.

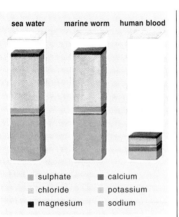

sea water   marine worm   human blood

■ sulphate   ■ calcium
□ chloride   □ potassium
■ magnesium   □ sodium

A comparison of the concentrations of salts. The concentration is highest in marine organisms that live in sea water where there is a high concentration of salt, and weakest in human blood because humans have adapted to living on land.

Salinity

The salt content of sea water is 300–400 times higher than fresh water. The concentration unit used to express the amount of dissolved mineral salts in sea water is parts salinity units (psu). Sea water, with a salinity of 35 psu, means that there are 35 grams of dissolved mineral salts in 1 kilogram of sea water. The average salt content in the world's oceans is about 35 psu.

The fluctuation in salinity in the sea is normally controlled by two factors. First, a decrease in salinity is due to fresh water, such as river or rain water, being added to the sea. Secondly, increases in salinity are due to the removal of fresh water from the sea. This occurs through evaporation. In Malaysia, the salinity of the Strait of Melaka is around 31 psu, which is significantly lower than that of the South China Sea and the surrounding seas. This is due to the heavy rainfall in the region and the large number of rivers, such as the Sungai Muda and Sungai Klang, which flow into the Strait of Melaka.

Why the sea remains salty

The chemical composition of sea water results from a balance between the rates of input and output of the various elements. A balanced system means that the rate at which dissolved matter is added to the ocean from the land and the atmosphere equals the rate at which it is removed from the sea by incorporation into sediments or by being returned to the atmosphere. Owing to the huge amount of sea water and the small amount of chemicals deposited into the sea, the amount of dissolved salts remains fairly constant. Numerous processes in the sea also help to maintain the constant chemical composition of the water. These include the recycling of nutrient salts by bacteria in the cycle of marine life (see diagram on right).

Origin of life

The fact that the seas contain mineral salts is of great significance to animal life. Marine organisms need many of these salts for growth. An indication that life on earth originated in the seas is that the body fluids of marine organisms have the same (or similar) concentrations of salts as sea water.

Of the total 22 major phyla (main groups) of animals, all have representatives in the sea, whereas only nine are represented on land. It took millions of years of evolution before living organisms evolved to colonize land. Of the 21 invertebrate phyla, which include more than 97 per cent of all known animal species, most have more species living in the sea than on land. Marine fish also comprise more than half of all vertebrates.

Salinity in the seas

Salinity levels in the seas depend on the amount of fresh water added and removed. If the evaporation rate is higher than the rate of river and rain water entering, the salinity will increase. The Dead Sea has very high salinity because it is small, only one river flows into it, and it is surrounded by desert, making the evaporation rate high. As the Red Sea is larger and has many rivers flowing into it, its salinity is lower. The South China Sea has an even lower salinity because it is fed by fresh water from monsoon rains and rivers.

VARIATION IN SALINITY

	SOUTH CHINA SEA (psu)	RED SEA (psu)	DEAD SEA (psu)
Sodium	10.8	12.2	40.1
Chlorine	19.4	22.0	224.9
Magnesium	1.3	1.5	44.0
Calcium	0.4	0.5	17.2
Others	3.1	3.8	13.4
Total (salinity)	**35.0**	**40.0**	**339.6**

Salinity is so high in the Dead Sea that a person can float naturally.

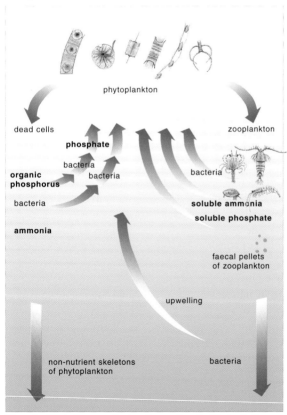

phytoplankton
dead cells
zooplankton
phosphate
bacteria
organic phosphorus   bacteria   bacteria
bacteria
soluble ammonia
soluble phosphate
ammonia
faecal pellets of zooplankton
upwelling
non-nutrient skeletons of phytoplankton   bacteria

The cycle of life in the oceans involves the recycling of nutrient salts. The chemicals in the dead cells of phytoplankton are usually broken down and recycled within the top layers of water. The heavier pellets of zooplankton also contain nutrients, but these sink to the bottom, decompose and the material is brought up by upwelling currents to be recycled by phytoplankton.

Salt production in Malaysia

A Malaysian salt factory

There are a number of salt factories in Malaysia. One of the largest is operated by Sulabayau Industries Sdn Bhd. Located at Kudat in Sabah, the factory produces different types of salt, such as fine sea salt, fine salt, refined iodized salt, coarse salt and even a low-sodium salt for the health-conscious. Industrial grade salt is also produced for salting fish and for preserving fresh livestock products.

When the company was first set up in 1992, salt was extracted manually from the sea. In 1997, a modern RM100 million factory was developed on a 400-hectare site. With the upgrading of facilities, the factory is now capable of producing large quantities of salt for export, although most of the products are sold locally. It now sells an average of 200 metric tons of salt a month.

1. The site of the Sulabayau salt factory, with its many evaporating ponds. Sea water is pumped into a reservoir, then to an irrigation channel and finally into the ponds.

2. Salt which has crystallized in the crystallization ponds is piled up in various places awaiting collection.

3. A view inside the factory, where salt is processed and then packed into bags.

4. Salt packed in bags ready for distribution.

Store and use of nutrients

More than 95 of the world's naturally occurring minerals have been detected in sea water. These include metals, such as lead, mercury and gold, as well as non-metals such as bromide and chloride. Some of these constituents of sea water, particularly trace metals, are also nutrients.

A nutrient is a mineral which is vital to the life cycles of organisms. For example, phosphate, nitrate and silicate are essential for the growth of microscopic marine plants known as phytoplankton (see 'Plankton'). Other marine organisms obtain most of their nutrients from phytoplankton, which form their basic food supply. Some nutrients are available in such large amounts that usage by living organisms produces very small changes in their concentrations. Although many of the other essential nutrients are present in very small amounts

in sea water, only minute quantities are required by living organisms. Others, which are not required as nutrients by marine organisms, can sometimes be absorbed by them.

A number of marine organisms are capable of concentrating particular nutrients in their bodies. For example, 1 kilogram of dry seaweed contains 5 grams of iodine, an element essential to human life, and the only source of which is sea water. The many species of seaweed growing in Malaysian coastal waters thus have great pharmaceutical value. Oysters accumulate zinc in their tissues because they have developed a system to do so without harming themselves. Thus, oysters are good indicators of water pollution. This ability of marine organisms to absorb certain minerals can be harmful to humans; for example, when poisonous mercury is ingested by eating contaminated shellfish.

Light in the sea

Light penetrates the seas to a depth of only about 200 metres. This defines the photic zone where light provides energy for marine plants to photosynthesize. Only in about 2 per cent of all water bodies does any light reach the bottom. Life in the deep oceans exists in permanent darkness. As most of the seas around Malaysia lie on the shallow Sunda Shelf, they receive enough light for marine life to thrive. Phytoplankton, algae and sediments in the sea absorb and scatter different wavelengths of light in different proportions, giving parts of the seas their characteristic colours.

A view of Pulau Sibuon, in the Semporna group of islands off Sabah, and its surrounding seas, showing the different colours of the water, from white in shallow areas to yellow, to light blue, then dark blue in deep waters. This is due to the different rates of absorption of light wavelengths in water.

Water in a swimming pool is usually clear blue as it is sediment free, and copper sulphate is often added to prevent algal growth. Next to it, the nearshore water appears dirty green because of sediments and phytoplankton.

Different light effects

The two photographs above are of an identical underwater scene in Malaysia. The top picture, taken with the available light, has an overall blue tinge because the few metres of water have differentially absorbed red light, and whatever light comes through is blue. All colour photographs taken underwater without a flash will have this blue tinge.

The bottom picture, taken with a flash, only has a blue tinge in the background (upper left). Although the flash supplied white light to the foreground, it was not intense enough to penetrate into the background. Artificial white light is thus needed to obtain the real colour (as perceived by the human eye) of underwater scenes.

Underwater light

Light travelling through water is absorbed or scattered. Absorption involves the conversion of the light energy into other forms of energy, such as heat or chemical energy (through photosynthesis). In sea water, the main absorbers are phytoplankton (see 'Plankton') which use the converted energy for photosynthesis, suspended particles, dissolved organic compounds and the water itself. Scattering refers to the change in direction of light due to reflections from suspended particles. Therefore, the more turbid the water, the higher the degree of absorption and scattering.

Why the sea is blue

The sea generally looks blue, although there are usually different shades of blue. Thus, the earth looks like a big blue marble from outer space because there is more ocean than land. The reason why the sea looks blue lies in the differential absorption of light in water.

Light visible to humans is in a spectrum of rainbow colours, with wavelengths of 400–700 nm (nanometres or 10^{-9} metres). By comparison, the thickness of the human hair is 100,000 nm or about 0.1 millimetre.

White light consists of a spectrum of different wavelengths which the human eye perceives as colours, ranging from violet, indigo, blue and green at one end to yellow, orange and red at the other end. Blue or violet light has the shortest wavelength of visible light and red light the longest. The human eye cannot detect light with shorter wavelengths, known as ultraviolet light, or longer wavelengths, known as infrared light. Infrared light can, however, be felt as heat.

When light passes through clean, fresh water, more of the longer wavelengths (yellow, orange and red) are absorbed than the shorter ones (violet, indigo and blue), which is why the water appears white or blue. Although water appears colourless or white when small amounts are viewed, it looks blue in a larger expanse, such as in the South China Sea.

Since the water in deep oceans is very clear and there are fewer phytoplankton, most of the blue wavelengths are reflected, making the water look deep blue. Except for the South China Sea, most of the seas around Malaysia are not deep, and therefore, do not appear dark blue. Thus, a shallow clean sea will appear white and as the water gets deeper, its colour quickly turns from white to yellow, to light blue-green, to light blue and, finally, to the deep blue typical of deep seas and oceans. Sea water containing a lot of phytoplankton will tend to look green because phytoplankton absorb most of the blue and red wavelengths and reflect the greens.

The macro algae (see 'Seaweeds') have adapted to changes in the type and availability of light by having appropriate absorptive pigments. Green algae

The red seaweed (*Halymenia* sp.), common in Malaysia, can live at greater depths under water than many other species because it absorbs the blue light that penetrates deeper under water and uses it for photosynthesis. At the same time, it reflects the red light that gives it its distinctive colour.

Clean, shallow water appears white. As the water gets deeper, its colour changes to blue and the blue becomes darker and darker with increasing depth.

Measuring light

To measure the quality (wavelength) as well as quantity (amplitude) of light, a complex instrument known as a spectroradiometer is required. The instrument shown on the right is a special battery-operated underwater spectroradiometer. Such instruments are expensive, so spectroradiometric measurements of light penetration in the sea are not common.

An easier way to measure light penetration in water is to use a simple device known as a Secchi Disk. This is a disk of 20–30 centimetres in diameter which is painted in black and white sectors, with a weight suspended from one face. The disk is lowered into the water until it disappears from view. It is then slowly raised until it becomes visible. The depth at which the disk becomes visible is the Secchi Disk reading.

Phytoplankton fix organic carbon through photosynthesis, using light as the energy source. As light diminishes with depth, the amount of photosynthesis decreases. The point where there is just enough light energy to produce carbon to balance that lost to respiration is known as the photosynthetic compensation depth. This is also the depth where about 1 per cent of the incident surface light remains. It has been found that this 1 per cent light penetration depth is about four times the Secchi Disk reading (depth).

ABOVE LEFT: The cylindrical container is the underwater housing for the spectroradiometer. The sensor is the white disk on the top of the cylinder. A cable connects the spectroradiometer to the readout deck unit.

ABOVE RIGHT: A Secchi Disk.

Effects of sedimentation

Heavy sediment loads in the water can rapidly shade out light which, in coastal areas, can lead to bottom communities like seagrasses (see 'Seagrasses') and corals (see 'Coral reefs') being starved of light and exterminated. Often this is caused by land-based activities. For instance, in Malaysia, soil erosion from forest clearing or coastal reclamation projects results in an increase of sediment loads. An increase in nutrient runoff from agricultural activities can also lead to phytoplankton blooms.

Decrease in light penetration also reduces photosynthesis and this, in turn, leads to reduced oxygen production. Should this happen in waters containing high organic matter—waters having a high biochemical demand for oxygen—dissolved oxygen is quickly used up. This leads to fish being killed or the water becoming unsuitable for most living organisms.

When all oxygen is used up, the water becomes anoxic (without oxygen), foul-smelling and toxic hydrogen sulphide forms. This is especially so for stagnant waters as flowing waters increase the mixing of water with atmospheric oxygen.

The coastal waters bordering this water village in Kota Kinabalu, Sabah, are a murky yellowish brown because they contain sediments. Water containing sediments scatters red, yellow and green light where these wavelengths have not been absorbed, making the water look greenish or yellowish brown.

with no adaptation usually live in shallow waters, but brown algae can live in deeper waters; and red algae which can utilize the blue light that penetrates deeper underwater even more effectively, can live down the deepest. Seaweeds of all three colours are found in Malaysia. Other factors, such as nutrient supply, also have an effect on the abundance of different seaweed species.

Roles of light

Light plays very important physical and biological roles in the seas. It is the main energy source. When light hits the water, parts of it are absorbed and converted to heat. Light is also absorbed by marine plants, using the absorbed energy to fix carbon by photosynthesis. Light, however, penetrates the seas and oceans to a certain depth only. In clear, oceanic waters, only 1 per cent of surface light penetrates to more than 100 metres. However, only 8 per cent of the seas are less than 200 metres deep, whereas 88 per cent are more than 1000 metres deep.

Therefore, only a relatively thin layer of the ocean, the photic zone, has light, while much of the ocean is in darkness (the aphotic zone). Almost all the production of organic carbon from inorganic carbon (carbon dioxide) or all of the photosynthetic production of oxygen occurs in the thin photic layer, using light from the visible band. This production of oxygen is vitally important in sustaining marine life.

Water and other cycles

Many of the important elements that support the earth's biosphere, such as water, carbon and nitrogen, circulate in biogeochemical cycles (literally, 'life–earth–chemical' cycles). In Malaysia, as elsewhere, these unending exchanges of water, carbon and other compounds between the ocean, atmosphere and land are fundamental in shaping the face of the land, determining the nature of the climate, and supporting life.

Global water distribution
Oceans and icecaps together account for more than 99 per cent of the total distribution of water.

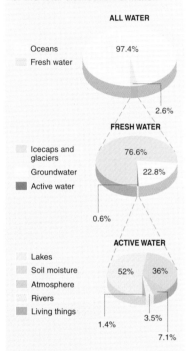

ALL WATER

Oceans 97.4%
Fresh water

2.6%

FRESH WATER

Icecaps and glaciers 76.6%
Groundwater 22.8%
Active water

0.6%

ACTIVE WATER

Lakes
Soil moisture 52% 36%
Atmosphere
Rivers
Living things

1.4%

3.5%

7.1%

Biogeochemical cycles

Although all living things are made up of chemicals, only 24 of the 103 known chemicals are required by organisms. Of these 24, six elements—carbon, oxygen, hydrogen, nitrogen, phosphorus and sulphur—are the major building blocks of all the organic molecules that make up the tissues of plants, animals and microbes. Carbon is the basic building block of organic compounds. Together with oxygen and hydrogen, it forms carbohydrates. Nitrogen, together with the other three, largely constitute protein molecules, while phosphorus is important in the transfer and use of energy within cells.

Growth, reproduction, death and decay of organisms is a continuous process of assembly and disassembly (decay) of various environmental elements. But for any form of life to persist, chemical elements must be available in the right ratios. Basically, a biogeochemical cycle is a series of storage reservoirs and pathways in which a chemical element (the 'chemical' aspect) moves through the earth systems—from the atmosphere, waters, rocks and soils (the 'geo' aspect) to organisms (the 'bio' aspect) and vice versa. These cycles include the very important elements of carbon, oxygen, nitrogen, phosphorus, sulphur and water.

The nitrogen cycle

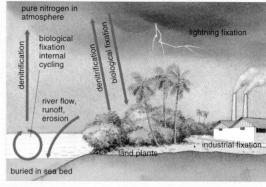

As nitrogen is necessary for the production of proteins, including DNA (deoxyribonucleic acid), the carrier of genetic information, it is essential to life. The nitrogen cycle is very complex. Although there is molecular nitrogen (nitrogen not combined with any other element) in the atmosphere, living things cannot use it directly. They require it to be in an organic compound, or as nitrate or ammonia.

Lightning and bacteria convert inorganic nitrogen in the atmosphere into nitrate or ammonia (nitrogen fixation). When nitrogen is converted into ammonia, it can then be taken up on land by plants and in the oceans by algae. These plants, algae and bacteria then convert the inorganic nitrogen compounds into organic ones. When the organisms die, other bacteria convert the organic nitrogen compounds back to nitrate, ammonia, or by chemical reactions, to molecular nitrogen, when it is then returned to the atmosphere. This process of returning fixed nitrogen back to molecular nitrogen is called denitrification.

Molecular nitrogen can also be converted by industrial processes into useful compounds, such as nitrogen in plant fertilizers. Industrial fixation is now a major source of commercial nitrogen fertilizers, a large source of fixed nitrogen in the nitrogen cycle. Many modern industrial combustion processes, including the burning of fossil fuels with diesel engines, produce oxides of nitrogen, which contribute to air pollution.

The water cycle

The water or hydrologic cycle is an important biogeochemical cycle. While water is vital for all organisms, it also functions as a medium for moving nutrients into and out of ecosystems.

The water cycle is the process of water exchange between oceans, atmosphere and land. The sun's energy powers the water cycle by heating the oceans, lakes and land. As a result, water constantly evaporates into the atmosphere, particularly from the oceans which comprise about 99 per cent of the earth's total water, where it remains aloft as vapour, clouds or ice crystals.

Moisture-laden air may either condense and fall back to the ocean as precipitation, where it is ready to begin another cycle, or be carried by winds to other parts of the ocean, or to the land where it condenses into clouds and produces rain and, at high altitudes, snow. If droplets of condensing water form in the atmosphere, the result is fog or mist. If the droplets form on the cool surfaces of vegetation, the result is dew.

Precipitation falling on the land then makes its way back to the ocean. Some of it soaks into the ground (infiltration), eventually seeping into lakes, streams or directly into the oceans. When the rate

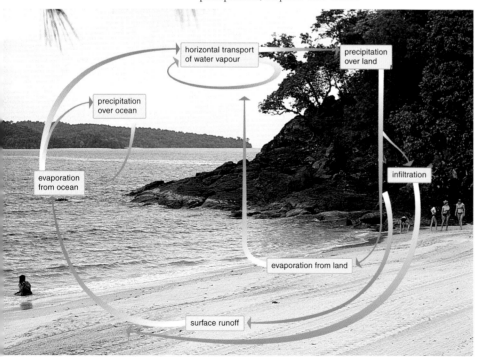

The water cycle basically consists of water rising to the atmosphere through either evaporation or transpiration, and leaving it through condensation and precipitation. When precipitation reaches the ground, it may infiltrate it, run off the surface, or evaporate.

The carbon cycle

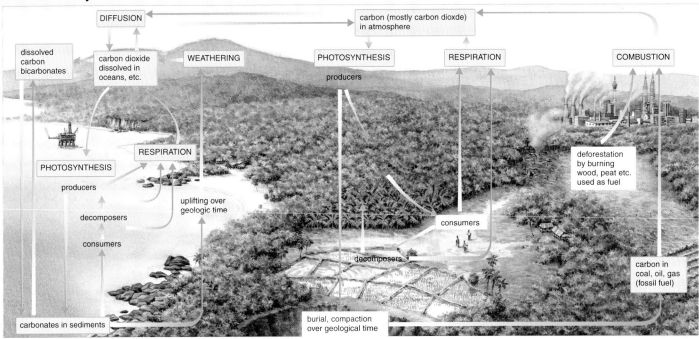

Most of the earth's carbon—10,000 times that of the total mass of all life on earth—is stored in ocean floor sediments and on continents where it enters the cycle very slowly.

This simplified model of the carbon cycle shows the movement of carbon through marine ecosystems (left) and terrestrial ecosystems (right).

The carbon cycle is based on carbon dioxide which makes up about 0.036 per cent by volume of the earth's troposphere and is also dissolved in water. It is especially critical in affecting climate and, ultimately, the type of life that can exist. If the carbon cycle removes too much carbon dioxide from the atmosphere, the earth will cool; if the cycle generates too much, the earth will get warmer.

Carbon enters the atmosphere through the respiration of living things, through fires that burn organic compounds, and by diffusion from the ocean. It is removed from the atmosphere by photosynthesis of green plants, algae and photosynthetic bacteria.

Carbon enters the ocean from the atmosphere by simple diffusion of carbon dioxide, which dissolves and is converted to carbonate and bicarbonate. A small amount of carbon is also transferred from the land to the ocean in rivers and streams as dissolved carbon and as organic particulates. Carbon occurs in the ocean in several inorganic forms, as dissolved carbon dioxide, and as carbonate and bicarbonate. It also occurs in the organic compounds of marine organisms and their products, such as seashells.

of rainfall is greater than the earth's ability to absorb it, the additional water flows over the surface into rivers and lakes (runoff) before returning to the oceans with sediments eroded by the rivers. Much of the water that soaks in or runs off eventually makes its way back to the atmosphere because of evaporation from the soil, lakes and streams or via transpiration by plants.

The phosphorus cycle

Phosphorus exists in the atmosphere only as part of dust because it does not have a gaseous phase on earth. Phosphorus compounds are not readily soluble in water and are not easily eroded as part of the water cycle. Phosphorus only becomes available on land very slowly through weathering. It occurs mainly in its oxidized state as phosphate, which combines with iron, potassium, magnesium or calcium to form minerals found in soils and waters.

In the global phosphorus cycle, phosphorus is recycled and released to the soil and land organisms by geological processes such as weathering of rocks, by birds that produce guano, and by humans. Algae, plants and certain bacteria take in phosphates, much of which is returned to the soil. Because the phosphates are relatively insoluble in water, they are very slowly removed from the soil by weathering and transported by rivers to the seas. Plankton, which take in phosphates, are eaten by fish which,

in turn, are eaten by sea birds. The birds nest on offshore islands where their phosphorus-laden excrement or guano is a major source of phosphorus for fertilizers.

The sulphur cycle

Much of the earth's sulphur is found in rocks and minerals underground or under the sea. Sulphur enters the atmosphere from natural sources (for example, hydrogen sulphide, a gas from active volcanoes and decay of organic matter, and sulphur dioxide from volcanoes). Particles of sulphate salts also enter the atmosphere via spray from the sea.

In the atmosphere, sulphur dioxide reacts with oxygen to produce sulphur trioxide, a gas which reacts with water vapour to produce droplets of sulphuric acid. Sulphur dioxide also reacts with other chemicals in the atmosphere to produce particles of sulphate salts which fall to earth as acid rain and which can harm plants and aquatic life. About one-third of the total sulphur entering the atmosphere comes from human activities, such as coal-burning plants or metal refining plants that produce sulphur dioxide as a result of burning sulphur.

AMOUNTS OF CARBON IN THE GLOBAL CARBON CYCLE	
SOURCE OF CARBON	AMOUNT OF CARBON (in gigatons or billions of metric tons)
Land: Vegetation	610 } 2190
Soils and detritus	1580
The atmosphere (carbon dioxide)	750
Ocean surface	1020
Marine organisms	3
Sea bed surface sediment	150
Intermediate and deep ocean	38 100

Human interference

It has become increasingly apparent that human activities can influence global biogeochemical cycles. The scale of resource utilization and modern technology is altering and transferring chemical elements in the cycles at rates comparable to those in nature.

While some of these activities are beneficial to man, others pose grave dangers. For example, the rapid increase in world population and resource use have disturbed the carbon cycle in two ways that have added more carbon dioxide to the atmosphere than oceans and plants have been able to remove: first, forest removal has left less vegetation to absorb carbon dioxide through photosynthesis and, secondly, burning fossil fuels and wood produces carbon dioxide that flows into the atmosphere.

Tides

A tide is the rise and fall of water level caused mainly by the gravitational attraction between the earth, the moon and the sun. Tides play an important role in Malaysia, surrounded as it is by seas. Knowledge of tides is essential, particularly for ships' captains and fishermen. Data about tides are needed to support the rapid growth of the coastal maritime sectors in Malaysia, and for this reason tide observation facilities are being set up at every port.

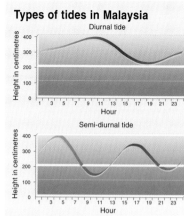

Types of tides in Malaysia

There are two main types of tides in Malaysia—diurnal and semi-diurnal. Diurnal tides complete a cycle of high and low water in one day, while semi-diurnal tides take only half a day; that is, there are two cycles in one day. Where the tides are semi-diurnal, large fishing boats and ships needing the extra depth of water can enter or leave a harbour twice a day.

Jetties are built into the sea to allow boats to come close to the shore at low tide. The jetty at Miri, Sarawak (top), is very long because it is also used as a tide monitoring station and has to project beyond the line where the waves break. The jetty at Pulau Perhentian Besar, off Terengganu (bottom), is short as it is used only as a landing pier.

The importance of tides

Knowledge of tides is essential in the making of navigational charts because ships' captains need to know the state of tides when entering or leaving a harbour. In order to produce an accurate chart, good tidal data are necessary. Inaccurate charts can result in the grounding of a ship, as they may show the charted depth to be deeper or shallower than it really is. Fishermen need to know about tides, too. They return to shore at high tide to avoid being stranded on the shoals. Local fishermen know that the best time to fish in coastal waters is during the new or full moon, which produces the highest tide (the spring tide, known locally as *air pasang besar*), rather than during the moon's first or last quarter when there is a small change in tidal heights (the neap tide, known locally as *air mati*). Knowledge of tides is also necessary for other marine activities, such as construction work along the shore, scientific research and development, as well as water sports.

Tides in Malaysia

The tides in Malaysia, like those in the rest of Southeast Asia, are among the most complex in the world because of the size, shape and depth of the seas, which have numerous bays, gulfs and straits varying greatly in depth. Most places in Malaysia have mixed tides, that is, they can be diurnal dominant (on most days diurnal) or semi-diurnal dominant (on most days semi-diurnal). The tides in the Strait of Melaka and as far as Kuantan on the east coast of the Peninsula are predominantly semi-diurnal while those on the northern east coast of the Peninsula and on the Sabah and Sarawak coasts are predominantly diurnal. The complexity of the tides means much effort has to go into monitoring and recording tide data for nautical charts.

Although tides are a self-renewing source of energy that can be harnessed, they are a difficult source to tap, and as yet there are no tidal power stations in Malaysia.

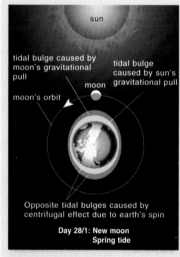

tidal bulge caused by moon's gravitational pull

tidal bulge caused by sun's gravitational pull

moon

moon's orbit

Opposite tidal bulges caused by centrifugal effect due to earth's spin

Day 28/1: New moon
Spring tide

Day 7: First quarter
Neap tide

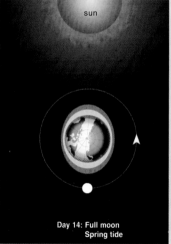

Day 14: Full moon
Spring tide

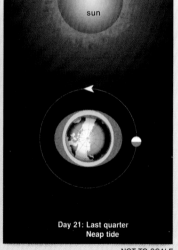

Day 21: Last quarter
Neap tide

NOT TO SCALE

What causes tides?

The gravitational attraction of the sun and the moon causes sea water to move horizontally towards a point on the surface of the earth directly below the heavenly body, resulting in a pile-up (tidal bulge) that raises the sea level of the area on the side of the earth facing the sun or moon. An opposing centrifugal force creates a similar tidal bulge on the opposite side. The extent of tidal fluctuations varies on both a monthly cycle that corresponds to the moon's orbit around the earth, and on an annual cycle, because of the earth's orbit around the sun.

The tides follow a 28-day cycle that reflects the changes in alignment of the earth, moon and sun, and the gravitational attraction forces of the moon, and to a lesser extent, the sun. When the sun, moon and earth are in line, this causes the strongest effect, that is, a spring tide ('spring' here means 'to rise up', not the season). Spring tides have the largest tidal range—the highest high tides and the lowest low tides. When the sun and moon are at right angles, this alignment produces the weaker neap tides with their smaller tidal range—the lowest high tides and the highest low tides.

The forces that cause tides are called tide-generating forces. However, the actual movement of the tides is not as simple as it seems. In addition to astronomical factors, seasonal effects, the shape of the landmasses surrounding the seas, as well as the sea bed all affect the type and range of tides.

Studies of tides

The gravitational attraction between the earth, the moon and the sun is not the only factor governing tides. There are other factors, such as seasonal effects and the shape and characteristics of the local landmass or sea bed. Therefore, tidal data need to be collected and analysed. Tidal data in Malaysia and elsewhere are collected using tide gauges.

The Royal Malaysian Navy (RMN) Hydrographic Service, the Directorate of National Mapping, and other authorities such as ports, maintain a network of tide gauges around Malaysia covering most major ports and several permanent tide stations on offshore installations or islands. As the national authority on hydrography and navigational safety, the RMN Hydrographic Service carries out both short- and long-term tide observations. The results are then used for the prediction of tides, which are published annually as Malaysian tide tables.

Tide gauges

Two types of gauges are used for the collection of tidal data: the mechanical gauge and the pressure gauge. These are housed in a tide station, which is usually an aluminium hut (see diagram below).

In the pressure gauge (left side of the tide station), the pressure sensor senses the pressure of the volume of water and records it in the data logger. Since any increase or decrease in atmospheric pressure will affect the reading, there is an atmospheric pressure compensator (below the data logger) to correct the reading. In the mechanical gauge (right side of the tide station), as the float moves up and down with the tide, the pulley above moves a pen placed on a chart recorder and records the tide level. The stilling well is a PVC tube which encloses the float and sensor, thereby reducing the effects of waves.

A staff member from the hydrographic department of the Royal Malaysian Navy carrying out routine maintenance at one of the many tide stations in Malaysia.

Studies of tides are necessary to determine tide patterns. Such studies help navigation, but also help to find solutions to problems caused by rising tides, such as this flood in the low-lying areas of Port Klang.

A tide station

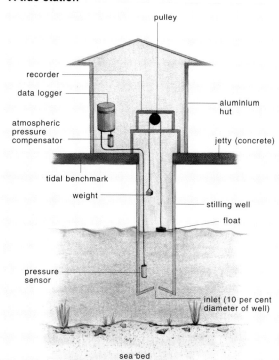

Location of tide stations

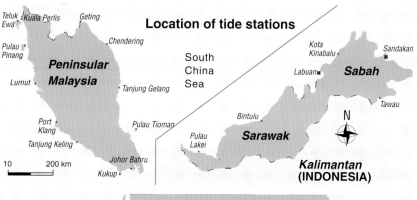

Tidal range

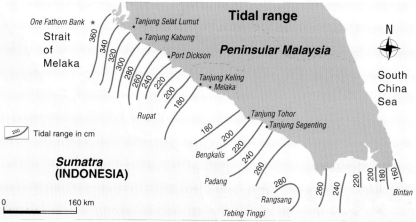

Tidal range in cm

A co-range chart shows places which have the same range of tides. Tidal range refers to the difference in height between low and high tides. It differs from place to place because the tide-generating forces, combined with local effects, such as the shape of the landmass and sea bed, produce different results.

Each line drawn across the Strait of Melaka (see map above) indicates places which have the same range of tides. For example, the 360 cm line shows that the range between the highest and lowest tides is 3.6 metres. It is necessary to know about such ranges in tides, for example, when constructing a jetty.

Source: Hydrographic Department, Royal Malaysian Navy.

Tidal bores

When a high tide enters a narrowing estuary, the water becomes concentrated into a narrow funnel. If, within the period of time it takes for the tide to complete one cycle, it does not have enough time to drain out to sea, and other high tides keep coming in, all the water eventually gets pushed up into a high wall called a tidal bore. Heavy runoff from monsoon rains can also be a factor. Tidal bores occur where a river is flat, narrow and often has a sand bar at the mouth, such as near Pulau Lakei, Sarawak.

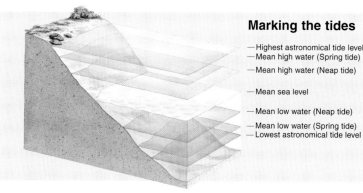

Marking the tides

— Highest astronomical tide level
— Mean high water (Spring tide)
— Mean high water (Neap tide)

— Mean sea level

— Mean low water (Neap tide)
— Mean low water (Spring tide)
— Lowest astronomical tide level

Waves

Malaysia has a long coastline formed by various natural phenomena, including waves, which erode, transport and deposit sediments. Waves are irregular, their different heights, directions and strengths being due to varying sea bed conditions, wind strength, the size of water bodies and water depth. In Malaysian seas, the size of waves is also affected by the monsoon winds, with huge waves being generated off the east coast of the peninsula during the northeast monsoon at the end of the year.

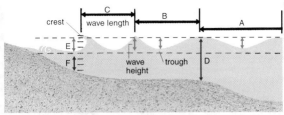

Breaking wave

The length of a wave (A, B and C) shortens as it approaches the shore due to the drag of the sea bottom, which begins to affect the wave when its height (D) is about half the wave length of (A). As the length of the wave shortens, its height increases until, when the height (E) reaches a ratio of 3 : 4 with the water depth (F), the wave breaks.

Many people flocked to the Teluk Chempedak beach in Kuantan to see giant waves during the northeast monsoon in January 2000. Although big waves are common during the monsoon, the waves were unusually large at that time.

Wave generation

Most ordinary waves are generated by winds sweeping over the surface of the water. Waves generated during the monsoons (in Malaysia, the northeast and southwest monsoons) are bigger because the monsoon winds are stronger.

Waves are also generated by other forces. The far-travelled descendants of giant waves (*tsunamis*) are generated by the sudden displacement of immense volumes of ocean water, usually caused by a submarine earthquake. Tsunamis occur regularly in the seas off Japan but have not been recorded around Malaysia.

Waves produced by the action of the wind are the most important type of sea waves. When the wind blows across a water surface, it subjects the surface to irregular, unequal pressures, as wind does not blow with constant velocity and pressure. The biggest waves are usually built up by the strongest wind. However, the height of the wave and its strength also depend on the fetch—the distance over which the wind blows. The greater the fetch, the more powerful the wave.

Waves in shallow water

Waves do not start to feel the drag of the sea bed until the water depth is slightly less than half a wave length. It is not until the depth is much shallower that any appreciable amount of sediment is transported, and deposition of sediment takes place.

When the waves are affected by the drag of the sea bottom, they gradually slow down as the water becomes shallower, each progressing more slowly than the ones behind, with the subsequent crowding of the wave crests reducing wave lengths. With this tendency to crowd, if the waves approach a shelving shore obliquely, the crest lines tend to swing towards a path almost parallel to the coast. This natural phenomenon is known as refraction.

When waves erode a coastline, the eroded particles are transported by currents and deposited offshore or further down the coast where they build new features (see 'Coastlines' and 'Moving sands'). Storm waves, which are stronger than ordinary waves, transport coarse eroded materials from the sea bed and other places and deposit them on the upper beach as they wash up a beach. When these waves recede, they have lost most of their energy and are unable to erode the part with the heavier coarse particles. They are only able to erode the lower part of the beach which has fine sand.

Consequences of wave action

Waves approaching the beach generate secondary flow motions such as longshore drifts (see 'Moving sands') and under-currents that dislodge, agitate and transport bottom sediment, resulting in beach erosion. The destructive impact of breakers against beaches is often far greater than realized. Although the force generated by waves in Malaysian waters, such as in the Strait of Melaka and the South China Sea, is not as great as in some other countries, the coastlines are still subject to intense shocks.

Cracks and crevices in rocks and coastal structures can be quickly opened up and expanded. Similarly, openings in the mangroves (for example, caused by illegal felling) provide opportunity for waves to attack the hinterland. Water, often in the form of high-pressure spray, is driven into every opening along the structures or coast, tightly compressing any entrapped air within the structure, or building up a concentration of water forces

Types of waves

Two distinct types of waves are produced by the wind: capillary and oscillatory. Capillary waves are more or less ripples. The smaller the wave length, the more rapidly it moves. Such waves are due to surface tension and the wind wrinkling the surface. Their impact on the local physical phenomena—such as erosion of the coastline— is negligible.

Oscillatory waves are due mainly to gravity. The greater the wave length, the faster it moves. In typical oscillatory waves in deep water, each water particle moves through a circular orbit, the particle moving forward on the crest of the wave. If the wind is strong, however, each water particle advances a little further than it recedes and the wave becomes strongly asymmetrical.

Similarly, in shallow water, where friction against the bottom begins to be felt, each particle recedes a little less

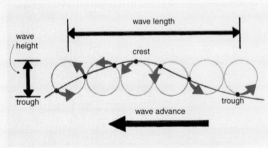

An oscillatory wave, showing how water particles move through a circular orbit.

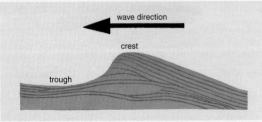

An asymmetrical oscillatory wave driven by a high wind.

than it advances. In both cases, the orbit, instead of being a closed circle, resembles a slightly open ellipse and a certain proportion of the water then drifts forward in the direction the wave is moving.

within the open area. As the wave recedes, the compressed air in structures bursts out, subjecting coastal features to enormous strains over time, and causing erosion. A beach or mangrove forest is a natural means of absorbing the energy of breaking waves and can protect a coastline from erosion. However, interference from human activities, such as converting mangroves into prawn ponds, usually causes erosion. Unfortunately, building structures to prevent erosion also results in unwanted deposition as well as erosion (see 'Moving sands').

The process of coastal erosion

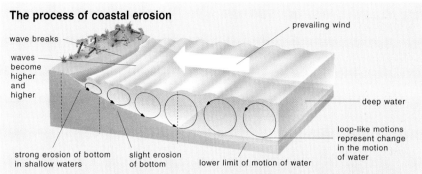

As waves enter shallow water, they increase in height, become unstable and break on the shore. The resulting uprush rides up the beach and carries sediments back out to sea in the backwash. When the incoming destructive wave is followed by less steep constructive waves, sediment is removed more quickly than it is replaced. This leads to erosion of the beach. If one part of the beach is protected, another will be affected.

An unprotected stretch of sandy beach eroded by waves.

Another unprotected stretch of beach in Melaka eroded by waves.

Breakers

Formation of breakers

As a wave enters the shallows, it changes from a deep column of water into a shallow one. Each wave increases in volume and becomes higher, while the wave front becomes steeper. Finally, a point is reached where the volume of water is insufficient to fill up the wave form, leaving the crest unsupported. Because the orbit is broken, the wave itself breaks.

The depth of the water at which the wave breaks ranges from 0.75 to 1.25 times the height of the unbroken waves following it. The four types of breaking waves—spilling, plunging, surging and collapsing—are shown (right) at Chendering in Terengganu.

Types of breakers

Chendering • South China Sea

PENINSULAR MALAYSIA

Strait of Melaka

1. The spilling breaker is characterized by 'white water' at the crest. It is generated along the gently shelving sea bed where a wave front steepens gradually, causing the wave to break gradually.

2. The collapsing breaker is the transition wave between plunging and surging. It occurs over the lower half of the wave. Minimal air pockets are formed and usually no splash follows. Bubbles and foam are usually visible.

3. The plunging breaker is generated when, along the sea bed which shallows rapidly, the advancing wave steepens quickly, rearing up or curling over a large air pocket and suddenly plunging down with great force or violence.

4. The surging breaker builds up as if to form a plunging breaker, but the base of the wave surges up the beach before the crest can plunge forward.

Other phenomena: Upwash and backwash

As the waves advance up the beach, the final movement of water up the beach is called the swash or upwash.

The return of the wave down the slope of the beach towards the sea is termed the backwash.

The formation of waves is accompanied by other natural phenomena which influence beach formation, such as upwash and backwash. Destructive waves are those in which the backwash is strong, such as those generated by plunging breakers. They churn up the beach and, as a result, beach material is swirled a little way back.

Constructive waves are those in which the backwash is weak. When a mixture of sediment is swept up the beach, the coarse material is left stranded at the top. Moreover, some of the swash percolates down into the shingle and sand, reducing the strength of the backwash further. The result of a long spell of constructive waves is the build-up of a broad berm (beach head) of coarse sand or shingle.

Currents and circulation

Currents are the movements of water in the seas and oceans. There are two main types of currents: surface currents caused by winds and the rotation of the earth, and deep ocean currents caused by differences in temperature and salinity. Warm water is moved away from the equator and cold water to it by these currents. Thus, the earth's temperature is distributed and climate controlled. Coastal currents, primarily caused by tides and waves, also occur. The monsoon winds are a key factor in explaining Malaysia's circulation pattern.

The world's oceans

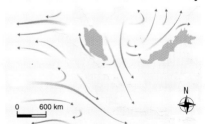

Arctic 4%
Atlantic 26%
Indian 21%
Pacific 49%

According to the relative sizes of the world's oceans, the Pacific is the world's largest ocean. (The International Hydrographic Bureau does not recognize the Antarctic Ocean.)

Causes of currents

When winds blow across the oceans, they drive the water under them by friction, imparting energy across the water surface as they do so and creating currents. Therefore, the paths of ocean currents closely follow the patterns of winds. These winds and currents are deflected from their original paths by the Coriolis force, which is due to the rotation of the earth. For instance, it has been found that in the open ocean the surface currents in the northern hemisphere are deflected by 45 degrees to the right of the wind direction. The Coriolis effect is small in Malaysia as the country lies only 2–7 degrees north of the equator; and the smaller the latitude, the lesser the effect. However, the direction of the monsoon winds in Malaysia is due to the Coriolis effect. Without it, the monsoons would come only from the north, not the northeast (northern winter) and from the south, not the southwest (northern summer).

The formation of waves is one effect of wind action. At the coastline, waves break and release their energy, resulting in coastal currents that cause deposition or erosion of beaches (see 'Waves'). Therefore, although currents cannot be seen, one indication of their presence is the direction in which a sand bar or spit grows (see 'Moving sands').

Circulation of currents in Malaysian seas

Northeast monsoon drift (northern winter)

Southwest monsoon drift (northern summer)

In the South China Sea and the Andaman Sea, the circulation of water is driven mainly by the monsoon winds. During the northeast monsoon (November–February), the northeast monsoon drift flows from the South China Sea through the Strait of Melaka and westward via the Andaman Sea into the Bay of Bengal in the Indian Ocean.

The circulation reverses during the southwest monsoon (May–September)

when the southwest monsoon drift flows west–east from the Indian Ocean to the Pacific Ocean and towards Malaysia. Both currents flow through the Strait of Melaka, but in opposite directions during different times of the year.

Although tidal and wave-induced coastal currents and thermohaline circulation also contribute to circulation in Malaysian seas, they play a smaller role than the monsoon currents.

Surface currents of the world's oceans

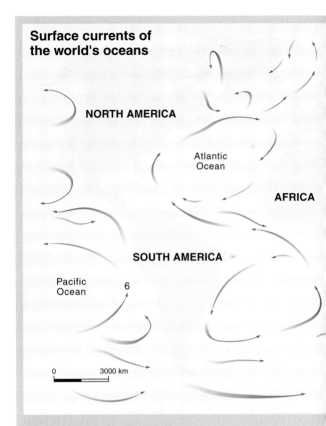

NORTH AMERICA

Atlantic Ocean

AFRICA

SOUTH AMERICA

Pacific Ocean

6

0   3000 km

Global oceanic circulation

The pattern of circulation of surface currents is driven by the Coriolis effect. This can be seen close to the equator where currents moving towards the poles flow clockwise in the northern hemisphere and anticlockwise in the southern hemisphere. The result is a series of spinning circles called gyres. The Coriolis effect piles water up on the left of each gyre, creating a narrow, fast-moving stream matched by a wider, slower returning current on the right. Warm currents move from

Currents are also generated by tides (see 'Tides'). Tidal currents are prevalent near coastlines and in estuaries. In the Strait of Melaka, which is straight and narrow, tidal currents are strongest at the centre because of the funnel effect.

Water density differences cause currents in the deep ocean where there are areas of hotter or colder water as well as areas of lighter, fresher water and of denser, more saline water. These differences in the temperature and salinity, or thermohaline, properties of water, give rise to water masses of differing densities and result in water movement. Denser cold water sinks to the bottom while lighter warm water rises to the surface. When water is too warm, evaporation occurs, increasing salinity and density.

Langmuir currents

Langmuir currents are vertical corkscrew motions, induced by winds, moving in opposite directions on the water surface. Their velocities are very small, and they can only be felt when other water movements, such as waves and tides, are weaker. They usually occur in enclosed areas, such as at the Sungai Merbok estuary in Kedah or in the more enclosed Penang Strait. A line of debris floating in the water between the corkscrew motions can indicate the presence of a Langmuir current.

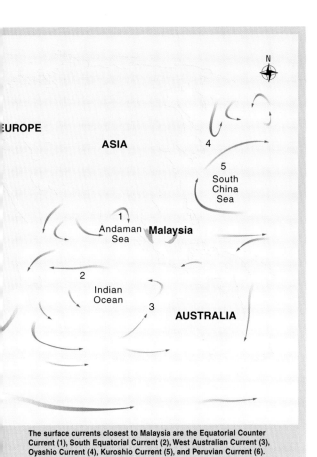

The surface currents closest to Malaysia are the Equatorial Counter Current (1), South Equatorial Current (2), West Australian Current (3), Oyashio Current (4), Kuroshio Current (5), and Peruvian Current (6).

the equator and cold currents return to it. These cold currents are important because they cause upwelling of nutrients which support fishes. Certain currents near the equator sometimes reverse their direction, affecting the onset of the Asian monsoon. A delay of the monsoon in countries like Malaysia and India can create drought and affect agriculture adversely.

Oceanic circulation

In each major ocean basin, there is a gigantic oval-shaped flow of currents, with currents on the western and eastern sides strongly influenced by the shapes of the adjoining landmasses and the rotation of the earth. Oceanic circulation therefore comprises many current systems that connect different seas and oceans, forming a global conveyor belt of water, heat and nutrients, as well as flotsam and jetsam.

Like the global winds that generate them, ocean currents play a major role in ensuring that the tropics do not overheat. Waters warmed in tropical countries like Malaysia, with a 30 °C average sea temperature (32 °C on land), flow northward to colder regions, while waters cooled at high latitudes flow south towards the equator.

Link between atmosphere and ocean

The dynamics of oceanic circulation are complex and depend upon a number of factors, including atmospheric circulation, the rotation of the earth, the presence of landmasses, and temperature differences in the seas. One example of the effect of landmasses is the monsoon system in Malaysia, which affects the circulation pattern of the seas. Another local atmospheric system are the diurnal land–sea breezes. While ocean circulation is driven by the same

A drogue

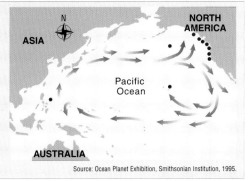

float

window shade drogue, an alternative to a parachute

weights

Measuring currents

Oceanic circulation is a continuum linked to the atmosphere which transcends national jurisdictions. Data collected is used for studying climate change, navigation and monitoring the ocean's species.

There are two methods of measurement: Lagrangian or Eulerain. The Lagrangian approach is to follow a body of fluid over time as it moves about. This is achieved by inserting dyes and drogues (floats with weights) into the water and tracking their speed and direction. The Eulerian approach is to describe the changes of fluid motion over time at fixed points in a grid system. Current meters are used to measure the speed of the current flow.

The Acoustic Doppler-effect Current Profiler can measure water currents at multiple depths, from the surface to the bottom of the sea. It gives a surface-to-bottom current speed and direction profile.

Tracing the flow

Recovery of objects that fall from ships, such as the 60,000 pairs of Nike shoes which spilled from a cargo ship in the northeastern Pacific in 1990, can confirm the circulation pattern of the oceans.

The map shows the surface ocean currents in the northeastern Pacific moving around in a slow circle (gyre). Oceanographers constructed a computer model that predicted the route of the shoes. The location of finds of shoes (indicated by red dots on the map) verified the model.

Source: Ocean Planet Exhibition, Smithsonian Institution, 1995.

elements and additionally by water density differences, it is more complex than atmospheric circulation because the expanse of the ocean is disrupted by landmasses against which water piles up. The relationship between the winds and the currents is close. If the passing currents are cold, the air temperatures of the landmass will drop; conversely, if the currents, such as those nearest to Malaysia, are warm, the air temperatures will rise. This link between ocean and atmosphere can also be seen in specific regional climatic and weather phenomenon, such as the El Niño Southern Oscillation (see 'El Niño: Oceanic aspects').

Importance of circulation

Oceans play an important role in climate change because of their ability to absorb as well as transfer heat. Ocean currents thus affect the climate of nearby landmasses. Oceans are also a great sink (store) for carbon and other excess greenhouse gases, helping to reduce the greenhouse effect by absorbing excess carbon.

Understanding oceanic circulation is essential for predicting long-term climate variability, monitoring biological species, and operating offshore structures. Understanding climate change depends on detailed scientific knowledge of the circulation of both ocean and atmosphere. Ocean circulation is an important input in the assessment of the transport and distribution of pollutants such as sewage wastes and chemical effluents.

Sailing solo around the world

Azhar Mansor setting out on his historic voyage around the world.

In 1999, Malaysian mariner Datuk Azhar Mansor attempted to become the first person to sail solo around the world non-stop on a new west–east route. To obtain the fastest route, he had to follow the paths of certain winds and ocean currents.

Unfortunately, on the 69th day of his voyage, the mast of his yacht, the *Jalur Gemilang*, broke in stormy seas. Nevertheless, he managed to sail on with a makeshift sail to the Falkland Islands for repairs, and then continued his voyage successfully. His attempt, covering 23,890 nautical miles and taking 188 days, was reclassified as a solo round-the-world voyage with one stop, and created a world record.

Monsoons and the seas

Many sea surface phenomena, such as waves and currents, result from the action of winds on the sea. As Malaysia and its surrounding seas lie within the monsoon belt, seasonal characteristics of the seas in terms of waves, currents and sea surface temperatures are largely shaped by the monsoons. Malaysia experiences two monsoons a year: the northeast monsoon, from mid-November to February, and the southwest monsoon, from mid-May to September. This phenomenon has shaped the country's development as well as its agriculture.

During the northeast monsoon, high waves are frequent in the stormy South China Sea off the east coast of Peninsular Malaysia. This adversely affects water sports and tourism activities.

Monsoon effects

The two annual monsoons exert a strong influence on Malaysia and its neighbouring seas. The Southeast Asian seas which border Malaysia are the Andaman, South China, Sulu and Sulawesi, and the Strait of Melaka. Of these, the South China Sea is the most important to Malaysia because the major part of the country's coastline faces it. Moreover, the alignment of the coastline is from southwest to northeast, parallel to the main wind direction during the northeast and southwest monsoons. Malaysia's location at the southwestern end of the South China Sea also exposes the country to both the oceanic and atmospheric effects of the northeast monsoon, which brings heavy rains, storms and floods.

Currents

Seasonal sea currents in the Southeast Asian seas are greatly influenced by the monsoons. Beginning from the autumn transition in October, the current called the north equatorial drift, which is driven by the Pacific trade winds, enters the South China Sea through the Bashi Strait between Taiwan and Luzon Island. This causes water to pile up in the Gulf of Tonkin which, in turn, leads to the establishment of a southward-flowing current. The current is thus mainly wind-driven and its strength is controlled by the intensity of the northeast monsoon. It is also caused by mean sea level differences. The current flows closely along the Vietnam coast on its way to the equator, taking with it cooler water into the equatorial region. Another branch of the north equatorial drift makes its way into the Sulu Sea. The

Heavy rains brought by the northeast monsoon, from mid-November to February, cause floods in the east coast states.

warmer current streams along the coastal waters of Sabah and Sarawak. Part of the current swings north as a counter current in the central South China Sea, while another part merges with the mean southerly stream that flows across the equator into the Java Sea. Part of the southerly current flows into the Strait of Melaka and the Andaman Sea.

During the spring transition in April, the southwesterly current in the South China Sea weakens quite considerably. A reversal of the current takes place in the

Causes of the monsoons

A monsoon is a massive cycle of air set in motion by temperature differences over land and sea. In summer, land heats faster because solar radiation does not penetrate its surface. Because sea water circulates, it stays cooler, although it stores heat in its upper layers for a long time. The monsoon winds are also directed by the tilt of the earth and its rotation about its axis.

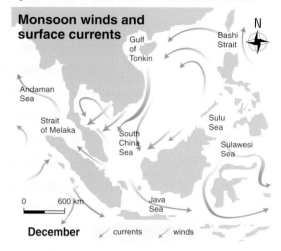

Monsoon winds and surface currents

December — currents — winds

The northeast monsoon (northern winter)

During the northern winter, the northern continents are cold because the sun is overhead in the southern hemisphere. The heavy cold air creates high pressure that forces the cold, dry, northeasterly winds to flow southwards. Where they cross the equator, they are deflected east by the earth's rotation. As they flow over the oceans, they gather moisture and bring heavy rains between November and February to countries such as Malaysia, Indonesia and northern Australia.

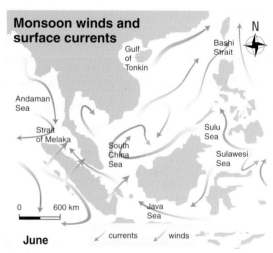

Monsoon winds and surface currents

June — currents — winds

The southwest monsoon (northern summer)

During the northern summer, the northern continents are warmer. As warm air rises, the pressure falls. This causes cooler air from the southern hemisphere to flow northwards. Where winds cross the equator, they are deflected to the east. The winds bring rain to much of Southeast Asia from May to September. In Malaysia, the southwest monsoon brings less rain than the northeast monsoon because the peninsula is sheltered by Sumatra lying to its west.

Java Sea and the South China Sea following the onset of the southwest monsoon around May. In the Java Sea, the current is caused mainly by the piling up of the water there as a result of the south equatorial drift. In the South China Sea, however, the monsoon contributes to a significantly larger wind-driven component to the current.

Mean sea surface temperatures

There is little variation in sea surface temperatures, which range mainly between 28 and 30 °C in the southern and central parts of the South China Sea during most of the year, except during the northeast monsoon. Associated with the cool, southwesterly current during the northeast monsoon, the sea surface temperature off the east coast of Peninsular Malaysia can drop to as low as 24 °C.

On the other hand, under the influence of the warmer current originating from the Sulu Sea, the coastal waters of Sabah and Sarawak are maintained in the range 27–29 °C. Thus, there exists a significant sea surface temperature difference, ranging from 2 °C to 5 °C, between the coastal waters of Peninsular Malaysia and those of Sabah and Sarawak.

As the sea surface temperatures in the South China Sea vary with the surge–lull cycle of the northeast monsoon, they exert a strong influence on the rainfall distribution in Malaysia during the northeast monsoon which brings about 50 per cent of the country's precipitation.

Rainfall is heaviest in Kelantan, Terengganu, and other east coast states of the Peninsula during November and December, and can cause severe flooding. However, during the late

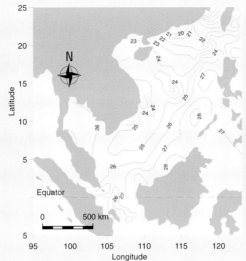

A map of Malaysian seas showing a typical sea surface temperature distribution in January during the northeast monsoon (in a non-El Niño year, 1996).

monsoon, the cooler waters off the east coast tend to reduce convection and rainfall while the warmer waters off Sabah and Sarawak enhance convection and rainfall there.

Source: Meteorological Department, Malaysia.

A satellite image illustrating a typical case of enhanced convection and rainfall over Sarawak during the northeast monsoon at the end of the year. The pink area indicates the densest clouds which bring the heaviest rainfall, while the purple, blue, green and white areas show progressively fewer clouds and thus less rainfall.

Sea level variations

The monsoons cause large seasonal sea level variations in Malaysia. Along the east coast of Peninsular Malaysia, the monthly mean sea level shows a peak during the northeast monsoon when the winds bring currents from the northeast, thus increasing the sea level; and a low during the southwest monsoon when winds from the southwest bring currents to the west coast, not the east. The difference varies from about 50 centimetres to the north to around 25 centimetres to the south. The maximum mean sea level along the east coast of the Peninsula occurs in November on the northern part and in December on the southern part.

Along the west coast of Peninsular Malaysia, there are two maxima (in June and November), and two minima (in February or March and September). The June peak is higher than the November one along the northern part of the west coast because it is exposed to the Bay of Bengal and the Indian Ocean, from where the southwest winds bring currents. The reverse is true in the southern part of the west coast where the winds bring currents from the northeast in November. This indicates the competing influence of the northeast and southwest monsoons along the Strait of Melaka. Moreover, the mean sea level variations decrease from north to south because the southern part of the Strait is sheltered from the monsoons.

There are relatively fewer seasonal sea level variations in Sabah and Sarawak than in Peninsular Malaysia because of the relatively weak seasonal currents in the nearby seas. As the main part of the coastline of the two states has a northeast–southwest alignment, significant sea level variation is seen only at the western end of Sarawak, where a maximum occurs during the northeast monsoon and a minimum during the southwest monsoon.

Monthly mean sea level variation

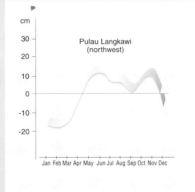

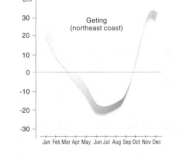

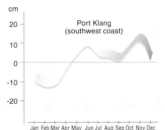

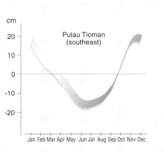

The monsoons cause monthly mean sea level variations from place to place in Peninsular Malaysia. Incomplete statistics only are available at present for Sabah and Sarawak.

Effects on waves

As with surface currents, waves are subjected to strong monsoonal influences. Waves are highest (2–4 metres) over the South China Sea during the northeast monsoon. Because of persistent north-easterly winds, swells (waves that do not break) are much more common than waves. Following monsoon surges, swells arriving from the northeast often exceed 5 metres. The rough seas hamper fishing activities. Coastal shipping and offshore oil drilling are also affected. Waves are relatively weaker (1–3 metres high) during the southwest monsoon.

They are larger over the coastal waters of Sabah and Sarawak than over the east coast of Peninsular Malaysia because of the wind fetch (distance) factor. During the spring transition, the sea is dominated by wind waves with heights of about 0.5–2 metres. Waves are much higher during the autumn transition.

Because of the northeast monsoon, seas off the east coast of the Peninsula are rough, forcing fishermen to stay on land and mend their nets.

El Niño: Oceanic aspects

Oceans, covering about 70 per cent of the earth's surface, act as huge reservoirs of heat energy from solar heating. The energy is then redistributed by oceanic currents to different parts of the globe. This distribution of energy, reflected in the temperatures of the upper layers of the oceans, interacts with the overlying atmosphere to influence climate. Abnormalities in these air–sea interactions can produce weather phenomena, such as El Niño. In Malaysia, the effects of El Niño are most pronounced in the eastern states of Sabah and Sarawak.

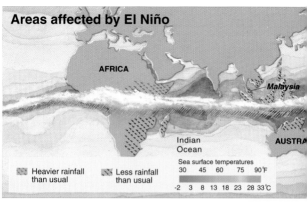

Areas affected by El Niño

Heavier rainfall than usual | Less rainfall than usual

Sea surface temperatures
30 45 60 75 90°F
-2 3 8 13 18 23 28 33°C

Malaysian boys wearing masks during the haze that enveloped the country for a few months in 1997. The haze was caused by forest fires aggravated by the drought which El Niño brought that year.

Weather phenomenon

In tropical regions, sea surface temperatures play an important role by driving the atmospheric wind circulation pattern, in addition to determining the most active rainfall areas or the regions of most active storms and typhoons. As the Pacific Ocean covers nearly half the earth's surface, any changes to the sea surface temperature of the Pacific will have far-reaching effects on the weather worldwide. Some of the major climate fluctuations that have had disastrous economic effects are caused by cyclical warming of the eastern part of the equatorial Pacific, part of the El Niño Southern Oscillation (ENSO) system, an atmosphere–ocean interaction.

The term 'El Niño', meaning 'the little one' in Spanish, after the Christ child, was used by Peruvian fishermen in the 19th century to describe the appearance of warm water at the end of the year (around Christmas) off the coasts of Peru, Ecuador and northern Chile. During this period, a warm northward current displaces the usually cool water, suppressing the upwelling of nutrients from below.

During El Niño years, the sea surface temperature becomes exceptionally high during the warm season (the cause of which is still unclear) and continues during the normally cold, upwelling season. Such unusual warming, lasting up to 12–18 months, is not a regular phenomenon, but occurs once in every 3–8 years.

The life cycle of an El Niño

The timing and intensity of each El Niño event varies. However, they follow a pattern, which can be divided into three phases: the onset, the mature phase and the decay or back-to-normal phase.

The onset begins around December, when the temperature of the warm ocean surface waters along the northwestern South American coast are above normal. Simultaneously, the atmospheric pressure falls in the eastern Pacific and rises in the west, causing the easterly trade winds to weaken. This, in turn, causes the warm surface waters that, under normal conditions have been piled over the western edge of the Pacific by the easterly winds in the equatorial Pacific, to move east.

This unusual warming continues into the following year, reaching peak intensity, or the mature phase, around the middle of the year. By now, the warmer waters have reached the Pacific coast of South America. This causes the sea level to rise by about 15 centimetres in the eastern Pacific, and to drop by about 10 centimetres in the western Pacific.

The increase in evaporation over the warmer ocean surface waters, coupled with a decrease in atmospheric pressure, causes convection rainfall over the eastern Pacific, triggering storms and floods in North and South America. Meanwhile, rainfall gets suppressed over the western Pacific, resulting in droughts in countries like Australia and Indonesia. Simultaneously, warmer ocean surface water

Changes in sea–air interaction during an El Niño

El Niño occurs when there is an unusual warming of the Pacific Ocean. This usually starts around December and continues for about a year, bringing drought to countries such as Malaysia in the western Pacific, but heavy rains to the Americas.

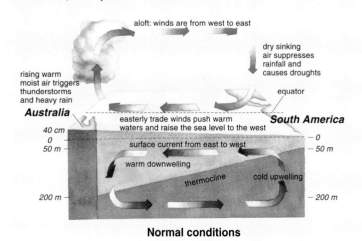

aloft: winds are from west to east

dry sinking air suppresses rainfall and causes droughts

rising warm moist air triggers thunderstorms and heavy rain

Australia

equator

South America

easterly trade winds push warm waters and raise the sea level to the west

40 cm
0
50 m

surface current from east to west

warm downwelling

thermocline

cold upwelling

200 m

0
50 m
200 m

Normal conditions

aloft: westerly winds weaken

dry sinking air suppresses rainfall and causes droughts

rising warm moist air triggers thunderstorms and heavy rain

Australia

equator

South America

easterly trade winds weaken or reverse causing warm water to flow back to the east

30 cm
0

15 cm
0

surface current reverses, causing thermocline to deepen in the east

50 m

thermocline

upwelling suppressed

50 m

200 m

200 m

El Niño conditions

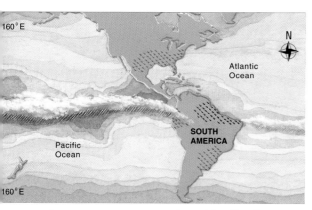

continues to moves westwards, and by October occupies the entire Pacific east of 160 degrees.

Almost a year after the onset, the back-to-normal phase begins when the easterly trade winds in the equatorial Pacific return to their normal speed, pushing the ocean surface waters back to the western Pacific and returning the thermocline closer to the surface in the eastern Pacific.

The atmospheric pressure seesaws back to its normal state of higher pressures over the eastern Pacific and lower pressures over the western Pacific. The sea level over the western edge of the Pacific is now about 40 centimetres higher than the eastern edge. When normal conditions are re-established, the countries in the western Pacific start receiving more rainfall, whereas those in the eastern part have less.

Effect on corals

Bleaching of *Acropora* corals off Pulau Tioman resulted from warmer waters in the South China Sea during the El Niño in 1998.

Higher sea temperatures during an El Niño cause corals to turn white. This 'bleaching' results when the zooxanthellae—algae living within coral tissues—are expelled by the stressed corals. Scientists are still uncertain as to how this expulsion occurs. Zooxanthellae lead a symbiotic existence within their host coral, providing it with food and oxygen. Since the algae give corals their colours, the corals' white skeleton is revealed when they are expelled. Bleaching, which can also be caused by water pollution, can kill large areas of corals as it causes them to lose their source of food—the zooxanthellae. However, corals can recover if temperatures return to normal.

In Malaysia, scientists at the Southeast Asian Fisheries Development Centre monitored the occurrence in the South China Sea in 1998 and discovered that about 15 per cent of the reefs were affected. In more severely affected areas, such as Pulau Labas near Pulau Tioman, up to 25 per cent of the reef was bleached. During that period, sea surface temperatures were 1–2 °C higher than normal, which is enough to trigger changes in the corals.

Sea surface temperatures and rainfall

Sea surface temperatures

In response to the strengthening or weakening of the easterly trade winds, the sea level fluctuates between the eastern and western Pacific simultaneously with sea surface temperature changes. During El Niño periods, the sea level tends to be higher over the eastern Pacific.

In spite of the large increase in sea surface temperatures over the eastern and central Pacific, very few changes in the sea surface temperatures take place over the western Pacific and South China Sea.

Effects on rainfall in Malaysia

A rice field dried up and cracked during the drought in Sabah in 1997, an El Niño year.

El Niño in drought-affected areas can aggravate forest fires, such as this one in Sarawak in 1998.

During an El Niño event, the northeast monsoon circulation is found to be less intense, resulting in weakened northeasterly trade winds. When the northeasterly winds are weak over the South China Sea, the sea surface temperature gradients also tend to be smaller. Since the sea surface temperature gradients over the South China Sea, especially those near the Borneo coast, are major driving forces behind the heavy rain spells during the monsoon season over Sabah and Sarawak, the impact of El Niño on the weather there is greater compared with Peninsular Malaysia. Rainfall in Sabah and Sarawak is greatly reduced. In March 1998, the drought in the north and interior of Sabah wiped out 5000 hectares of crops.

The result of sea surface temperature variations and sea level changes during an El Niño is a shift in the rainfall regime from the western Pacific to the central and eastern Pacific region, with disastrous economic consequences caused by the resulting droughts or floods. Although El Niño has been blamed for causing haze, El Niño itself does not cause haze. It causes drought, which can aggravate the forest fires that do cause haze.

In 1982–3, El Niño was estimated to have caused more than US$13 billion in damages and killed 2,000 people worldwide. These figures were eclipsed by the 1997–8 figures (about US$33 billion in property damage and 2,100 dead) as the 1997–8 El Niño turned out to be the worst in 150 years.

HOW EL NIÑO AFFECTS RAINFALL IN FOUR MALAYSIAN TOWNS

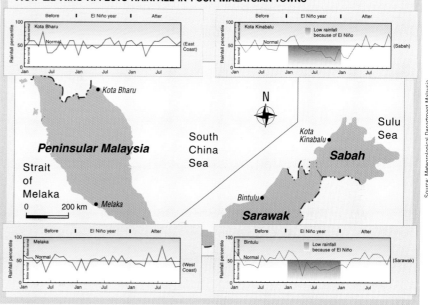

Source: Meteorological Department Malaysia

The result of coastal weathering, shattered granite creates a distinctive coastal form along the Penang coast.

A stranded coral platform on the beach at Tanjung Kemang in Port Dickson reveals that the sea level there was once higher.

A sand barrier is a feature caused by deposition of sediments (see 'Moving sands'). There is a settlement on this barrier at Marang in Terengganu.

A pebble spit at Teluk Nyiur on Pulau Langkawi is a result of deposition of materials by longshore drift.

The coastline of Pulau Rawa, a small island near Pulau Perhentian, is a popular scuba diving spot. The cracks and fissures of Pulau Rawa's underwater wall are home to many marine organisms.

GEOLOGY OF THE SEAS

Malaysia's lands and seas form the northern part of Sundaland—an amazing geographical region stretching down to Java and across to Sumatra and Borneo. The region was once entirely land, but much of the lower lying central portion was drowned during a major rise in sea level which occurred after the last Ice Age. Thus, the islands and landmasses we see today were formed. Malaysia's seas—the Strait of Melaka and the South China Sea—lie on the Sunda Shelf. The depth of water over the Sunda Shelf is very shallow, less than 200 metres. This feature has given rise to unique ecosystems, and has also allowed the geology of the sea bed to be explored. Drowned valleys on the Sunda Shelf reveal that the area was once land, drained by rivers. The valleys often have paired terraces indicating that over time the sea level did not simply rise but fluctuated—rising and falling over the period before the last major inundation. In Malaysia, there is much evidence of these fluctuations, especially from the most recent rise, 5,000 years ago, known as the Holocene transgression. Geological data and coastal formations in Malaysia, such as marine notches, show that the mid-Holocene reached its maximum height around 5,000 years ago when the sea level was 5 metres above its present level.

Apart from physical features, such as drowned river valleys and beach ridges, core samples of rocks and sediments from the west coast of the Peninsula have been analysed. The findings reveal fossilized plant remains, such as pollen of different types of vegetation, from 10 metres under the current sea level to some kilometres inland of today's coastline where mangrove remains have been identified. The basic outline of Malaysia was formed at the height of the Holocene transgression, but this original shape has been modified by the subsequent fall in sea level, by minor tectonic movements and, significantly, by coastal processes—the actions of tides and waves. Sedimentation and mangrove colonization have characterized large parts of the Malaysian coastline, especially around river mouths. In other areas, sandy beaches, spits and bars have been deposited by the action of the waves. In other places, again depending on the action of the waves, beach deposits and cliffs are being eroded and material transported along the coast. In fact, the evolution of the country's coastline is continual. In recent times, the hand of man can also be seen in the configuration of the coastline. Development close to the sea shore has exacerbated erosion in some areas; groynes and breakwaters have had some positive impacts but also interfered with the natural longshore drift process, ultimately causing unwanted build-ups of sediment; and mangroves have been destroyed exposing areas to erosion. Malaysia now has regulations prohibiting development too close to the high tide mark and people are realizing that often the cheaper and less destructive approach is to work with nature rather than against it. A clear understanding of geomorphological processes becomes vital in determining how future development can best take place.

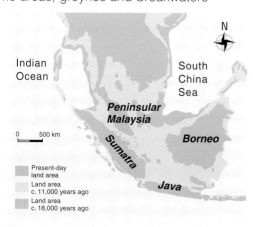

This map shows today's land areas as well as parts of the seas which were once land (Sundaland).

Sundaland

Sundaland is a geographical region comprising land areas of Peninsular Malaysia, Borneo, Sumatra, Java, all the smaller islands and shallow seas around these places, as well as the undersea area known as the Sunda Shelf. During the Pleistocene period from 1.6 million to about 10,000 years ago, the sea level was 100 metres below its present level and Sundaland was an extensive landmass. Subsequent rising sea levels have resulted in the separate islands and land formations present today.

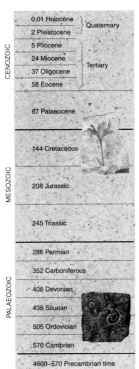

CENOZOIC	0.01 Holocene	Quaternary
	2 Pleistocene	
	5 Pliocene	
	24 Miocene	Tertiary
	37 Oligocene	
	58 Eocene	
	67 Palaeocene	
MESOZOIC	144 Cretaceous	
	208 Jurassic	
	245 Triassic	
PALAEOZOIC	286 Permian	
	352 Carboniferous	
	408 Devonian	
	438 Silurian	
	505 Ordovician	
	570 Cambrian	
	4600–570 Precambrian time	

Geological timescale in millions of years.

The Sunda Shelf

The Sunda Shelf, an area of 1.85 million square kilometres, is the most extensive continental shelf in the world. It lies in the southern part of the South China Sea between Peninsular Malaysia and Borneo, and in the Java Sea between Java and Borneo. Much of the surface of the shelf is flat, with an average depth of about 50 metres. Its outer edges, which are about 180–200 metres deep, drop suddenly into deep water.

Wide, drowned valleys, incised up to 20 metres deep, have been identified on the shelf. These reveal that during the last glacial period 80,000–18,000 years ago, the shelf was drained by three gigantic river systems—the East Sunda, the North Sunda and the Thai rivers.

Present-day rivers, such as Sungai Pahang and Sungai Kelantan in Peninsular Malaysia, and even the longest river in Southeast Asia, the Kapuas in Kalimantan, were mere tributaries then. As the whole region was one large landmass, both humans and animals could move freely between the Asian continent and the present islands of Borneo, Sumatra and Java. This explains some of the patterns of fauna and flora found in the wider region.

Present-day processes operating on the Sunda Shelf

Certain features found on the Sunda Shelf in the Strait of Melaka indicate that various processes are reshaping the undersea part of Sundaland today.

< 20 fathoms (<10 metres)	
20–25 fathoms (10 metres)	
25–30 fathoms (14.5 metres)	
30–35 fathoms (15 metres)	
35–40 fathoms (17.5 metres)	
> 40 fathoms (>20 metres)	
islands	

0   4 km

In the Pulau Sembilan group of islands, off Lumut in Perak, and near Pangkor, there are deep channels unrelated to the old drainage systems of Sundaland. Instead, they have been excavated by tidal scouring (erosion by tidal currents) between the islands.

Negeri Sembilan

Strait of Melaka

0   2   4 km

Port Dickson •

There are migrating elongated sand waves (sand ridges) along the bottom of the Strait of Melaka. These sand ridges, which are caused by deposition, are moved by currents along the sea bed and thus are being reshaped.

The drowned valleys, some 40–50 kilometres in width, often show paired terraces, suggesting that they are products of sea level fluctuations (see 'Sea level changes'). Rich concentrations of tin ore mined from depressions and potholes in current and buried river beds have been traced to the drowned and buried extensions of the corresponding rivers.

In addition to drowned valleys, there are also over-deepened parts unrelated to drainage systems. These 'blind' channels occur at and near entrances of narrow straits and among island groups such as Pulau Sembilan off Lumut in Peninsular Malaysia, and the Riau and Lingga groups to the south of Singapore. These channels could have been caused by tidal scouring or by fractures in the solid basement rocks.

There are other areas of the shelf with irregular bottom topography that indicate Sundaland was not flat. One such area, at the Strait of Gelasa between Bangka and Belitung islands, marks a regional divide that separated the East Sunda River from the North Sunda River. Blind channels and depressions upon these higher parts were probably also scoured by tidal currents when the sea was shallower.

Effects of the rising sea

The rising sea during the Holocene period not only inundated low lying areas but also converted the former single landmass into peninsulas and islands. When the sea rose, most of the corals fringing Sundaland were drowned because the water became deeper and the corals did not get enough light. However, corals along the shelf edge in the Strait of Makassar and the Sulawesi Sea, where conditions

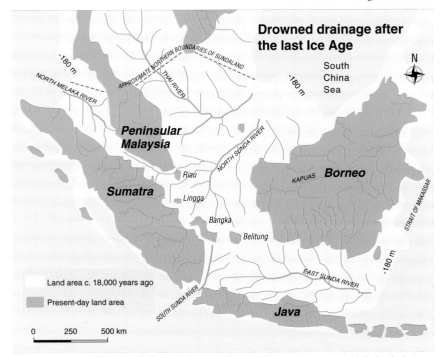

Drowned drainage after the last Ice Age

Drowned valleys on the Sunda Shelf indicate that there were rivers and that the area was once land. During the last glacial period (80,000–18,000 years ago), Sundaland was drained by three large river systems—the East Sunda, North Sunda and Thai rivers—as well as smaller rivers such as the South Sunda River and North Melaka River.

had been optimal for growth throughout geologic time, survived. These coral remnants now form a discontinuous barrier reef stretching from the Dent Peninsula in Sabah to the southern entrance of the Strait of Makassar.

Drowned hills were also seeded with new corals, some of which survived the rising sea to form patch reefs, atolls and cays. Off the west coast of Sabah, the Deluar shoals, Kalampunian Besar and Everett Reef are examples of cays, while the corals just east of Pulau Manukan form a patch reef.

When the marine inundation ended, some of the land margins, especially on islands, were fringed with corals. However, when the sea dropped to its present level from its Holocene high of about 5 metres above the present sea level, many corals fringing the mainland died because of permanent exposure to air. An exception are the corals off Tanjung Tuan (Cape Rachado) in Melaka, which survived because the waters around Tanjung Tuan, which was once an offshore island, were clearer.

Along the more sheltered coasts of Sundaland, such as along the Strait of Melaka, the rising sea drowned the mangroves, which retreated landwards. Subsurface studies offshore have revealed the presence of mangrove peat buried beneath recent deposits, usually of silt and mud. Beaches and barriers also migrated landwards, leaving a trailing wedge of sand deposits.

Subsurface structure

In the search for minerals and petroleum, various methods, including drilling and the use of artificial seismic waves, have been used to gain information about the subsurface structure of Sundaland.

Offshore tin exploration has established that the soft sedimentary cover of the Sunda Shelf consists of three units that together may reach 100 metres in thickness. The youngest, uppermost layer, around 20 metres deep, was deposited under marine conditions. Below this are river sediments. Conditions under which deposition occurred in the lowermost unit are unclear, but no marine fossils have yet been found. In most places, this soft sedimentary cover rests on hard pre-Tertiary rocks more than 65 million years old. From depressions on their surface,

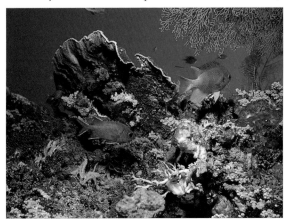

Pulau Sipadan, off Sabah along the Sundaland margin, became fringed with corals when the sea level rose after the last Ice Age, about 18,000 years ago.

Evidence of submergence and emergence in Sundaland

Various physical features in Sabah are the result of submergence (sea level rise or sinking land), or of emergence (sea level drop or land uplift), or both.

1. A cliff in Semporna, Sabah, formed largely by corals that emerged when the land was raised (during tectonic uplift).

2. The chain of reefs and islands off east Sabah, from Mabul extending to Ligitan and into the Meridian reefs in the Philippines, is part of a barrier reef formed by submergence (sea level rise).

3. The double-tiered wave-cut terrace at Bako, Sarawak, is caused by wave erosion as a result of a drop in sea level (emergence).

rich concentrations of tin ore have been extracted. In certain areas, known as geological basins, this cover overlies thick Tertiary sediments. Since 1976, substantial amounts of petroleum and natural gas have been produced from these Tertiary layers in the Malay basin (more than 10 kilometres thick and located off the northeast coast of the peninsula). To date, no commercial quantity of hydrocarbons has been found in the Penyu basin to the southeast, the other Tertiary basin in Malaysian territory.

Earthquakes and volcanic activity

The earth's surface is made up of several plates which converge, diverge or slide laterally against each other. These movements are driven by heat circulation in the earth's lower mantle and by gravitational forces at the plate boundaries, and are responsible for volcanic activity, earthquakes and the distribution of minerals and rock types.

The western and southern rims of Sundaland are bordered by deep submarine trenches on the ocean side. These are believed to be locations where one ocean crust moves beneath that of another plate.

Sundaland forms part of the southern portion of the Eurasian plate and is bordered on the west and south by the Indo-Australian plate. The Eurasian and Indo-Australian plates have been moving towards each other and the colliding margin has created the deep Java Trench off Java and Sumatra. As rocks deep below the islands readjust to compensate for the subduction process, geological activity is unleashed. Earthquakes result, the effects of which are sometimes felt on the west coast of Peninsular Malaysia. However, except for a small area in central and east Sabah, Malaysia is not prone to earthquakes.

Subduction also causes the development of volcanoes parallel to the trenches. However, as Malaysia lies towards the middle of a continental plate and not on the edge, the effects of volcanic activity are indirect, such as when Mount Pinatubo in the Philippines erupted in 1991 and deposited ash on Sabah and Sarawak.

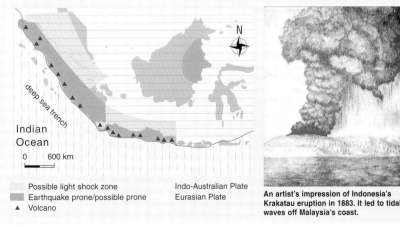

Possible light shock zone
Earthquake prone/possible prone
▲ Volcano

Indo-Australian Plate
Eurasian Plate

An artist's impression of Indonesia's Krakatau eruption in 1883. It led to tidal waves off Malaysia's coast.

Sea level changes

Apart from sea level changes due to tides, the mean level of the sea fluctuates, but because of the slow rate at which this occurs, the changes cannot be observed in a human lifetime. On a geological timescale, however, the sea level has recorded innumerable rises and falls. Information on the fluctuating sea has been gathered from marine sediments millions of years old. In Malaysia, there is much evidence from the most recent sea level rise, the maximum Holocene transgression, which occurred about 5,000 years ago.

A raised beach, such as this one at Sungai Ular in Pahang, indicates a drop in sea level.

Causes

Many factors cause long-term sea level changes (those occurring over thousands of years), in contrast to tidal or seasonal changes (those occurring over hours or months). These include glacio-eustatic changes (melting and growth of ice sheets and glaciers), glacio-isostatic changes (adjustment of the earth's lithosphere to changes in ice and water loads), plate tectonics and seafloor spreading (changes in the volume of ocean basins caused by changes in the spreading rates of the earth's crust and in the areas of ocean and land).

Another major factor is geoidal change. The geoid is the level surface of equal gravitational potential that the sea surface would assume in the absence of external disturbing forces, but because of the uneven distribution of mass in the earth, the geoid has undulations. Sediment compaction and subsidence also cause sea level changes.

Latest changes

During the height of the last glacial period (Ice Age), around 18,000 years ago, large tracts of ice sheets covered North America, Europe and Asia. The large amount of water stored as ice lowered the sea by at least 100 metres below its present level. Today, we are in an interglacial phase—a warm phase in which the ice sheets have retreated, thus releasing water back into the sea and raising it to its present level. The sea level rise, also termed the

Measuring change: Collecting data

To determine past sea level positions, the ground surface in which core samples are to be taken is levelled and then tied to the nearest benchmark level (a level determined by the Department of Survey and Mapping). The core sample elevation is then determined by relating it to the levelled ground surface. The surveying instrument that is used, called a level, basically consists of a telescope raised on a tripod stand with a spirit level attached, and a long pole with ruled measurements. Once the depth of the core has been determined, a core sample (a cylindrical specimen of sediment) is taken by drilling, then it is processed, analysed and carbon-dated (see 'Geological evidence: Core samples').

A level is used to measure the height of a coastal swamp at Penur, Kuantan.

Malaysia's changing sea level

Maximum height sea level reached	Bathymetry (m)
Present coastline	Political boundary
River	

The effect of the mid-Holocene high sea level on coastal areas is seen in many places in Malaysia. For example, in Perak shorelines 5,000 years old have been found 26 kilometres inland.

Holocene transgression, has been recorded at coastal and offshore areas in many parts of the world, including Malaysia.

A peat layer recorded at about 68 metres below the present sea level at offshore Terengganu, and radiocarbon dated to $11,170 \pm 150$ years ago, indicates that during that time, the coastline of Peninsular Malaysia extended far east in the South China Sea, while the present-day Strait of Melaka, Karimata Strait and part of the Java Sea were non-existent. A continuous landmass, Sundaland, covered the whole region of Peninsular Malaysia, Sumatra, Java and Borneo (see 'Sundaland').

Research done at various coastal sites in Peninsular Malaysia and in neighbouring countries, such as Thailand and Singapore, has revealed similar trends in sea level changes. For example, core samples taken from the Seberang Perai coastal plain on the northwest coast of the Malay Peninsula revealed that, like most plains in Malaysia, it had evolved after the mid-Holocene high sea level.

Records from Peninsular Malaysia show that the Holocene transgression reached its maximum height of about 5 metres higher than the present-day sea level about 5,000 years ago. Subsequently, the sea level has fallen slightly to its present position. The impact of Holocene sea level changes can be clearly observed in Malaysian coastal areas where the coastal lowlands of the east and west coasts of Peninsular Malaysia have largely evolved within this recent 5,000-year period.

Indications of sea level changes in Malaysia

A study of mollusc fossils (right) and foraminifera, a protozoa (such as an *amoeba*) with a shell (far right), as well as carbon-dating reveals their age from which an indication of sea levels over time can be made.

Evidence of long-term sea level changes is principally derived from a variety of indicators, physical, chemical, biological or archaeological in nature. These include raised beaches, sedimentary structures, beach rock, peat beds, soil formation in subaquatic deposits, prehistoric occupation levels and other geological and ecological data.

The well-preserved remains of hard-shelled molluscs and other fossils found in sedimentary rocks from the Palaeozoic (c. 570–245 million years ago), Mesozoic (c. 245–65 million years ago) and Cenozoic (c. 65 million years ago to the present) eras provide strong evidence of the fluctuating sea.

In the South China Sea and the Strait of Melaka, evidence of marine incursions is indicated by submerged peat layers, erosion and depositional features, mangrove sediments, raised marine terraces, marine notches, emerged coral reefs, marine molluscs and other features.

1. A rock island of limestone, drowned karst, off Pulau Langkawi. The island emerged because of a drop in sea level.

2. Owing to sea level changes, beach ridges can be seen along the coast of Miri in Sarawak.

3. The abrasion terraces found on these cliffs at Miri, Sarawak, reveal that there have been several sea level changes.

4. The beach rock at Pulau Singa Besar, Langkawi, was formed when the sands became cemented by calcium carbonate, organic matter and iron. The calcium carbonate in sea water dries and precipitates to form a cementing agent. When organic matter or iron in the sands oxidize, they also cement the sands.

5. A marine notch cut into a sandstone cliff at Kampung Air in Sandakan, Sabah, reveals that the sea level there was once higher than it is today.

6. Stranded coral heads are corals that emerged because of a drop in sea level.

Future trends

Predicting sea level trends

Projection of sea level trends depends very much on future climatic changes. Apart from the natural variability of the global climate, there is considerable evidence pointing to the increasing influence of human activities on the environment. The burning of fossil fuels, land use changes and agriculture are increasing the atmospheric concentrations of greenhouse gases—mainly carbon dioxide, methane and nitrous oxide— in some regions. These changes will alter regional and global climate and temperature and the amount of precipitation experienced in some places.

The Intergovernmental Panel for Climatic Change predicts that global mean sea level will rise by 3–10 centimetres per decade over the next century. It is estimated that even if greenhouse gas emissions are stabilized or reduced, sea level rise will continue for decades or even centuries because of the long response time of the global ocean system. It is, however, expected that regional sea level changes may differ from the global average owing to land movements and ocean circulation patterns, though these variations cannot be accurately predicted at present.

The bustling town of Kuantan in Pahang on the east coast of Peninsular Malaysia could be inundated if the sea level rises rapidly in the future. This is because it lies only 3–6 metres above the mean sea level.

Implications of sea level rises

Sea level is predicted to continue to rise worldwide. The long-term implications of this scenario will be quite disastrous, with existing tidal wetlands likely to be most affected. Peninsular Malaysia has wide stretches of coastal plain, most of which is less than 2 metres above the mean sea level. These precious areas are presently fully utilized either for agriculture, industrial activities or urban centres, and plans need to be formulated for if they are submerged.

Flooding, as a result of a rise in sea level, such as has occurred at Rungup in Perak (left), is likely in low lying areas in the future if sea levels rise. Bunds (far left) can be built to protect coastal areas.

Geological evidence: Core samples

Geological evidence in the form of undersea features, coastal landforms such as coastal plains and raised beaches, the position of coral reefs, and the analysis of rock and sedimentary deposits, all contribute towards providing a picture of how the earth changes over time. Sea level fluctuations can be charted and the world's changing climate recorded. Scientists in Malaysia have extracted core samples from sediments. By dating them and analysing the data collected, scientists have been able to reconstruct a picture of Malaysia through geological time.

A large mechanical drill (above left) can be used to obtain cores. A hand auger, called a gouge auger (above right), is also often used to drill for cores. Samples can be taken directly as well from an exposed cliff or mine exposure (right). Fossils such as this 480-year-old seashell (see inset), discovered near Pantai Remis, Perak, have been extracted from such mine exposures.

Core samples

A core sample is a cylindrical specimen of rock or sediment recovered by drilling. Locally, cores are obtained from coastal as well as offshore sediments. Suitable samples are then selected for various types of analyses. One type is pollen and spore analysis (palynology)—the microscopic study of the preserved remains (fossils) of pollen and spores.

From the cores retrieved, samples are selected from various depths and processed. Once processed and mounted on glass slides, the samples are analysed microscopically and the pollens and spores identified. To determine a sample's age, the radio-carbon (Carbon-14) dating technique is employed.

By correlating the information—from the depth of sampling, the sample analysis and the dating—the scientist can find out about the climate and environment, as well as the changing sea levels, at the location from which the core was taken at different times in history. From such analyses it can be shown that most coastal plains found in Peninsular Malaysia evolved 6,000–5,000 years ago when the last major high sea level—about 5 metres above the present-day level—was recorded throughout the region.

The effects of these sea level changes can be observed in many coastal areas of Malaysia today. One such location is on the Seberang Perai coastal plain, where a detailed study of core samples has been undertaken and the findings published.

Fossilization

❶ 10 million or so years ago
A dead animal or plant sank to the bottom of the sea. Its soft tissues rotted.

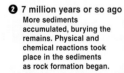

❷ 7 million years or so ago
More sediments accumulated, burying the remains. Physical and chemical reactions took place in the sediments as rock formation began.

❸ Today
Subsequent land movements raised the rock formation above sea level, and as a result of erosion the fossil became exposed.

Analysing core samples

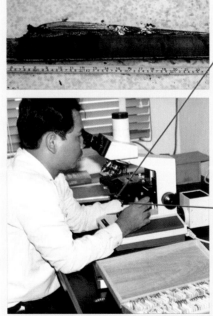

This close-up of a section of a core sample (top) from Pontian Kechil, Johor, shows peat and mud layers. The core sample is 0.5 metres long. A microscope (above) is used for looking at processed samples.

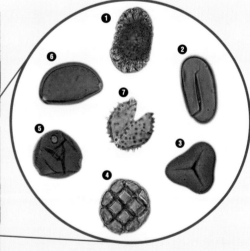

These microscopic views (shown at 1,000 times magnification) of pollen grains and spores from Malaysian plants reveal interesting shapes and patterns.

1. Tree pollen grain (*Dacrydium faloiformc*).
2. Fern spore (*Christella arida*).
3. Fern spore (*Acrostichum aureum*).
4. Tree pollen grain (*Acacia auriculiformis*).
5. Tree (durian family) pollen grain (*Durio macrophyllus*).
6. Palm pollen grain (*Daemonorops verticillaris*).
7. Nipah palm pollen grain (*Nypa fruticans*).

Interpreting a core sample from the Seberang Perai coastal plain

The Seberang Perai coastal plain is situated on the west coast of mainland Peninsular Malaysia facing Penang Island. Like most Malaysian coastal plains, it evolved after the mid-Holocene high sea level, which occurred 5,000 years ago (see 'Sea level changes).

Its main features are a series of low-profile beach ridges separated by swales or shallow depressions, which form broad, flat plains. Locally termed *permatang*, these ridges are aligned north–south, parallel to the present-day coastline. The Holocene coastal plain extended about 6–15 kilometres inland from the present coastline, and is widest in the areas bordering the main river channel of the area, the Sungai Muda.

The Quatenary (the most recent period of geological time, covering the last 1.6 million years) sediments obtained from this coastal plain comprise fluvial, beach, estuarine, lagoon and swamp deposits.

Radiocarbon dating performed on a peat sample collected from the base of the beach sand deposit (C), recorded an age of approximately 6,472 years. The peat layer (2 metres above the present mean sea level) represents an intertidal mangrove swamp deposit, indicating an approximate sea level position during its accumulation. This implies that the sea level 6,472 years ago was about 2 metres above the present level. Subsequent beach ridges were formed as a result of later fluctuations in sea level.

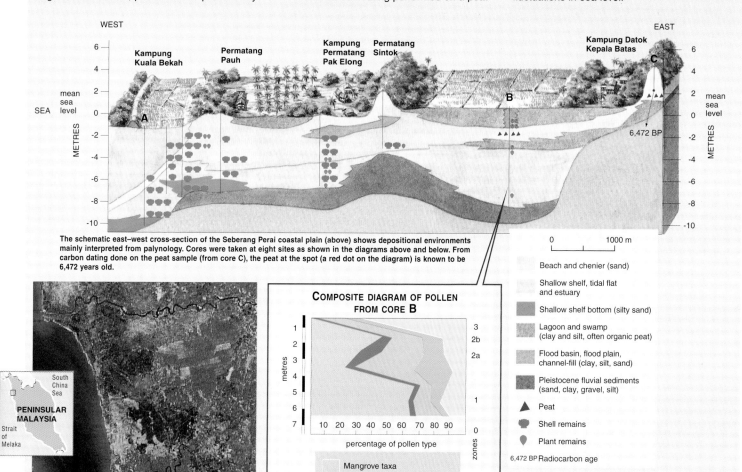

The schematic east–west cross-section of the Seberang Perai coastal plain (above) shows depositional environments mainly interpreted from palynology. Cores were taken at eight sites as shown in the diagrams above and below. From carbon dating done on the peat sample (from core C), the peat at the spot (a red dot on the diagram) is known to be 6,472 years old.

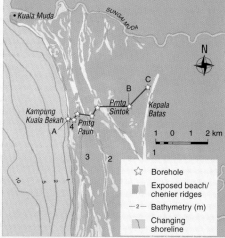

A satellite image of the Seberang Perai coastal plain.

Changing shoreline alignments on the Seberang Perai coastal plain occurred because of fluctuating sea levels after 6,472 years ago. The line A–C refers to the west–east cross-section in the diagram (top of page).

COMPOSITE DIAGRAM OF POLLEN FROM CORE B

percentage of pollen type

- Mangrove taxa
- Back mangrove
- Other pollen
- Unidentified
- Spores (excluding *Acrostichum*)

Legend:
- Beach and chenier (sand)
- Shallow shelf, tidal flat and estuary
- Shallow shelf bottom (silty sand)
- Lagoon and swamp (clay and silt, often organic peat)
- Flood basin, flood plain, channel-fill (clay, silt, sand)
- Pleistocene fluvial sediments (sand, clay, gravel, silt)
- Peat
- Shell remains
- Plant remains
- 6,472 BP Radiocarbon age

Palynological analyses of these sediments, from a representative core B (see diagram above), revealed four main pollen zones.

The bottommost zone (zone 0) was devoid of any pollen or spores; even if present during the sedimentation process, subsequent conditions were anaerobic and not conducive to preserving pollen remains. The horizon is represented by the mottled clay layer, which indicates an oxidizing depositional layer.

Zone 1 indicated a predominance of mangrove pollen, mainly from the *Rhizophora* species, but pollen from *Sonneratia*, *Avicennia* and the fern *Acrostichum* were also identified. Their presence showed that the sediment had been deposited in an estuarine or shallow area.

In Zone 2 (2a and 2b), mangrove floral components continued to predominate, but were much reduced compared with Zone 1. Instead, much of the pollen came from back mangrove taxa (plants thriving at the back of mangrove areas). These included mainly *Phoenix* and *Pandanus*, as well as terrestrial species such as *Castanopsis* or *Lithocarpus* pollen types, *Eugenia*, *Macaranga* and Gramineae. Their presence indicates that this sediment accumulated in a lagoon or swamp.

Zone 3 showed the disappearance of the mangrove pollens, a low frequency of terrestrial pollen, but more fern spores. This indicates that the sediment accumulated in an open, swampy environment which was disturbed. This sequence most likely marked the start of disturbance by humans to this environment. This can be deduced by the yellow-orange mottling in the sediment, which indicates there were some periods of exposure.

Some pollens and spores in the core sample could not be identified because they were corroded, folded, torn or obscured.

Coastlines

Malaysia's coastline is around 4800 kilometres long. The coastline is very varied and harbours changing environments. Over thousands of years, the coastline has evolved in various places into different shapes, with protruding deltas or indented inlets, and into different types, such as rocky or sandy. On the east coast of the Peninsula, where the waves are strong, there are many sandy beaches. In Sabah, the sea level rise during the Holocene period created a highly indented coastline. Mangroves fringe many parts of the coastline, especially where rivers meet the sea.

Penang Island has many sandy beaches popular with tourists.

Coastline evolution

Many factors cause coastlines to evolve. A key factor is sea level change, but waves, currents and tides also play their part. Whether the coastal rocks are hard or soft will determine how badly they are eroded by waves. So will the rock structure, as it is easier for waves to erode horizontal layers of rock. Coastline development also depends on whether there are protective mangroves.

Around 18,000 years ago, during the Pleistocene period, when the sea's surface was more than 100 metres below its present level, the outer edge of Sundaland formed the land–sea boundary. At the end of the glacial epoch, the sea began to rise rapidly and drowned the old coastal plains and river valleys of Sundaland. Borneo became separated from the Malay Peninsula. The general coastline configuration of Malaysia was formed at the height of this Holocene marine transgression—about 5,000 BP when the sea stood at 5 metres or so above its present level. This original outline was modified by the subsequent sea recession which has occurred, and by coastal processes and minor tectonic and volcanic activities—giving the Malaysian coastline its present form.

In Peninsular Malaysia, the sea recession initiated the filling in of estuaries and lagoons followed by barrier-lagoon formation on the east coast and mangrove advance interrupted by chenier (sand with shells) and beach ridge deposits on the west coast. The infilling process is ongoing in the Merbok estuary, but in the Klang and Pahang deltas, the coastline has protruded seawards. South Johor

Coastline shapes in Malaysia

Offset coastline: Kemaman, Terengganu

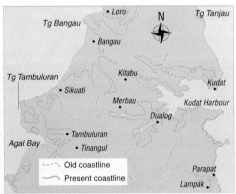

Coastline advances over thousands of years have converted former islands into headlands alternating with inverse J-shaped bays, creating the offset coastline of southern Terengganu. Rivers drain into the sea at the northern end of each bay in response to the south-flowing drift.

Ria coastline: Kudat Peninsula, Sabah

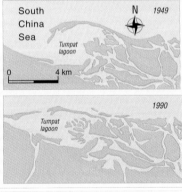

This ria coastline, with its highly indented shape, at the Kudat Peninsula in Sabah, was formed when river valleys were drowned as a result of rising sea level and/or subsiding land.

Man-made coastline: Melaka

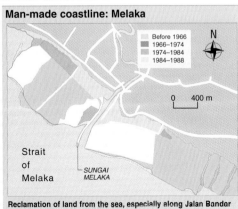

Reclamation of land from the sea, especially along Jalan Bandar Hilir, has created this man-made coastline in Melaka. The reclaimed area is now a thriving commercial centre with hotels, shopping complexes and restaurants.

Lagoon coastline: Tumpat, Kelantan

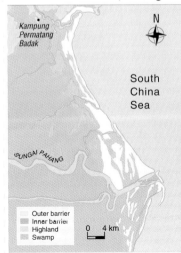

The dynamic nature of a barrier-lagoon environment is illustrated in Tumpat, Kelantan. The barrier spit developed westwards and attached itself to the mainland, initially enclosing the lagoon and creating a sheltered environment suitable for recreational activities and cage culture. When the end of the spit attached to the mainaind started to break up, large waves entered the lagoon and made such activities no longer possible.

Delta coastline: Pekan, Pahang

This delta coastline is at Pekan, on the east coast of Pahang. Sediments brought down by a river are usually transported out to sea by currents. A delta is formed when there is a surplus of such sediments. Initially, the sediments are laid down in the river mouth and estuary. When these are filled in, the coastline protrudes seawards in various formations. The Pekan delta has a cuspate (pointed) form in which the flanks of the delta have a concave outline. It has a complicated history, and the present shape is the result of several shifts in the mouth of the Pahang River.

A depleting sandy beach at Pantai Batu Buruk, Kuala Terengganu, awaits renourishment with sands dredged from offshore and channelled along pipes.

and part of Pulau Langkawi still have the appearance of a drowned coastline.

In Sarawak, the sea recession resulted in general mangrove advance, especially along the large delta at the mouth of the Rajang and Baram rivers, and minor raised beaches at Sematan, Bintulu and Miri.

In Sabah, the sea transgression resulted in a highly indented ria coastline, and transformed some high coastal ridges into islands. An example is the present Klias Peninsula, which became an island but later was rejoined to the mainland when the sea retreated following the Holocene transgression maximum. The infilling process that usually accompanies sea recession is incomplete in Sabah, where the coastline remains highly indented with many natural harbours. Small sectors of coastline advance include the beach ridge plain and small Papar delta along Kimanis Bay and the beach ridge plains of Karambunai, Kota Belud and Sikuati.

Coastline progradation (advances over thousands of years) in Malaysia has been intermittent. Many ancient coastlines are recorded in the form of old beach ridges. By analysing these progressive changes, a coastline can be reconstructed. As evolution occurs, bays are filled and headlands eroded, and coastlines shortened and straightened.

Human impact on the coastline

Of the Malaysian coastline, 52 per cent has beaches and slightly less is fringed by mangroves. Only a very small proportion is rocky or reclaimed.

In places, mangroves, which lie below the high tide level, have been converted to agricultural land, and such areas have to be protected by bunds. Such reclaimed land occupies large areas of coastal Kedah and west Johor. In some locations, the mangroves in front of the bunds are narrowing or have even disappeared. The bunds then come under direct wave attack, and where it is not economical to protect the coastline, the bunds have been relocated landwards and some agricultural land has been abandoned to the sea. In recent years, coastal land reclamation has been carried out extensively in towns such as Kota Kinabalu and Melaka.

About 30 per cent of the Malaysian coastline is eroding, at varying rates. This can cause problems. Both mangroves and beaches can be affected. Causes are a mixture of natural and human. Attempts to stabilize coastlines include structural measures such as sea walls and breakwaters. Coastline change is usually gradual and hardly detectable unless monitored over decades. However, in river mouths where sediment supply is large, change can be dramatic.

Where is the coastline?

Although a coastline is commonly understood to be the boundary demarcating land and sea, there is much confusion regarding what it represents and its actual position on the ground. There is even a lack of agreement among experts over the definition of the term 'coastline'. Moreover, the term is often confused with 'shoreline', which is more commonly used in the United States of America.

The coastline has been variously defined as the position of the high water mark, the mean sea level or mid-tide, or the land margin in the backshore zone. In the National Land Code of Malaysia, the position of the high water mark during spring tides is regarded as the 'shoreline'. In some international encyclopedias, the coastline is referred to as the low water limit and sometimes the high water limit.

For practical purposes, the high water mark, indicated by the presence of strand deposits or the seaward margin of land-based vegetation, represents the position of the coastline. Such a working definition is necessary in order to be able to monitor changes along a coastline. The position of the coastline is a fairly permanent feature compared with that of the shoreline, the position of which advances and retreats with the daily movements of the tides.

A typical coastal profile on the east coast of Peninsular Malaysia

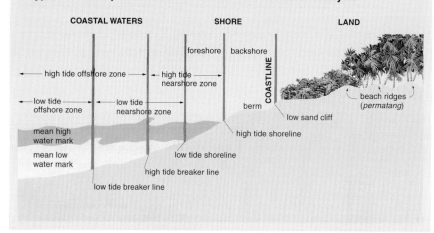

Types of coastline in Malaysia

A slumping cliff coastline at Miri, Sarawak, provides sand for the beach below.

A mangrove-fringed coastline at Johor, on the west coast of Peninsular Malaysia.

A rocky coastline at Pulau Perhentian, off the east coast of Peninsular Malaysia.

An eroding sandy coastline along the old coastal road between Miri and Kuala Baram in Sarawak.

There are many types of coastline in Malaysia, with sandy, rocky beaches forming the main type. Large stretches of mangroves also fringe some coastlines, especially around Peninsular Malaysia and Sabah. Other types of coastlines include rias and cliff-faced shores.

MALAYSIAN COASTLINE TYPES AND LENGTHS (km)

	MANGROVE	BEACH	OTHERS	TOTAL
Peninsular Malaysia	921	1024	27	1972
Sabah	973	703	126	1802
Sarawak	238	777	20	1035
Total	2132	2504	173	4809

Moving sands

The features seen along Malaysian coasts are the result of erosion and deposition. They reflect the dynamic equilibrium between the various forces at work in the coastal environment, such as tides, waves and currents. Constant movement of sand and shingle is a key process which creates some of Malaysia's characteristic coastline formations—golden strands of beach, barrier islands and mangrove-lined estuaries.

In Malaysia, there are beaches with sands of different colours (white, golden and black) depending upon the mineral composition of the rocks in the area. Beaches with golden sand, such as this one in Terengganu, are found all along the east coast of Peninsular Malaysia.

Beach sediments

Weathering and human activities such as forest clearance cause soil erosion whereby sediments are carried by rivers into the sea.

The sediments found on the beach as well as offshore are mostly derived from rocks through the processes of weathering, transportation and deposition. By far the largest supply is that brought in by rivers which transport and ultimately deposit their suspended load of sediments in the sea. These sediments are the products of erosion of rocks inland. The other source of sediments on the beach is the erosion, by wave action, of rocks along the coast. Such sediments are subsequently dispersed along the shore by longshore drift. The actual proportion of sediments from these two sources varies from locality to locality.

In addition to sand, which is the most common sediment and which is usually associated with beaches, the sediments found in the coastal zone may also include coarser grain sizes such as pebbles, cobbles and boulders, as well as finer grains of silt and clay. As a consequence of wave action offshore and on the beach, sediments gradually become sorted according to grain size. Thus, coarse sand is usually found on the upper portions of a beach. This grades into fine sand near the shoreline and eventually into silt and mud farther offshore.

Typical depositional features along a coast

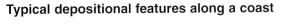

A spit with a crescent-shaped bar at Pantai Hiburan, Rompin, in Pahang. A spit is formed by longshore drift carrying sediments along a beach.

mangroves

An elongated spit around a lagoon on reclaimed land at Port Dickson. A spit is a long ridge of sand or gravel extending out from a beach into open water.

beach

bay

lagoon

barrier islands

spit

cliff

tidal inlet

A settlement on a barrier at Marang, Terengganu. A barrier is a long, narrow, low lying offshore island of sediments parallel to the shore. It is separated from the mainland by a lagoon.

A small baymouth barrier in Sarawak. A baymouth barrier is formed when a spit grows until it extends completely or almost completely across the mouth of a bay.

TOP: The black sand beach at Pasir Hitam, Pulau Langkawi, gets its colour from the minerals ilmenite and tourmaline, derived from the erosion of ilmenite-rich rocks in the area.

BOTTOM: This white beach at Sungai Sembilang, Selangor, is made up of shell fragments which consist of calcium carbonate.

In terms of mineral composition, most beach sands consist principally of quartz, the most common durable mineral in rocks. The less resistant minerals are mostly removed by weathering. White mica or muscovite is sometimes found in varying proportions, depending on the locality, as fine white flakes. The other common component of beach sands is shell fragments which are made of calcium carbonate. One beach with abundant shell fragments is Pantai Remis, south of Jeram in Selangor.

A sand bar at Tanjung Rhu, Pulau Langkawi. There are various types of bars which are usually exposed during low tide and submerged during high tide.

tombolo

baymouth sand bar

A tombolo is formed when a sand bar links an island or a stack to the mainland. This example can be seen at Kemasik, Terengganu.

A bayhead beach at Teluk Senajang, Terengganu. This is formed when there are different types of rocks being eroded at different rates, thus forming an indentation.

Man-made structures on the beach

Effects of human activity

A number of structures have been built along the Malaysian coast to protect it from waves. Unfortunately, these man-made structures disturb the state of dynamic equilibrium between sediment deposition and erosion on the beach. Since they interfere with the natural transport of materials along the beach by longshore drift, these structures often cause undesirable deposition and erosion, not only in their immediate vicinity but much farther downdrift. Dredging can temporarily minimize the problems but does not solve them and is sometimes difficult and expensive.

Groynes

A groyne is a low structure built on a beach, often at right angles to it, in order to check erosion on that particular stretch of the beach. Usually constructed in a series, forming a groyne field, groynes impede the normal longshore drift of sand and cause it to be trapped on the updrift sides, thus eventually building a wider beach there. As a result of the interruption in the supply of sediment, severe erosion occurs farther downdrift. This effect can be seen at several beaches along the west coast of Peninsular Malaysia.

Breakwaters

A breakwater is a structure built out in the sea or into it to intercept waves and protect a harbour. It may be attached to the beach or detached from it. Such a structure interferes with the natural longshore transport of sediments because longshore currents are weaker behind it. Consequently, sediment deposition occurs there whilst severe erosion can take place downdrift. Sand trapped updrift of an attached breakwater may eventually block the entrance to a harbour. This build-up has to be removed by dredging, which is expensive. Breakwaters have been built at various Malaysian river mouths and harbours, such as at Chendering in Terengganu.

Jetties

A jetty is often built at the mouth of a river to protect it from waves, to stabilize the channel, and to minimize the deposition of sediments there. However, increased deposition occurs on the updrift side and may eventually obstruct the channel. On the downdrift side, erosion takes place and causes further problems. One example of this is at the mouth of the Melaka River before the recent land reclamation project.

Longshore drift

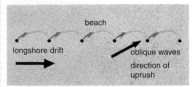

beach

longshore drift

oblique waves

direction of uprush

Longshore drift is the process that occurs when waves are driven obliquely against the coast. Sediments are washed up on the beach in a forward sweeping curve. The backwash then drags the material down the beach slope until it is caught by the next cycle of waves. By repetition of this zig-zag movement, sediments are moved along the shore.

beach

groyne

erosion

sea

deposition

A groyne at Bagan Tamsang, Butterworth.

The deposition of sediments on one side of a groyne causes the unprotected side of the coast to be deprived of these sediments and to be eroded by waves.

A breakwater with sediments inside the harbour at Chendering, Terengganu.

A

beach

erosion

deposition

sea

B

beach

erosion

deposition

sea

breakwater

In diagram (A), one end of the breakwater is attached to the coast. As it breaks the force of the oncoming waves at some distance from the coast, it creates a zone of quiet water behind it. Sediments get trapped in this zone, while erosion occurs farther downdrift where the coast is unprotected. In diagram (B), the breakwater is built away from the coast, but the same process happens and sediments get trapped in the quiet zone behind and erosion occurs farther downdrift.

A structural jetty made of rocks at Melaka.

Marine biodiversity in coral reefs

The greatest marine biodiversity in Malaysia is found in coral reefs which support a vast variety of organisms.

1. Bottlenose dolphin (*Tursiops truncatus*)
2. Barracuda (*Spyraena qenie*)
3. Porcupine fish (*Diodon hystrix*)
4. Spotted eagle ray (*Aetobodus narinari*)
5. Plate coral (*Montipora* sp.)
6. Green turtle (*Chelonia mydas*)
7. Cave soft coral (*Dendronephthya* sp.)
8. Barrel sponge (*Xestospongia testudinaria*)
9. Razor fish (*Xyrichtys* sp.)
10. Moray eel (*Muraenidae* sp.)
11. White-tip shark (*Carcharhinus longimanus*)

12. Banded pygmy angelfish (*Genicanthus* sp.)
13. Lion fish (*Dendrochirus* sp.)
14. Blue trigger fish (*Odonus* sp.)
15. Whip coral (*Ellisella* sp.)
16. Brain coral (*Goriastrea* sp.)
17. Emperor angelfish (*Pomacanthus imperator*)
18. Gorgonian coral (*Subergorgia mollis*)
19. Butterfly fish (*Heniochus* sp.)
20. Bubble coral (*Cycloseris* sp.)
21. Cleaner shrimp (*Lysmata amboinensis*)
22. Cup coral (*Tubastrea faulkneri*)

23. Royal dottyback (*Pseudochromis paccagnellae*)
24. Reef crab (*Carpilius maculatus*)
25. Blue-spotted stingray (*Tasniura lymma*)
26. Giant clam (*Tridacna maxima*)
27. Anemone fish (*Amphiprion percula*)
28. Sea anemone (*Heteractis crispa*)

The segmented worm (*Protula magnifica*) lives in a tube completely buried in coral.

MARINE BIODIVERSITY

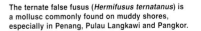

A frigate bird flies off with a fish it has robbed from a common tern.

The term biodiversity, short for biological diversity, generally refers to the variety of living organisms and the habitats in which they live. The simplest way of quantifying biodiversity is to count the number of species. However, species diversity is not just about numbers. Also important is the range of evolutionary and ecological adaptations species display in the environments in which they live.

Of the 33 main groups of animals, 28 have representatives in marine systems and 13 are entirely marine. Malaysian seas are home to many of these major groups. Species diversity increases towards the tropics in almost all groups of animals. The reasons for this include the length of time the species have existed in tropical regions, the more stable climate over geological time, warmer temperatures, and the greater amount of sunlight which allows high levels of photosynthesis in phytoplankton and other plants—thus building up large food reserves at the bottom of the food chain.

Of the tropical seas throughout the world, those of the Indo-West Pacific region, where Malaysia's seas are situated, are the most diverse. An indication of this is that of the world's 20,000 fish species 4,000 are found in Malaysian seas compared with only 500 in the Bahamas, in the tropical Atlantic region. This high species diversity in the Malaysian seas is even more marked in marine reptiles. Of the 50 species of sea snakes worldwide, 22 are found in Malaysia, and 4 out of the 7 sea turtles species nest on Malaysia's shores.

The seas and coastlines of Malaysia support many different ecosystems, each with its unique range of species, contributing to the country's overall high levels of biodiversity. There are the numerous worms and molluscs on the mud flats, uniquely adapted tree species in the mangrove-lined estuaries, and a myriad of coral and fish species in the coral reefs. The communities of the coral reefs exhibit the highest concentrations of biodiversity. The glorious technicolour hard and soft coral species range from branching staghorn and ridged brain coral to shimmering sea fans and whips, moving with the currents. A vast and varied range of fish live in this designer habitat, their colours and patterns complementing those of the coral.

Many organisms have adapted to survive in specific environments. Marine organisms of the intertidal zone are good illustrations of this fact. The creatures of these areas have devised ways of surviving both in and out of the water. Barnacles keep themselves hydrated—enclosed within waterproof plates—when the tide goes out, and ghost and fiddler crabs have tufts of abdominal hair to absorb the water from damp sand. Yet other organisms have adapted to living in the darker depths of the sea—red seaweeds, for example, have pigments that allow them to make use of the blue light that penetrates to these depths.

Included in the roll-call of marine creatures are mammals such as Fraser's dolphin and the oceanic and shore sea birds which thrive off the rich pickings of Malaysia's productive seas.

The ternate false fusus (*Hermifusus ternatanus*) is a mollusc commonly found on muddy shores, especially in Penang, Pulau Langkawi and Pangkor.

Plankton

Plankton are generally tiny organisms with limited locomotive ability which live in natural bodies of water. Plant plankton (phytoplankton) and animal plankton (zooplankton) are vital organisms as they form the basis of the food chain in the sea. Many of the world's numerous species of plankton exist in the Malaysian seas. Phytoplankton live in the surface waters where they can photosynthesize, while the larger zooplankton are found throughout the water column. Since plankton provide food for fish and other marine organisms, as well as for each other, phytoplankton is now artificially cultured as feed for fish and prawns.

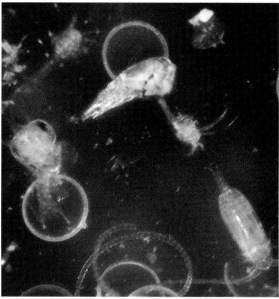

Various species of plankton drift along with the currents. Many cannot swim and can only make short, darting movements, mainly vertically.

Characteristics

The word 'plankton' comes from the Greek word *planktos* which means 'to wander'. Plankton are, in fact, limited in their ability to move horizontally, such movement being determined by currents. They are thus often associated with specific water masses. One group of zooplankton, arrow worms (Chaetognatha), are used as indicator organisms for particular currents or water masses. Many plankton are able to control their movement vertically, moving up or down tens or even hundreds of metres through the water column, and many species exhibit a regular pattern of daily vertical migration.

There are two main types of plankton: phytoplankton (plants) and zooplankton (animals). They vary greatly in size, from sub-micron nannoplankton to macroplanktonic jellyfish and colonial salps which can grow up to 1 metre or more. Few plankton are easily visible. Even the larger ones, such as jellyfish and salps, are hard to see because they are almost transparent. However, their presence can often be indicated by the colour of the water.

A phytoplankton net, used for collecting plankton, with 0.21 millimetre mesh pore, is made of basket weave monofilament nylon, which gives it strength as well as high porosity, reducing clogging.

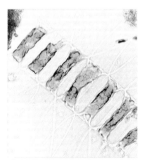

Skeletonema, phytoplankton common in Malaysia. In order to capture as much sunlight as possible, they have evolved to form chains which allow them to stay suspended, exposing as great a surface area to the sunlight as possible in relation to their volume.

Chaetoceras species of phytoplankton dominate the coastal phytoplankton in Malaysian seas. They exceed other genera not only in the number of species but also in the number of individuals. Like other species, they form chains to stay suspended in the water.

Artificial culture of phytoplankton

Scientists have long been able to identify individual phytoplankton and grow them in artificial media or nutrient-enriched filtered sea water. Many marine biological laboratories maintain various species of phytoplankton in artificial cultures. Such cultures are being grown in ever larger volumes as feed for fish and prawn larvae in the aquaculture industry.

The picture above shows cultures of phytoplankton in three large glass carboys, at different stages of development, with the densest and oldest culture (just over a week) on the left. Sometimes artificial light is used. Air is bubbled into the bottle to keep the plankton dispersed as well as to supply them with oxygen and carbon dioxide.

For instance, the greenish colour of coastal waters is the result of large numbers of green phytoplankton. Occasional red tides occur when certain species of dinoflagellate with red eye spots bloom. Fish eggs and early larvae are planktonic and these form a special class known as ichthyoplankton.

Phytoplankton

Many species of phytoplankton are found in the Malaysian seas. Among the most common are *Chaetoceras*, *Coscinodiscus* and *Rhizosolenia*. Phytoplankton are the main primary producers in water bodies and form the base of the food chain in the oceans. The production of phytoplankton depends on a number of factors, the most important of which are light (for photosynthesis to occur) and mineral nutrients (for growth). Where nutrient supply is adequate, as in many coastal waters and in upwelling regions of oceans, phytoplankton productivity will usually be high. In some places, plankton are present in such large quantities that they can directly support some of the world's largest mammals, such as baleen whales.

Diatoms—microscopic unicellular plants belonging to the algae class called Bacillariophyceae—constitute the major part of phytoplankton. They occur individually and in colonies. Enclosed in a siliceous cell wall, each cell consists of two parts that fit into each other to form a case for the living cell within. In the protoplasm are chloroplasts containing the green pigment chlorophyll and a brown pigment, giving the phytoplankton their characteristic golden green colour.

Many species of diatoms have adaptations to help them stay suspended in the water. These include the ability to link together to form long chains of individuals. The smaller plankton, called nannoplankton, are found in greater abundance than the larger phytoplankton and form the basis of the food supply for the larger zooplankton and the developing larvae of other species.

Zooplankton

Zooplankton are animals which drift along with the currents. The largest group are crustaceans and their larvae, such as prawns or crabs, which live at greater depths as adults. Of the crustaceans, the copepods are the most abundant. Many species of copepods are found in Malaysia, including *Undinula vulgaris*, *Labidocera acuta*, *Eucalanus subcrassus*, *Centropages furcatus*, *Euchaeta concinna* and *Oithona plumifera*. Some of the larger crustaceans—copepods, crab larvae and shrimp larvae—as well as jellyfish and arrow worms are visible to the naked eye. The rest are microscopic.

Many of the zooplankton are herbivores (feeding on phytoplankton); others are carnivorous (feeding on other zooplankton); while yet others are omnivorous. The zooplankton use their appendages to create currents of water which carry the plankton towards their mouths.

Arrow worms (*Sagitta* sp.) are another common type of zooplankton found in Malaysian seas. They belong to the phylum Chaetognatha and are transparent, elongated animals, They can grow up to 15 millimetres in length. They are voracious predators and have spines on both sides of their heads to catch their prey.

Zooplankton thrive in coastal Malaysian seas, such as the South China Sea, where nutrients are readily available and warm conditions prevail. Most zooplankton rise towards the surface of the sea at night and move down during the daytime. The precise reasons for this are not known, but the cover of darkness might make them less prone to being taken by predators.

Eutrophication

When phytoplankton find themselves in ideal growth conditions they bloom (multiply very rapidly) almost overnight. Like most living organisms, these microalgae consume oxygen, and in high concentrations can deplete all the dissolved oxygen in the water. This happens only at night because during the day these plants produce oxygen as they photosynthesize. Depletion of dissolved oxygen can be fatal to other organisms, such as fish, living in the same body of water. When nutrients become persistently abundant (for example, runoff from agricultural fertilizers), the density of phytoplankton in a body of water can remain high over a long period of time. This overabundance of plankton and consequent depletion of oxygen is known as eutrophication.

Another aspect of the eutrophication process is a change in species composition of phytoplankton. Sometimes the new and abundant species are not suitable food for the zooplankton grazers and the number of zooplankton drops despite the overall higher productivity in the water. With fewer grazers, the animals higher up the trophic level, such as fish, are also adversely affected.

Red tides

Most plankton blooms colour the water green because of the presence of the photosynthesizing pigment chlorophyll. Occasionally, when certain species of a group of plankton, known as dinoflagellates, are in bloom, the colour of the water turns red. This is because of the dinoflagellates' red eye spots which cause a 'red tide'. As many species of dinoflagellates contain a toxin deadly to humans, there is a real danger for those who consume seafood (especially shellfish) which has fed on plankton during a 'red tide'. The precise reason for the occurrence of red tides is not known. In many places, dinoflagellates are usually present in very small numbers, and in most places they do not bloom into red tides. Since nutrients are a requirement for plankton blooms, this is likely to be one of the main causes. In Malaysia, most red tides occur off the coast of Sabah and Sarawak and are rarely seen off the coast of Peninsular Malaysia.

Sabah on red tide alert

KOTA KINABALU: A new-wide red tide alert has been issued by the Fisheries Department here following a recent outbreak in coastal waters around Sabah.

Above: The skeleton of *Pyrodinium bahamese*, the dinoflagellate which causes 'red tides'.

Left: Red tides cause concern over the contamination of shellfish.

A selection of zooplankton and phytoplankton

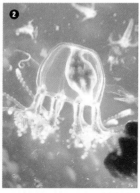
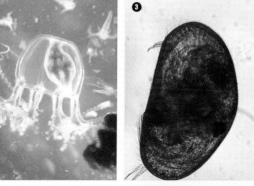

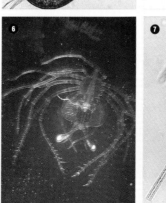
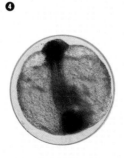

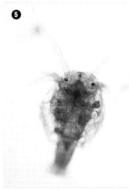
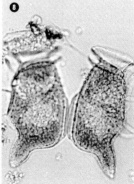

1. A copepod is a tiny crustacean with a segmented body and antennae on its head. It can grow up to 3 millimetres.
2. The newly formed adult jellyfish, called a medusa, is considered zooplankton.
3. A barnacle cypris is in the larval stage of its life cycle. It drifts for a brief period before attaching itself to a surface to develop.
4. Fish eggs are considered zooplankton. However, identification of such eggs requires laborious culture through their juvenile stages.
5. Shrimp protozoa, the early stage in the life cycle of shrimps, are zooplankton.
6. The phyllosoma of the flathead lobster (*Thenus* sp.) is a crustacean larva.
7. Dinoflagellates, including *Ceratium* sp., have two whip-like attachments, called flagella, with which they propel themselves through the water.
8. This dinoflagellate (*Protoperidinium* sp.) occurs in abundance near the coast. This is thought to be due to the enrichment in nutrients of the coastal waters due to runoff from land-based activities.

Seaweeds

Marine macroalgae, commonly referred to as 'seaweeds', fall into four divisions determined by colour. There are about 240 species of seaweeds in Malaysia, where they have traditionally been used as sources of food, medicine and industrial chemicals. Coral reefs support the highest diversity of species, followed by rocky shores and sandy or muddy areas. Seaweed beds contribute greatly to the productivity of the seas, as well as provide feeding and breeding grounds for marine life.

Seaweed is cultivated on a small scale in Sabah. The seaweed is dried and used in cooking.

Microscopic species

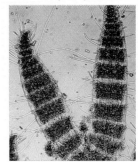 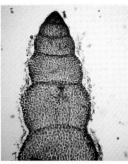

Some tiny species can barely be seen with the naked eye. Among these are (left) *Wrangelia biscuspidata*, a filamentous red seaweed, and (right) *Ceramium*, an epiphytic red seaweed, as seen under a microscope. They grow on larger species of red seaweed below the water's surface as they have pigments that can harvest the light that penetrates deep down.

Origin

Algae first appeared on earth about 1,500 million years ago, when life consisted mainly of bacteria and primitive marine invertebrates. The early Palaeozoic era, specifically the Cambrian period around 553 million years ago, saw the advance of the algae, especially the marine forms. Over time, some species left the sea and adapted to life on the land, while others remained in the sea. Some freshwater species evolved to give us some of the existing land plants, while others returned to a marine habitat.

Structure

The colours determining the four divisions of seaweeds are red (Rhodophyta), brown (Phaeophyta), green (Chlorophyta) and blue-green (Cyanophyta). The plant body is made up of filaments which can branch or be differentiated into prostrate and erect stems. Larger forms have a holdfast or rhizoid leading up to a stalk which may carry an expanded leaf, like the green *Ulva*, or a mass of cylindrical branches, like the red *Gracilaria*.

The blue-green seaweed (*Nostoc commune*) consists of aggregations of sticky filaments. The brown seaweed *Sargassum* is highly differentiated into a holdfast, stem, branches, leaves, air bladders and fruiting bodies ('receptacles').

Seaweed habitats

Common seaweed habitats include rocky shores, mud flats, coral reefs and mangroves. Many seaweeds are epiphytes, that is, they grow on larger host species as well as on the roots and trunks of mangrove and estuarine vegetation, and even on fallen leaves. Some also attach themselves to live fish and invertebrates. This is mutually beneficial as the colour of the seaweed acts as a protective camouflage for these hosts.

Malaysia's long coastline, extensive coastal shelf, and many islands harbour a great diversity of seaweed habitats. The sea offers two distinct habitats for seaweeds: the littoral or intertidal region, which is regularly covered and uncovered by the tides, and

Reproduction

Unique method of propagation in a Malaysian alga

Sargassum stolonifolium Phang et Yoshida was first discovered in 1994 and collected from Batu Ferringhi on Penang Island. This new species, found only in Malaysia to date, exhibits a phenomenon recorded for the first time in the genus *Sargassum*. It has the unique ability to propagate itself from its primary leaves, a method of reproduction that is distinctly different from the life cycle of other species. The special feature is the transformation of its cauline or primary leaves into stolons. When the tip of a stolon touches the ground, a haustorium is produced and a new plantlet formed. This unique form of vegetative reproduction is an adaptation for colonization of slippery rock surfaces at the splash zone of rocky shores.

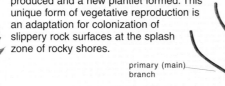

Sargassum stolonifolium a brown seaweed

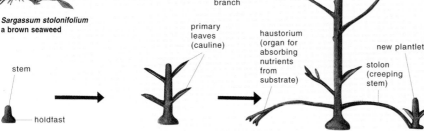

stem

holdfast

primary leaves (cauline)

haustorium (organ for absorbing nutrients from substrate)

primary (main) branch

new plantlet

stolon (creeping stem)

Life cycle of seaweeds

Most species of seaweeds exhibit an alternation of generation in their life cycle. The diploid sporophyte generation—having double the number of chromosomes—produces the asexual spores, while the haploid gametophyte generation—having only a single set of chromosomes—produces the gametes (sperm and eggs) involved in sexual reproduction. The gametophyte bears the sexual organs that produce the gametes.

At fertilization, sperm are carried by water to the carpogonium (structure bearing the eggs). When a sperm adheres to the tip of the carpogonium, the wall dissolves and the male nucleus enters to fuse with the egg. The fertilized egg produces many filaments, each of which produces spores. These spores germinate into a plant which produces other spores (asexual reproduction). The new spores then germinate to form either male or female plants, and the cycle continues.

Like most species of seaweeds, the red seaweed (*Gracilaria* sp.) reproduces in both a sexual as well as a non-sexual way. *Gracilaria* grows in intertidal areas.

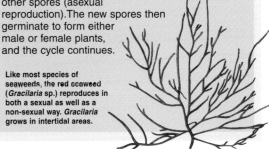

the sublittoral or subtidal region, which is permanently below the low tide mark and in which plants remain submerged. Species inhabiting the littoral region must be capable of surviving periods of exposure with the accompanying changes in temperature, salinity and pH level. The largest seaweeds, the brown ones, dominate the intertidal zones and shallow coral reefs. *Sargassum* and *Padina*, for example, are found on the intertidal coral reefs around the Port Dickson area, along the west coast of Peninsular Malaysia. In the sublittoral zone, the quantity and quality of light determines the species present. Species of red seaweeds, which have specialized pigments adapted to harvesting the wavelengths of light penetrating the depths, are the deepest living species of seaweeds.

Malaysian species

The 240 species of seaweeds growing in Malaysia are similar to those found in other parts of the Indo-Pacific region. The red seaweeds are the most common, ranging in size from microscopic species which are epiphytic, to larger ones like *Halymenia*.

Exhibiting great diversity of form, these red seaweeds yield many useful products. *Eucheuma*, a rich source of carrageenan, is cultured on a small scale around Semporna in Sabah, while *Gracilaria changii*, which produces high-quality agar, is grown experimentally in Peninsular Malaysia.

Almost as common are the green seaweeds, which are the least known because of limited utilization by man. However, many green seaweeds, like *Ulva* and *Enteromorpha*, thrive under polluted conditions and serve as biological indicators of marine pollution. Species of *Chaetomorpha*, *Cladophora* and *Boodlea*, which inhabit the surfaces of rocks and dead corals, are known as 'turf algae'. Other species of green seaweeds include the grape-like *Caulerpa,* the lobed, calcified plants of *Halimeda* and the luminescent filaments of *Chlorodesmis*.

Common Malaysian species

Sargassum binderi is a species of brown seaweed that has air bladders to help it float.

Like other brown seaweeds, *Sargassum siliquosum* is a good source of iodine.

The red seaweed *Halymenia* is a good source of agar, which is used in jellies and desserts.

Amphiroa, a red seaweed, often has calcium carbonate on its surface. It is used in Chinese medicine.

The filamentous green seaweed *Chaetomorpha* grows epiphytically on mangrove tree roots.

Caulerpa racemosa ('sea grapes') is a green seaweed growing among staghorn corals at Pulau Perhentian.

LOCAL USES OF SEAWEEDS

SPECIES	PRODUCT	USES
Graciliaria changii *Graciliaria tenuistipitata* *Gelidiella acerosa* *Gelidium amansii* *Agardhiella tenera*	Agar	Jellies, desserts, bacteriological agar
Eucheuma spinosum *Eucheuma cottonii* *Kappaphycus alvarezii* *Hypnea musciformis* *Acanthopora spicifera*	Carrageenan (a stabilizing and gelatinizing agent)	In pet food, toothpaste, cosmetics, ice-cream, frozen foods, salad dressing
Colpomenia sinuosa *Hormophysa triquetra* *Hydroclathrus clathratus* *Padina tetrastromatica* *Sargassum polycystum*	Alginate/alginic acid (an emulsifier)	Surface coating agent in textile printing and paper industries
Halimeda, Corallina, Ulva, *Caulerpa, Graciliaria, Hypnea,* *Sargassum* sp.	Whole plant in dried or powdered form, or fresh for salads	Traditional remedies against gallstones, worms and other infections

Symbol of prosperity

The blue-green seaweed (*Nostoc commune*), known as *fa' tsai* or *fatt choy* to the Chinese, is consumed as a delicacy in vegetarian dishes. It is sold in a dried form and looks like a mass of tangled black hair. Popular among Malaysian Chinese, it is a 'must' for the family reunion dinner at Chinese New Year. This is because in Chinese the name of the seaweed sounds like the word 'to prosper'.

Seagrasses

Seagrasses are submerged marine flowering plants which, unlike seaweeds, produce flowers, fruits and seeds. Of the 67 species presently known worldwide, 13 are found in the coastal waters of Malaysia. Ruppia maritima, a rare seagrass, was found in Seberang Perai in 1935 by I. H. Burkill, the then Director of the Singapore Botanic Gardens. Since then, it has not been found in Malaysia. Seagrass beds are important because they support marine life and aid coastal stability.

A bed of *Halodule univervis* in the lagoon (a shallow reef atoll) of Pulau Layang-Layang in the South China Sea.

Of the animals which live among the seagrasses, (1) the sea horse (*Hippocampus kuda*) is the most unusual in that the male gives birth to and carries the young! (2) This sea cucumber (*Holothuria scabra*) prefers to stay at the bottom of the seagrass bed.

The structure of seagrasses

Seagrasses are marine plants belonging to the subclass Monocotyledoneae within the class known as Angiospermae. They have the ability to complete the generative cycle under submerged conditions, and thrive in saline conditions.

Structurally, seagrasses are similar to terrestrial grasses, having leaves, stems, roots and reproductive structures (flowers and fruits). Seagrass plants have two flowering forms; either male or female flowers are borne on the same plant, or male and female flowers occur on separate plants.

The leaves can be non-petiolate with linear, grass-like blades or petiolate—having a petiole or leaf stalk with elliptic to ovate blades. Unlike most other aquatic plants, there are no stomata (pores) in the leaves of seagrasses. The leaves perform a photosynthesizing function and absorb water, carbon dioxide and nutrients directly from the water.

All seagrasses are typically rhizomatous, that is, they have prostrate underground stems (or rhizomes), with developed air channels, which can grow and branch out. These serve as a means of vegetative propagation. Arising from the lower surfaces, generally from nodes of the prostrate stems, are branched or unbranched roots. These roots serve some of the functions of those of terrestrial plants, such as anchoring and absorbing nutrients. They do not play a significant role in water uptake.

The importance of seagrasses

Underwater beds or meadows of seagrass form part of the Malaysian marine coastal environment. These beds, like their terrestrial counterparts, are known to be highly productive. They support marine life such as echinoderms (sea cucumbers, sea urchins and starfish), molluscs (shellfish), crustaceans such as crabs and prawns, fishes, and even large marine animals, including turtles and dugongs.

Local seagrass beds serve as nursery areas for young fishes, including those of commercial importance such as the dusky jack (*Caranx sexfasciatus*), blue trevally (*Caranx ferdau*), longarm mullet (*Valamugil cunnesius*), bony bream (*Anodontostoma chacunda*), silvery belly (*Leiognathus splendens*) and greenback grey mullet (*Liza subviridis*).

Fishes found in seagrass beds can be categorized according to their mode of feeding. Herbivores, which feed on seagrass and seaweed, include the rabbit fish (*Siganus guttatus*, *Siganus virgatus*) and longarm mullet (*Valamugil cunnesius*). Carnivores, which feed on other fishes, crustaceans, molluscs and other animals found in the seagass beds include

Marine life supported by a seagrass bed

Seagrasses such as (from left) spoongrass (*Halophila ovalis*), toothed seagrass (*Cymodocea serrulata*) and tropical eelgrass (*Enhalus acoroides*) serve as food for turtles, and also as food, shelter and nurseries for fish, invertebrates and the dugong.

1. Dugong (*Dugong dugon*)
2. Neretid (*Clithon oualaniensis*)
3. Puffer fish (*Tetraodon nigroviridis*)
4. Creeper shell (*Batillaria zonalis*)
5. Bivalve (*Paphia gallus*)
6. Sea cucumber (*Holothuria scabra*)
7. Shrimp (*Parapenaeopsis tenella*)
8. Black-lipped conch (*Strombus ureceus*)
9. Rabbit fish (*Siganus guttatus*)
10. Green turtle (*Chelonia mydas*)
11. Starfish (*Protoreaster nodosus*)
12. Swimming crab (*Species unknown*)
13. Spider conch (*Lambis lambis*)
14. Sea horse (*Hippocampus kuda*)

NOT TO SCALE

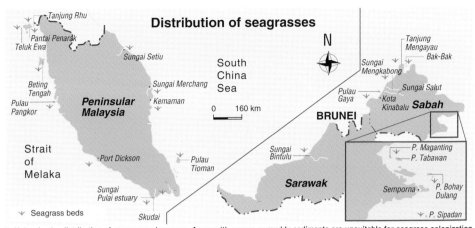

Distribution of seagrasses

N

South China Sea

Peninsular Malaysia

Strait of Melaka

BRUNEI

Sabah

Sarawak

Tanjung Rhu
Pantai Penarak
Teluk Ewa
Sungai Setiu
Sungai Merchang
Kemaman
Beting Tengah
Pulau Pangkor
Port Dickson
Pulau Tioman
Sungai Pulai estuary
Skudai
Sungai Bintulu
Tanjung Mengayau
Bak-Bak
Sungai Mengkabong
Sungai Salut
Pulau Gaya
Kota Kinabalu
Semporna
P. Maganting
P. Tabawan
P. Bohay Dulang
P. Sipadan

0   160 km

✓ Seagrass beds

In Malaysia, the distribution of seagrasses is sparse. Areas with coarse or muddy sediments are unsuitable for seagrass colonization. Seagrasses thrive where coastal habitats consist of lagoons, sandy beaches, mangroves and coral reefs. To date, no seagrass inventory has been compiled for Sarawak.

Seagrass fruit
The tropical eelgrass (*Enhalus acoroides*) bears a single small fruit, which is 4–6 centimetres in diameter and has six or seven edible seeds. The skin of the fruit is dark green and ribbed, while the seeds are white. High in carbohydrates, these seeds taste like water chestnuts and can be eaten raw. In Malaysia, very few people, except some villagers in Johor, eat these seeds, although they are eaten by the Australian aborigines and certain coastal inhabitants in the islands of the Philippines.

the sagor catfish (*Arius sagor*), puffer fish (*Tetraodon nigroviridis*), common pony fish (*Leiognathus equulus*) and one-spot snapper (*Lutjanus monostigma*). Omnivores—animals which feed on both plants and animals—include the Indian whiting (*Sillago sihama*) and the silvery belly (*Leiognathus splendens*).

The green turtle (*Chelonia mydas*) and hawksbill turtle (*Eretmochelys imbricata*) are known to eat seagrasses, as is the rare marine mammal the dugong (*Dugong dugon*). The tropical eelgrass (*Enhalus acoroides*) is thought to be the main food for the *Dugong dugon*. But it is also known to feed on various other types of seagrasses, which are abundant in Malaysian waters around four islands—Pulau Tengah, Pulau Tinggi, Pulau Besar and Pulau Sibu— off Mersing in the southern state of Johor.

Seagrasses are also valuable coastal resources as they assist coastal stability. They act directly to reduce soil erosion by physically binding the sediment and reducing turbulence near the surface of the soil. They can also accelerate the sedimentation process, facilitating the accumulation of silt and clay on the sea bed. These physical benefits, together with their habitat role, mean that destruction of seagrass meadows can therefore have serious environmental consequences. Natural threats include heavy monsoon rains, which may reduce the salinity of the water in which the seagrass is growing, and strong waves, which detach the plants or smother them with sand. Man-induced threats include construction near the coast, which can cause pollution and excessive sedimentation.

Uses of seagrasses

Traditionally, seagrasses have many uses in a number of Southeast Asian countries, particularly in the Philippines. They are woven into baskets, made into roof thatch, used as stuffing for mattresses and upholstery material, and used as fertilizers. A durable fibre, good for making fishing nets, can be produced from the softer parts of the tropical eelgrass (*Enhalus acoroides*) if it is allowed to rot. Seagrasses can also be used as sewage filters, for making paper, medicine, food and as an insulation material. Although there are no records of traditional uses of seagrasses in

Some Malaysian seagrasses

Tropical eelgrass (*Enhalus acoroides*)
The largest and most common of all seagrasses, this plant is characterized by its dark green, linear leaves with many parallel veins. Its rhizomes are thick with long bristles and cord-like, hairless roots. It has an edible fruit.

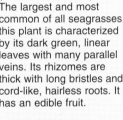

Curled-base spoongrass (*Halophila spinulosa*)
The plant is 'fern-like', with dark green compound leaves. Each leaf comprises 10–23 pairs of oblong-linear serrated leaflets arranged obliquely around the stalk. The rhizome nodes bear single roots with numerous root hairs.

Spoongrass (*Halophila ovalis*)
A common species, it has a pair of petiolate bright green oval to elliptical leaves borne on each node of the rhizome. Each leaf has 10–25 pairs of cross-veins. Although bigger than *Halophila minor*, it is structurally similar.

Dugong grass (*Thalassia hemprichii*)
A common species forming seagrass beds, it has a thick rhizome prominently marked by several shoot scars between successive erect shoots. Its ribbon-like leaves, which are slightly curved laterally, grow up to 16 cm long.

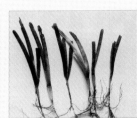

Toothed seagrass (*Cymodocea serrulata*)
This is a common species with a cluster of 2–4 dark green leaves (up to 5.8 cm long) attached by a flattened and triangular leaf sheath to the erect stem. The leaf tip is distinctly serrated, giving the plant its unusual name.

Estuarine spoongrass (*Halophila beccarii*)
This uncommon species grows in estuaries and mangrove mud flats. The world's first specimen was discovered in 1867 at the estuary of the Sungai Bintulu in Sarawak by Odoardo Beccarii, and named after him.

Malaysia, because of their scarcity, their potential uses are now being studied and one day may encourage their conservation.

The tropical eelgrass and dugong grass have potential as forage crops for beef cattle and fodder for sheep, while the syringe grass (*Syringodium isoetifolium*) has potential as an organic fertilizer. Various experiments have shown that, when applied as a mulch around young tomato and strawberry plants, seagrasses can increase the fruit yield, suppress weeds and give cleaner, tastier fruits.

Starfish and sea cucumbers

Starfish and sea cucumbers belong to a group of marine animals called echinoderms which form a large and important component of sea bed organisms. Apart from starfish (Asteroidea) and sea cucumbers (Holothuroidea), the group also includes feather stars (Crinoidea), sea urchins (Echinoidea) and brittle stars (Ophiuroidea). Most of these organisms live at the bottom of the sea and are distributed from the shallow intertidal areas to the deep ocean floors. In Malaysia, starfish and sea cucumbers are mainly found on coral reefs.

A group of colourful feather stars (*Oxycomanthus* sp.) perched high on a piece of coral expose themselves to the strong currents which bring a plentiful supply of plankton within reach.

Starfish

The colourful starfish is among the most visually striking of sea bed creatures. A number of species are found in Malaysia, with the *Fromia* being the most common. The starfish exemplifies the basic body plan of echinoderms in having a number of arms radiating out from a central body. Although most starfish have five arms, some have more, and while those in most species are long and narrow, some have short, rounded arms.

The starfish's mouth is found at the centre of the underside and is linked through its stomach to the anus which is directly above. Starfish feed by thrusting their stomachs out through their mouths and digesting their prey externally. Many starfish feed on detritus, while others feed on sponges and molluscs. There are also species, such as the crown-of-thorns starfish, which feed on corals. Some predatory species, such as *Coscinasterias*, use their tubed feet to hold onto prey and to prise open live shells in order to feed on the flesh inside.

The tubed feet on the arms of starfish which inhabit sandy areas are pointed to help them burrow in the sand. In contrast, starfish which inhabit rocky and coral areas have suckered feet to help them climb onto rocks and also to prevent them from being swept away by strong currents.

Starfish have separate sexes and can reproduce sexually. They are able to regenerate body parts when bits are broken off. For example, a new arm grows when one is lost. An arm can also generate a new body. Divers on reefs occasionally see a lopsided starfish, an indication of regeneration.

Feather stars

Feather stars or crinoids are common in Malaysian seas. They have small, central bodies surrounded by many (usually 10–20) delicate arms. Like starfish, feather stars also have tube feet. However, unlike other echinoderms, they do not use their tube feet for moving, but instead use cirri (slender tentacles on their undersides) to grasp substrates and move slowly. Since they are filter feeders, their mouths are positioned on the upper side.

To reproduce, male feather stars release sperm while females release eggs into the water where fertilization occurs, producing larvae.

Brittle stars

Brittle stars, also common in Malaysia, have a central body with many arms. Unlike other echinoderms, they have whip-like arms lined with spikes. These arms bear tube feet without suckers which emit a mucus to trap food. The mouth is located under the central disc and also serves as an anus. As part of their self-defence system, they can detach a part of an arm, or even the whole arm, if seized by a predator, and regenerate a replacement part.

1. The brilliantly coloured blue Linkia starfish (*Linckia laevigata*) can grow up to 40 centimetres in diameter.

2. The red-tipped starfish (*Fromia monilis*) feeds mainly on sponges.

3. The granular starfish (*Choriaster granulatus*) has reddish gills protruding through the skin of the upper parts of its body.

4. Unlike most members of its species, this *Linckia laevigata* has only four arms.

Destroyer of corals

One particular species of starfish, *Acanthaster planci*, commonly known as the crown-of-thorns starfish, feeds on corals, its favourite being the branching corals of the genus *Acropora*. Large tracts of corals have been attacked and destroyed by this starfish. The newly attacked corals appear bleached, then die and become overgrown with algae. In Malaysia, swarms of *Acanthaster* have been reported on the coral reefs of Pulau Redang and its surrounding islands off Terengganu. Many attempts have been made by divers to remove them from

A crown-of-thorns starfish feeding on coral.

the reef. One reason suggested for the increase in the *Acanthaster* population is pollution from runoff. Another is the over-collection of a type of shellfish—*Triton tritonis* or the triton, as it is commonly called—which is a natural predator of the *Acanthaster*. The triton is collected for the ornamental shell trade.

As tough and resilient as it may seem, the coral reef is a finely balanced system, and the removal of a component, in this case a predator of the starfish, can result in the degradation of the whole system.

Common Malaysian sea cucumbers

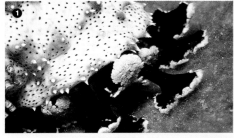

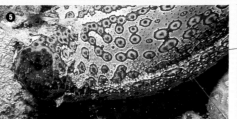

A symbiotic relationship
One species of fish (*Encheliophus homei*), commonly known as the assfish, lives in the gut cavity of the leopard sea cucumber (*Bohadschia argus*), as well as some other species of sea cucumber. It enters and exits through the sea cucumber's anus and feeds on its internal organs without causing them any serious damage.

1. A sea cucumber (*Pearsonothuria graeffei*) using its oral tentacles to collect food.

2. A *Holothuria* species of sea cucumber. As a defence mechanism, it expels some of its internal organs to provide food for the predator, thus allowing itself to escape.

3. Like most species, the *Sinopsis* species of sea cucumber is sluggish by nature and easy to catch.

4. A close-up of a *Stichopus* species of sea cucumber. Some *Stichopus* species have pharmaceutical value.

5. A *Bohadschia* species, also known as the leopard sea cucumber because of its spots.

Sea urchins

There are over 800 species of sea urchins worldwide, many found in tropical reefs such as those in Malaysia. Although they have the basic shape of a starfish, sea urchins have a hard structure with external spines, some with venomous tips. Most are herbivorous but some are carnivorous.

To reproduce, they release sperm and eggs into the sea where fertilization takes place. Sea urchin eggs have been studied in conjunction with human fertilization research. Marine laboratories in some countries are also testing sea urchin eggs for compounds with potential medicinal use.

Sea cucumbers

Sea cucumbers, or holothurians, are divided into three main groups: Aspidochirotes, Dendrochirotes and Apodus holothurians. The cylindrical shape of their bodies (which gives rise to their name), the number and shape of their tentacles, and their spicules or skeletons are among their main distinguishing features.

In the rocky or fringing coral intertidal areas throughout Malaysia, two common species of sea cucumber—*Holothuria atra* (the most common species in Malaysia) and *H. edulis*— are found scattered on the sea bottom. The diversity of sea cucumbers increases in subtidal waters. Some species crawl on the bottom, others live on coral, and a few bury themselves in sand or mud with only their feeding tentacles swaying in the water to capture plankton. As many species are nocturnal, they hide within coral crevices and boulders during the day and crawl out of their homes to feed at nightfall. One species, as yet unnamed, found in the South China Sea around Pulau Aur and Pulau Besar off Johor, has so synchronized its activity that the whole population leaves its coral refuge at almost the same time every evening. At dawn, the animals disappear back into their homes.

The brittle star (*Ophiothrix* sp.) (left) and the pencil sea urchin (*Theonella cylindrica*) (right) are two common echinoderms found in Malaysian seas.

Some sea cucumbers found in Malaysia are hermaphroditic (a single individual having both sexes). At Pulau Payar, south of Langkawi, the sea cucumber *Stichopus chloronotus* spawns twice a year. Both sperm and eggs are produced at the same time and fertilization occurs in the water. Sea cucumber young are seldom noticed on the reefs as many mimic the colour of sea slugs to protect themselves.

Ecologically, sea cucumbers are important. In areas where the sea bottom is predominantly mud, their burrowing introduces oxygen into the substrate, making the area accessible to other marine organisms. They are also food to some fishes.

For centuries, sea cucumbers have been harvested worldwide for food and medicine. In Malaysia, the Malays use sea cucumber extracts for medicine (see 'Pharmaceuticals'), while the local Chinese eat the creatures.

Increasing demand is causing a decline in populations. Sea cucumber collecting is also causing the destruction of many reefs as collectors break and overturn coral heads to look for the animals at low tide. Fortunately, research into the artificial breeding of sea cucumbers is under way.

Starfish move and feed—and flip over—with the assistance of hundreds of tiny suckered feet.

A Chinese delicacy
Sea cucumber is a popular but expensive delicacy among Malaysian Chinese although some species contain a deadly toxin. The cucumber is usually cooked with vegetables in herbal soups and stews. The flesh is tough and needs to be soaked in water overnight or longer before cooking.

Hard corals

The seas of Southeast Asia, including Malaysia, contain the most diverse coral ecosystem in the world and the hard coral colonies of the Malaysian reefs thus exhibit a great variety of shapes and colours. Hard corals (Scleractinia) belong to the phylum Cnidaria, which also includes soft corals, jellyfish, anemones and sea pens. Hard corals are the dominant builders, their skeletons forming the foundation of reefs. However, some deep-dwelling Scleractinia do not build reefs.

A stamp issued by Pos Malaysia Berhad to commemorate the International Year of the Reef, 1997, features a brain coral (*Symphillia* sp.)

Location

Coral reefs are found in well-lit tropical seas the world over, including Southeast Asia, the Caribbean and Australia. Although coral reefs are found in many parts of Malaysia, they are particularly developed in the South China Sea and the Sulu Sea where the waters are clear and salinity levels high. Thus, there are many fringing reefs around islands such as Pulau Redang, Pulau Perhentian and Pulau Tioman off the east coast of Peninsular Malaysia, and Pulau Sipadan off Sabah. These are major tourist attractions for diving activities.

The depth of reefs in Malaysia is very much dependent upon water clarity. The clearer the water, the deeper the light can penetrate to the bottom. In the South China Sea, corals are found to depths of 25–30 metres. In comparison, the highly sedimented waters of the Strait of Melaka only allow coral growth to depths of 1–5 metres.

Diversity

Though relatively small in area, Malaysia's coral reefs are high in biodiversity. The country lies in the Indo-Pacific region which has an estimated 500–600 species of hard corals. Typical estimates of coral genera found in Malaysia are 35 at Pulau Payar in the Strait of Melaka, 70 at Pulau Redang and Pulau Tioman in the South China Sea, and 70 at

Same species, different environments

Acropora gemmifera in sheltered areas grow into large, staghorn-shaped colonies.

The shapes of coral colonies are influenced by environmental variables such as water clarity and depth. For instance, *Acropora* living on a shallow reef are usually exposed to strong wave action and thus exhibit short, stubby branches.

Pulau Sipadan in the Sulu Sea. In comparison, the number of coral genera on Australia's Great Barrier Reef is estimated at about 70 and in Indonesia between 70 and 80, whereas in the Caribbean, the richest coral area in the Atlantic Ocean, there are only 20 genera of corals.

The coral polyp

General characteristics

Most corals live together in colonies but some, such as mushroom corals, are free-living. The actual coral animal is a tiny coral polyp which sits in a skeletal case that it secretes called a corallite. Polyps range in size from about 1 millimetre to more than half a metre depending on the species. Each polyp has a fleshy sac topped with a crown of tentacles surrounding the central mouth opening.

Nematocysts are found on the tentacles and are used for self-defence and for trapping food. A nematocyst is a double-walled structure comprising a spiral spring-loaded venom sac filled with thread with a tiny barb on the tip. A tiny sensor is positioned at the rim of the nematocyst. When the sensor is stimulated, the capsule explodes launching the thread, the barb penetrates the victim's skin and injects the poison to paralyse it.

The outer layer of the coral colony is alive with millions of tiny polyps. This layer overlies dead coral skeletons deposited over time. The build-up of these skeletons forms the foundation of the reefs.

A budding coral polyp.

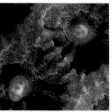

A magnified view of a sperm and egg bundle of coral polyps.

A magnified view of coral eggs and sperm separating as they move towards the surface.

Spawning and reproduction

Most hard corals produce asexually, although sexual reproduction is not uncommon. Asexual reproduction involves the production (budding) of new polyps from older ones. In some species, pieces of corals broken off from an established colony can form new colonies.

Sexual reproduction in corals is a spectacular affair. Colonies of corals can produce sperm or eggs or they can be hermaphroditic—producing both sperm and eggs—although not at the same time. At a specific time each year, colonies of corals synchronize their spawning. Over a period of only 3–5 nights a year, these spawning corals release millions of their eggs and sperm onto the reefs. The sea appears a luminescent green as the eggs and sperm of these animals fill the water column and form a nutritious 'soup' for other reef organisms.

This mass spawning increases the chances of fertilization. Some of the coral larvae which survive will find a suitable substrate on which to develop and begin life as a new colony. This spawning of hard corals is known to peak in April and May at the Pulau Payar Marine Park in the Strait of Melaka.

Patterns and colours of hard corals

Reef-building hard corals

Hard coral colonies exhibit an extraordinary multitude of patterns and colours. For instance, the genera *Symphyllia* and *Lobophyllia* are referred to as brain corals since the shapes of their colonies resemble brains. Close-up views reveal the many other interesting patterns of hard corals, including floral and geometric designs that make them look like sculptures.

Coral reefs also look spectacular because of their brilliant colours, which are determined by the hues of the zooxanthellae living within them. These range from brown and green to yellow, orange and pink.

1. *Favites* sp., which has a distinctive design, is found not only in clear waters but also in turbid waters, such as at Tanjung Tuan, Melaka.
2. This brain coral (*Platygyra* sp.) has the typical outline of a brain coral with ridges and valleys containing polyp mouths.
3. The staghorn coral (*Acropora valida*) has small tubular pink tips which distinguish it from other branched corals.
4. The mushroom coral (*Fungia* sp.) is a single polyp and corallite. Thin partitions covered in living tissue radiate outwards from the central mouth.
5. Dome-shaped coral (*Diplaastrea heliopora*) colonies are massive and look like floral sculptures.

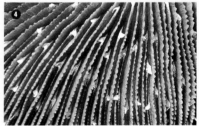

Non-reef building hard corals

Some species of hard corals live much deeper down beneath the sea where there is little light. They have bigger polyps, with tentacles, specialized for capturing zooplankton. The beautiful bright orange or pink coral (*Tubastraea* sp.) with large, fleshy polyps belongs to this group. It does not form coral reefs.

1. *Tubastraea faulkneri* grows in small clumps.
2. The green tree coral (*Tubastraea micranthea*) with extended tentacles, found south of Pulau Pangkor.
3. *Cynarina lacrymalis* has a symmetrical pattern.

Acropora coral growing in deeper water near Pulau Tioman form large plates.

In sheltered areas, *Acropora* develop into more familiar staghorn-shaped colonies. However, the same species inhabiting deeper, darker waters forms plates as these provide a larger surface for the harvesting of light energy for photosynthesis.

A symbiotic relationship

Hard corals consist of a thin layer of living organisms (the coral polyps) overlying a hard skeleton. The skeleton is made of aragonite (calcium carbonate) which is secreted by the living corals. There are two main types of hard corals—reef building and non-reef building.

The success of corals in forming reefs is due to their symbiotic relationship with algae, known as zooxanthellae, which live within their tissues. The algae (*Symbiodinium microdriaticum*) uses light to photosynthesize, providing food for the living coral. The need for light means that most hard corals are restricted to the shallow, well-lit areas of the seas. However, there are some species which have adapted to the darker, deeper waters. In addition to food supplied by the zooxanthellae, the corals extend their tentacles to trap food particles in the currents. Some even secrete a sticky substance and mobile filaments from their stomachs to catch food. Their tissues are interconnected and they share food.

Azooxanthellate hard corals in deeper waters do not need light to survive and do not depend on zooxanthellae for their food. Instead, they feed on zooplankton. As there is little light in deeper waters, these corals tend to be smaller, seldom growing into large colonies. Thus, they are non-reef building.

Soft corals

The term 'soft corals' is broadly used and often includes sea fans, sea pens and sea whips although, unlike true soft corals, sea fans and sea whips have hard skeletons. They all belong to a subclass called Alcyonaria, which belongs to the same phylum (Cnidaria) as hard corals. In certain parts of the Malaysian seas, soft corals form the dominant group and, with their multi-hued colonies, make up the more visual elements of the coral reef. Many marine organisms depend on soft corals for their food and shelter.

A rich diversity of colourful soft corals is found in the warm tropical waters off Pulau Layang-Layang in the South China Sea.

The fluffy white flowerets (inset) on the vertical stems of the harp coral (*Ctenocella pectinata*) are the polyps. These open up during strong currents to trap food.

Diversity and geographical distribution

In Malaysia, the diversity of soft corals, including sea fans, sea pens and sea whips, totals around 200 species, the same as for Indonesia. More than half belong to the Alcyoniidae family, which includes the common species of *Sinularia* and *Nepthea*. Soft corals are found throughout Malaysia, from the Strait of Melaka to the South China Sea, and eastward to the Sulu Sea. Unlike hard corals for which diversity varies greatly, the range of soft corals is high throughout Malaysian waters—though the Strait of Melaka has fewer species than the South China Sea with its clearer waters. Many species are found in the Langkawi and Pangkor group of islands in the Strait of Melaka despite the turbidity of the water.

Sea fans (gorgonians) are the most widespread type in their distribution. As they do not require light for growth, they suffer little competition from hard corals and flourish in darker waters. Large colonies of soft corals, including sea fans, are found on the deeper parts of the reefs in the South China Sea and the Sulu Sea. In some places, such as off some of the Johor islands, they are the dominant organisms. They are also common in the murky, turbid waters of the Strait of Melaka.

Vertical distribution

Soft corals which have the symbiotic algae zooxanthellae living on them are found in shallow waters. In Malaysia, such corals thrive on the exposed side of islands, on the north and eastern side of the east coast islands of Peninsular Malaysia, including Pulau Redang and Pulau Perhentian. Attaching themselves to rocky boulders, these corals are tolerant of the strong, high waves pounding these areas during the monsoons. In such an environment, they can compete with hard corals.

Sea fans are usually found in deeper waters where there are strong currents and in turbid waters where light is limited. Many healthy stands of gorgonians are found at Tanjung Tuan and Pulau Langkawi in the Strait of Melaka.

Importance of soft corals

Soft corals provide homes for some animals, including fish, shrimp and algae. Certain shrimps mimic the colours of the sea fans they live alongside for camouflage. In 1995, a rare species of winged oyster (*Pteria scabriuscula*), not reported since its discovery in 1857, was rediscovered on a sea fan in Johor. Other animals, such as feather stars, perch on sea fans to gain better access to passing currents, enabling them to take better advantage of the food supply. Certain species of soft corals provide food for nudibranchs (see 'Molluscs') which are found on the soft folds of *Sinularia* and *Lobophyton* corals.

The zooxanthellae living on some soft corals give colour to the reefs. The rich composition of colours, shapes and patterns on the reefs is what makes the ecosystem so appealing to divers.

Sea fans, sea pens and other soft corals, particularly Malaysian species, are poorly studied. However, some soft corals have now been found to contain chemicals, which fend off encrusting animals and serve as a deterrent to predators. Such chemicals have high potential as pharmaceuticals and are being investigated in the search for cures for diabetes and cancer.

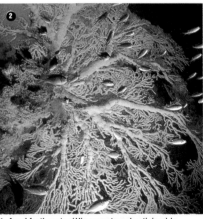

1. A red feather star (*Himerometra robustipinna*) is perched on top of some soft corals so that it can obtain food from the currents flowing by.

2. Many small fish seek shelter around a crimson sea fan (*Melithaea* sp.).

3. A small underwater cave, covered with various species of soft corals, is home to many fish.

Types and characteristics

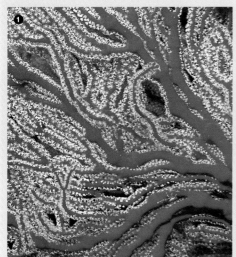

Some common species in Malaysia

1. A Gauguin sea fan (*Melithaea squamata*), found near Pulau Perhentian. The white flowerets are the polyps.

2. A leather soft coral (*Sinularia* sp.), seen here with tentacles retracted, is among the most common species.

3. The sea pen (*Virgularia* sp.) looks like a quill. The function of the top half, called the rachis, is to capture food.

4. A sea pen (*Pteroeides* sp.) with its polyps extended. A stalk anchors this animal to the substrate.

5. A red soft coral (*Dendronephthya* sp.) found off Pulau Labas, near Pulau Tioman, provides shelter for small fish.

6. Red sea whips (*Ellisella* sp.) have many long, thin branches that give them their name.

7. A white sea fan (*Melithaea* sp.) is rare. Most are red or orange in colour. This one was found in the Strait of Melaka.

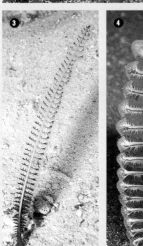

Types

There are many types of soft corals, ranging from those which look like trees or flowers to those which resemble fans, whips or pens. Most are named after their shapes.

Soft corals

Soft corals are structurally similar to hard corals but they lack the support of a hard limestone skeleton. Instead, they have a fleshy stem and a support comprised of very tiny calcareous particles (sclerites). Different species have a distinctive pattern of distribution of these 'skeletons'. Identification of soft corals depends on the pattern of their sclerites and the shape of the colonies they form.

As their name suggests, soft corals have a soft body, which can be inflated in water to trap plankton. Unlike hard corals, they have tentacles with pinnules (branches) along each side. The total number of tentacles is eight, which is why soft corals are also known as octocorals. When their branches are extended to capture food, soft corals look like colourful flowers.

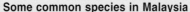

Soft corals have a support of tiny calcareous particles called sclerites. In the *Dendronephthya* sp. these sclerites are large enough to be seen with the naked eye in live specimens.

Sea pens

Sea pens are octocorals that form colonies. The bottom half of the 'pen' is the stalk that anchors the animals in the sand or mud where they are commonly found. The top half of the animal resembles a quill, known as the rachis. Secondary polyps arise from the rachis. As sea pens do not have branches, one function of the rachis is to capture food.

Sea fans

Although sea fans, which belong to the family Gorgoniaceae, are also called soft corals, their skeletons are not soft. Under water, sea fans align themselves at right angles to the water currents so that their intricate frame can sieve and trap plankton efficiently.

Sea whips

Sea whips are usually found on sandy sea bottoms beyond the extent of the reef. As their name suggests, they are long, slender branches of semi-rigid corals. They may have a single long stem, as in the species *Juncella fragilis*, or they may look more like trees with many branches, as seen in the genus *Ellisella*.

Modes of feeding

Most soft corals, particularly those living in shallow waters, have symbiotic algae known as zooxanthellae living on them. The algae manufacture food through photosynthesis, providing food for the corals in exchange for being hosted. As they are coloured, the algae also give the corals their different colours.

Some species do not have zooxanthellae but depend entirely on the capture of zooplankton for food. Others are suspension feeders and depend on the currents to bring suspended food particles to their filter structures. The tentacles of soft corals, extending from the polyp, with their comb-like branches, trap small particles, plankton and dissolved organic nutrients from the water. During feeding time, the polyps stretch their tentacles out forming a living net to capture any passing food particles.

Reproduction

As soft corals have separate sexes, reproduction occurs by releasing sperm and eggs into the water. Fertilized eggs hatch into larvae, which float as plankton for a brief period before settling on a reef. The larvae, which avoid being eaten by animals higher in the food chain, manage to find a place on a reef, then metamorphose into polyps which, in turn, start budding into other polyps, thus forming a new colony.

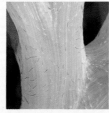

This soft tree coral (*Dendronepthya* sp.), found off Pulau Perhentian, can change its size, becoming bloated when feeding.

Molluscs

Molluscs are soft-bodied animals. Most molluscs often have beautiful calcareous shells, a large muscular foot and a rasping tongue called a radula. Although these three characteristics have enabled them to adapt to a wide range of habitats, the majority live in the sea. The phylum Mollusca includes a large variety of forms and, comprising more than 100,000 species, is second in number only to insects. There are six classes of molluscs, all of which are found in Malaysia's seas.

Oysters are cultured for pearls on a farm off Pulau Bohey Dulang, Sabah.

The tiger cowrie (*Cypraea tigris*) is usually found under overhanging ledges and among seaweeds at Pulau Tioman, Pulau Sembilan and other Malaysian islands.

Habitats

The habitats molluscs are commonly found in include rocky shores, sandy beaches, mud flats, coral reefs, rivers and mangroves. Those living in coral reefs show greater diversity compared with those in other habitats. The rock oyster (*Saccostrea cucullata*) and the polished nerite (*Nerita polita*) are commonly found on Malaysian rocky shores, where they are exposed to air during low tide, both on the east and west coasts of Peninsular Malaysia. The blood cockle (*Anadara granosa*) and angel wing clam (*Pholas* sp.) are two common species found in muddy areas in Kedah and Penang.

Diversity of Malaysian molluscs

There is a greater diversity of molluscs on the east coast of Peninsular Malaysia than on the west coast because the pollution and high turbidity level of west coast waters reduce the level of dissolved oxygen and thus limit the mollusc population. The diversity of molluscs in Sabah and Sarawak is higher than anywhere in Peninsular Malaysia. This is because they are surrounded by the South China and Sulu seas which are both rich in living organisms. For example, only four species of giant clams are found in the Johor islands and Pulau Redang whereas seven (out of a total of eight species in the world) are found in Sabah.

The diversity of Malaysian molluscs is, however, generally lower compared with that in Thailand, Indonesia or the Philippines. In 1997, only 39 species of gastropods and 22 species of bivalves were reported at Pulau Pemanggil in Johor, compared with 382 species of gastropods and 91 species of bivalves in the Gulf of Thailand.

Conservation

Endangered species

Endangered species of molluscs in Malaysia include the giant clam (*Tridacna* sp. and *Hippopus* sp.), the trumpet shell (*Charonia tritonis*), the donkey's ear abalone (*Haliotis* sp.) and the chambered nautilus (*Nautilus* sp.). Most of these have become endangered as a result of fish bombing activities, over-harvesting of their shells and meat, as well as pollution and degradation of the environment.

One conservation method is protection of the natural environment. Other measures include captive breeding and artificial spawning in the laboratory and then release of the young.

Over-collecting has led to the *Nautilus* species becoming endangered.

Saving giant clams

The largest bivalve molluscs in the world are the giant clams (Tridacnidae). Of the total of eight species of giant clams worldwide, seven live in Malaysian seas. These include *Hippopus porcellanus* and *Tridacna derasa*, *which are* found only in Sabah. *H. hippopus* and *Hippopus porcellanus* live on reef flats while *Tridacna crocea* populations are considered stable and live embedded in dead and live corals. However, *Tridacna squamosa* and *T. maxima* are considered endangered, and *Tridacna gigas* is almost extinct in Peninsular Malaysia. Because of this, the Department of Fisheries Malaysia has listed giant clams as protected species.

The habitats of giant clams are mainly in the shallow seas around islands off the east coast of the Peninsula—Pulau Redang, Pulau Pemanggil, Pulau Besar, Pulau Tinggi and Pulau Aur, and also in Sabah. This is because they rely on sunlight to survive. The giant clam can grow to a size of approximately 1 metre in shell length and is capable of living for a very long time, up to 70 years.

Artificial breeding

A project to save a species of giant clam (*Tridacna squamosa*) in Malaysia was launched in 1997 after research by the Reef Research Group of Universiti Sains Malaysia discovered the precarious status of the molluscs in Johor. Realizing the importance ot the clam as a natural heritage, its position as a world record holder, and its tourism potential, the Johor state government collaborated with the university to breed the clam artificially. Giant clams were injected with serotonin to induce them to spawn in their natural environment. Plastic bags were used to collect the larvae and bring them to land to be cultured. Upon reaching a certain size, the hatchery-cultured young were released into the sea. In October 1999, 600 young were released into the marine parks of Pulau Tinggi, Pulau Rawa and Pulau Pemanggil.

1. *Tridacna gigas*, the largest giant clam in the world, is found only in the South China Sea.

2. Three-year-old cultured young giant clams (*Tridacna squamosa*) being released on the reefs off Johor in October 1999.

3. *Tridacna squamosa* is an endangered species in Malaysia. Artificial breeding is helping to save it.

Classes and characteristics

CLASS	SHELL/SHAPE	MAIN CHARACTERISTICS
Gastropoda e.g. cowrie, cone, murex and olive shells and nudibranchs	Mostly a one-piece (univalve) shell usually coiled in a right-handed spiral. Of various sizes, shapes and colours. Also those which have no shell, like the nudibranch.	Eyes, radular teeth, tentacles, a mantle and a broad foot. Some species have a siphon. On the foot of some, a horny cover called an operculum acts like a door to plug up the shell's aperture when the animal withdraws into it. As the name 'gastropod' implies, the animal crawls on its stomach.
Bivalvia e.g. oysters, mussels, cockles and clams	Two outer shells hinged and joined by a supple ligament. Many bivalve shells are fragile but others are thick and heavy.	No eyes and no radular teeth. A large foot and two siphons, one for drawing in water and the other for expelling waste. Gills for filtering food particles from the water drawn in over the gills through the siphon.
Scaphopoda e.g. tusk shells 	A single, long and hollow shell. Ivory or creamy coloured, resembling an elephant's tusk.	No head, no eyes and no gills. Strong radular teeth and a broad foot which sticks into the sand from the broader end of the shell.
Cephalopoda e.g. cuttlefish, squid, octopuses, nautilus shells	Mostly no shells, except for a few species of *Nautilus*. Instead of shells, squid and cuttlefish have internal bone-like rods for support.	A head, large eyes, long tentacles, strong radular teeth and parrot-like beaks. Very fast movement through a kind of jet propulsion. Some species of squid eject an inky fluid to repel predators. Some male squid change their colour to attract females during courtship.
Monoplacophora e.g. limpets	A fragile, conical-shaped shell which looks like a miniature volcano.	Segmented bodies, a row of radular teeth, but no eyes or tentacles. Paired gills and internal organs.
Polyplacophora/ Amphineura e.g. chitons	A series of eight shell plates arranged in a row and held by a girdle.	Radular teeth but no eyes or tentacles. Although they have no eyes, they have light-sensitive organs within their shell plates.

General characteristics

The shell shapes of molluscs are highly variable and suited to the lifestyle of specific species. Those which live on the sea floor, for example helmet shells and muricids, tend to have heavy and ornamented shells. Those which need to swim have modified feet and smaller, lighter, more delicate shells. Nudibranchs (molluscs which lack shells) have brightly coloured bodies to deter predators. Some of the smallest species, such as eulimids, live parasitically on other organisms, while others live among the sand grains of the intertidal zone. Molluscs can crawl, glide, burrow, leap or even swim with their single foot (radula), but they cannot walk as they have no legs.

Different molluscs feed on different types of food, and thus have different styles of feeding. Those which are herbivorous use their radula to rasp microalgae off hard or soft substrates, while carnivorous species, such as muricids, immobilize their prey by a toxin secreted and administered by a radula tooth that flicks out on the end of a long proboscis. Other species, especially bivalves, are filter feeders, straining microorganisms from the water.

Rock oysters (*Saccostrea cucullata*) exposed during low tide at Pulau Pemanggil, off Johor in Peninsular Malaysia. These bivalves are used for making oyster omelettes.

Reproduction

Most molluscs have separate sexes. Many gastropods are hermaphrodites, that is, each has a complete set of male as well as female sex organs. A few species change sex (from male to female) when they mature.

Some gastropod eggs develop inside the mother or are hatched by being sat upon for a few days. Other eggs are protected within gelatinous capsules, clusters of which are deposited and attached to other objects. The eggs of most bivalves are simply shed into the water without any protective covering. The fertilized eggs change into free-swimming larvae which fall prey to other marine animals. Hence, molluscs usually produce millions of eggs to offset the high mortality rate.

Economic importance

Molluscs are commonly consumed as food in Malaysia. The tropical oyster (*Crassostrea iredalei*) harvested from Kelantan and Terengganu, and *C. belcheri* from Perak, Kedah and Johor, are well known in the half-shell trade and are served in local restaurants and five-star hotels. On the other hand, rock oysters (*Saccostrea cucullata*), which are mainly collected from rocks during low tide, are used only in oyster omelettes at local hawker stalls.

Blood cockles (*Anadara granosa*) are abundant in Malaysia, which is the world's main cockle exporter (see 'Cockles and mussels'). Other edible molluscs include razor clams and wedge shells (*Donax* sp.), most of which are harvested for local consumption.

Although molluscs are also made into trinkets, such as boxes and jewellery (see 'Seashells'), this trade is slowly dying because of the limited number of shells to be found in Malaysian waters, as well as the regulations set by the National Advisory Council for Marine Parks and Reserves for their collection.

Tubercular nudibranch (*Phyllodesmium kabirasnum*) have finger-like appendages which are non-retractable.

The nudibranch *Phyllidia varicosa* is found off Pulau Pemanggil, Johor.

Nudibranchs

Some molluscs, such as cephalopods (see 'Squid, cuttlefish and octopuses') and nudibranchs have no shells. There are about 3,000 species of nudibranchs worldwide, many of which are found in Malaysian seas. The name 'nudibranch' means 'naked gills' and are so called because they have exposed respiratory organs along their backs. These small, highly colourful aquatic creatures live in a variety of habitats ranging from intertidal rock pools to sea walls 100 metres deep. Most nudibranchs are carnivorous, feeding on fish eggs, anemones and other organisms. Some species have varied diets while others have very specific ones.

Nudibranchs are able to store living cells and toxins from their prey and use these to attack their predators. Thus, most fish and other organisms are adept at avoiding them. Their brilliant colour also provides camouflage amidst their colourful surroundings. They are hermaphrodites, which are first male and then female in turn during mating. All species die after spawning only once.

This common nudibranch (*Phyllidia* sp.) has a tough, warty, outer covering.

Squid, cuttlefish and octopuses

Many species of squid, cuttlefish and octopuses inhabit the shallow seas around Malaysia. They are molluscs belonging to the class Cephalopoda, and have internal skeletal rods instead of shells for support. They vary greatly in length (8–35 cm). Most squid and octopuses inhabit the shallow seas around the continental shelf, while cuttlefish live nearer the coast. Mainly a by-catch of fish and prawn trawlers, these cephalopods constitute around 5 per cent of the annual commercial marine landings in Malaysia and are popular in local cuisine and as dried food products.

The oval squid: from eggs to adult

The male oval squid (*Sepioteuthis lessoniana*) can change its body colour in a split second to attract the female, to indicate alarm and aggression, or for camouflage. Its colour changes are achieved by three layers of chromatophores (cells filled with coloured pigments) and other cells which act as reflectors. As the cells expand and contract, the colours change.

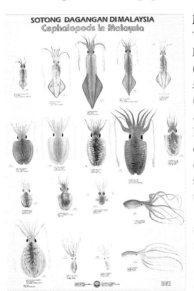

A poster from the Fisheries Department showing the wide range of cephalopod species in Malaysia.

Malaysian species

The main species of squid found in Peninsular Malaysia are *Loligo chinensis*, the mitre squid (known locally as *sotong jarum*, *sotong candat* or *sotong torak*), *L. duvaucelli*, the Indian squid (known locally as *sotong ketupat*) and *Sepioteuthis lessoniana*, the oval squid (known in Peninsular Malaysia as *sotong arus* on the west coast and as *sotong mengabang* on the east coast). Although these species inhabit the shallow seas away from the coast, they migrate to coastal waters to spawn.

The most common local cuttlefish species are the *Sepia aculeata*, *S. pharaonis* and *Sepiella inermis*. Found mainly off the east coast, the *S. aculeata* is the main species of cuttlefish in Peninsular Malaysia. The *S. pharaonis* is known locally as *sotong harimau* or 'tiger cuttlefish' because of the tiger-stripe pattern on its body.

Octopuses present in Peninsular Malaysia belong to a number of species and are generally known as *sotong kurita*. They are edible and are sold mainly as dried products. Based on commercial landings, the species of squid, cuttlefish and octopuses found in Sabah and Sarawak differ little from those in Peninsular Malaysia.

Spawning

The main spawning and nursery areas for squid and cuttlefish of the *Loligo* and *Sepia* species are the coral reefs off the east coast of Peninsular Malaysia, near Pulau Redang, Pulau Kapas, Pulau Perhentian and other islands. During mating, the male transfers the sperm from its body into the female's body with a modified arm. The eggs are laid encased in gelatinous, finger-like capsules attached to seagrasses, seaweed, rocks or other hard objects on the sea bed.

The mitre squid spawns throughout the year, with the peak period between April and July when groups migrate inshore. This species is among the common commercial squid found in the South China Sea, off the east coast of the Peninsula. On the west coast, this species can also be found in the

The oval squid trap (*bubu sotong arus*)

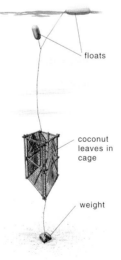

floats

coconut leaves in cage

weight

The *bubu sotong arus* is a traditional wooden trap used for catching oval squid. Coconut leaves are tied on two sides as lures. Squid eggs or transparent pieces of plastic that look like squid eggs are placed inside as bait. Once a squid enters the valve-like opening at the top (which narrows into the trap), it finds it very difficult to squeeze back up to escape and thus is trapped.

Catching cephalopods

Out of the squid, cuttlefish and octopus catch in Malaysia, squid make up the majority: 60–70 per cent of the total. A high percentage of the total catch comes as a by-catch from the fish and prawn trawler industry. About half of the squid and cuttlefish are landed on the west coast of Peninsular Malaysia. Total annual landings for 1997 in the Peninsula were 60 352 metric tons. Landings of squid and cuttlefish in Sabah and Sarawak are small compared with those in the Peninsula. In 1997, total landings of squid, cuttlefish and octopuses in Sarawak amounted to 8299 metric tons and only 2020 metric tons in Sabah.

Most squid are a by-catch, but some form the target catch. Jigging is a popular method used on the east coast of Peninsular Malaysia to catch mitre squids (*Loligo chinensis*). The jig, a lure, is moved up and down by hand. Fishermen go out at night in small boats and shine lamps to attract the squid, and then move the jigs. Traps, known locally as *bubu sotong arus*, are also widely used to catch oval squid during the peak spawning period, especially in Kedah and Perlis waters. Although other traps are used on the east coast to catch the cuttlefish (*Sepia pharaonis*), the use of cuttlefish traps is not common. Cuttlefish are mainly caught in trawl nets. Most octopuses are also a by-catch of prawn trawlers, but there are isolated fishing activities through which small species inhabiting intertidal areas are caught during low tide with bare hands.

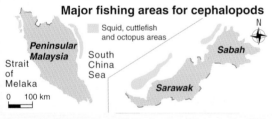
Major fishing areas for cephalopods

Squid, cuttlefish and octopus areas

Peninsular Malaysia

Strait of Melaka

South China Sea

Sabah

Sarawak

0   100 km

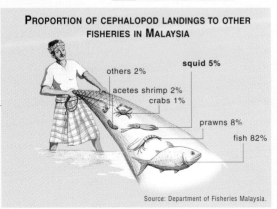

PROPORTION OF CEPHALOPOD LANDINGS TO OTHER FISHERIES IN MALAYSIA

squid 5%
others 2%
acetes shrimp 2%
crabs 1%
prawns 8%
fish 82%

Source: Department of Fisheries Malaysia.

TOP: The eggs of the oval squid are enclosed in cylindrical sacs.
BOTTOM: Young oval squid.

southern part of the Penang waters. The oval squid displays the same pattern of migration during spawning. Although this species also spawns throughout the year, its peak spawning period is between May and June off the east coast of Peninsular Malaysia and between September and December on the west coast. The eggs of the oval squid take 3–4 weeks to hatch. Upon hatching, the larvae swim to the surface of the sea and remain as semi-planktonic organisms until they grow larger and descend to settle at the sea bed. Often young squid are caught in fish traps set in mangroves.

Cuttlefish move to shallower places near the coast to spawn. They migrate in small groups, and pairs of males and females can often be seen moving together. On the west coast of Peninsular Malaysia, the *Sepia aculeata* spawns throughout the year, but the most active spawning period is between November and February. Like other species, the *S. pharaonis* migrates towards the coastal areas off Kelantan, Terengganu, Pahang and northwest Johor during the spawning season.

Little is known about the spawning activities of octopuses in Malaysia. Octopuses sometimes

The reef octopus (*Octopus cyaneus*) is a common Malaysian species.

undergo distance mating where the partners remain separated, with only an outstretched arm introduced into the female's body. Egg-laying may be accomplished within a few days or last several weeks, depending upon the number of eggs and the temperature of the water.

Main characteristics of cephalopods

General features

Squid, cuttlefish and octopuses belong to the class Cephalopoda, which are molluscs with a head bearing a crown of arms. They have beak-like jaws and a radula (a tongue-like projection covered with small teeth) in their mouth. Squids have a soft, elongated body. The outer covering of the body, called the mantle, is supported by a skeletal plate. Cuttlefish have broad, sac-like bodies supported by the cuttlebone. Both squid and cuttlefish have eight short arms with two or more rows of suckers, plus two long, retractile tentacles. Octopuses, in contrast, have short, sac-like bodies or mantles, with no fins. They have eight arms with suckers. As the octopus has no shell or bone, it can squeeze itself into small spaces. It is a master of camouflage, changing the colours and patterns on its skin to blend in with the background, to frighten off an enemy, or to attract a female.

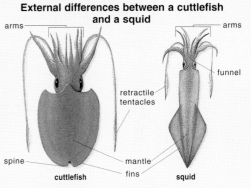

External differences between a cuttlefish and a squid

arms — retractile tentacles — spine — mantle — fins — **cuttlefish**

arms — funnel — **squid**

Squid, cuttlefish and octopuses take a wide variety of prey, such as fish, crustaceans and other cephalopods. Large cephalopods like the adult *Sepia* squid and octopus use an ink cloud as a mode of defensive behaviour. When a squid is disturbed, it ejects ink through its anus. The ink irritates the predator's eyes and paralyses its olfactory sense. This disorientates the predator and gives the squid time to abruptly change its direction and flee.

Movement

Squid can manoeuvre themselves very easily in the water. They draw water into their mantle cavity and then move by jet-like expulsion by expelling the water through a funnel. The funnel can be directed forward, backward or in any direction. They are propelled in the direction opposite to that of the jet of water. They use their fins for stability and steering.

Most Malaysian species of cuttlefish are bottom dwellers, meaning they crawl along the sea bed. Only some species use a water jet, like squid. Although there are octopuses that also use water jets to move, most Malaysian species of octopuses crawl.

A squid swimming in its usual position. It propels itself by expelling water from its funnel.

Water rushes in behind the squid's head when it expands its mantle cavity. This increases its moving power.

To move forward, the squid points its funnel towards its back. By forcing water out from the funnel, the squid will be propelled forward.

To move backward, the squid swings its funnel around towards the front. By forcing water out of the funnel, the squid will be propelled backward.

Food products

Although fresh squid and cuttlefish are sold in markets in Malaysia, much is also salted and dried and made into food products. Dried salted squid and cuttlefish are also commonly used in Malaysian cuisine. A popular hawker dish, called *sotong kangkong*, combines preserved cuttlefish with the water convulvulus. Squid and cuttlefish are also dried and sweetened to make crunchy snacks which are very popular.

Mitre squid are dried in the sun on a special frame.

Dried and sweetened cuttlefish are popular packaged snacks.

Seashells

Seashells are the cast-off coverings of soft-bodied animals known as molluscs (see 'Molluscs') which themselves are often referred to as 'seashells'. Since prehistoric times, the beauty and variety of seashells have enticed people to collect and use them for commercial purposes and adornment. Although a large variety of seashells is found in Malaysia, some species are becoming endangered because of over-collection. Therefore, shell collecting is now prohibited in Malaysian marine parks.

A fisherman sits beside seashells sorted out from his nets.

Shells have long been used in traditional societies in the region. These cowrie shells (*Cypraea moneta*), found at Kuala Selinsing in Perak, are thought to have been used as currency by the mangrove dwellers.

Types of seashells

Seashells come from the Gastropoda and Bivalvia classes of Molluscs. By far the largest group are the Gastropods and many of the species have wonderfully patterned and shaped shells. Cowries and the spiral-shaped *Murex* species are some of the most comonly found. Cowries are usually active at night when they can be seen feeding on algae on rocky surfaces.

Distribution

Seashells are found throughout the world, in both tropical and temperate areas. It is in the Indo-Pacific region, the world's largest, which comprises most of the Pacific Ocean, the Indian Ocean and the countries and islands around them, including Malaysia, that the greatest number and variety of seashells are found. This is because the warm, tropical climate is ideal for the growth of molluscs. Shells found in the tropics are most colourful.

Shells are found in a number of key habitats, principally rocky shores and coral reefs, mud flats and mangroves, and sandy shores.

Commercial and traditional uses

Traditionally, seashells such as cowries are used to make handicrafts. This practice is carried out in Malaysia, particularly by the Iban of Sarawak who decorate caps, jackets and other clothing with cowries and various types of seashells. The Iban also produce armlets made of brass decorated with shells. Many local species of shells, such as the popular *Melo melo* and *Cymbiola nobilis*, are sold loose and made into modern handicrafts such as picture frames, mirror frames, trinket boxes, ash trays, key chains and other decorative souvenir items which are in great demand from tourists. In Sabah, animal motifs traditionally used for handwoven Bajau and

①

Shell habitat zones in Malaysia

Shell habitats vary from rocky, sandy and muddy shores to mangrove swamps, coral reefs and bays. Changes in water salinity, different depths of the shoreline, and the force of waves and currents determine the varieties and numbers of shells found in each habitat. While some habitats are unsuitable for certain species, a limited area may sometimes harbour huge numbers of a particular species.

SHELL HABITAT ZONES

COMMON NAME	SCIENTIFIC NAME	LOCATIONS IN MALAYSIA	HABITATS
			Rocky shores and coral reefs
1. Cock's comb oyster	*Lopha cristagalli*	Pulau Payar	On rocks
2. Humpback cowrie	*Cypraea mauritania*	Pulau Payar	Under or in between rocks
3. Onyx cowrie	*Cypraea onyx*	Pulau Pangkor, Pulau Kapas, Mersing	On intertidal sands and stony coral slabs
4. Tiger cowrie	*Cypraea tigris*	Pulau Tioman, Pulau Sembilan	Under overhanging ledges, amongst seaweeds
5. Green turban shell	*Turbo marmoratus*	Pulau Pangkor	Under overhanging ledges, amongst seaweeds
6. Leopard cone	*Conus leopardus*	Sabah	Under overhanging ledges
			Muddy and mangrove shores
7. Midas ear shell	*Ellobium aurismidae*	Sitiawan (Perak)	In mangroves along upper reaches of rivers
8. Judas ear shell	*Ellobium aurisjudae*	Sitiawan (Perak)	In mangroves along upper reaches of rivers
9. Telescope snail	*Telescopium telescopium*	Kota Baru, Kuala Selangor and Sitiawan	On mud banks of mangrove-lined rivers
10. Burnt-end ark	*Anadara uropygmelana*	Tanjung Bungah and Gertak Sanggul (Penang)	On intertidal sandy mud bottoms
11. Discus shell	*Dosinia* sp.	Tanjung Bungah and Gertak Sanggul (Penang)	On sandy mud shores
			Sandy and sand-mud shores
12. Ternate false fusus	*Hermifusus ternatanus*	Penang, Pulau Langkawi and Pulau Pangkor	Offshore in muddy areas
13. Chiragra spider conch	*Lambis chiragra*	Pulau Perhentian, Pulau Sembilan	On intertidal rocks, sand and coral
14. Ramose murex	*Murex ramosus*	East coast, Peninsular Malaysia and Sabah	On sandy mud bottoms
15. Sunburst carrier shell	*Stellaria solaris*	Penang Channel and Tanjung Bungah	On sandy bottoms 30–60 metres deep
16. Noble volute	*Cymbiola nobilis*	Pulau Pinang, Pulau Perhentian, Pulau Pangkor, Mersing	On intertidal rocks, sand and stony reefs and sandy and muddy bottoms 2–20 metres deep
17. Horned helmet	*Cassis cornuta*	Pulau Perhentian, Pulau Tioman and Mersing	On coral sand 6–20 metres deep

Iranun textiles include stylized forms of seashells. Such motifs are also used in the wood carvings of the Bajau Laut at Semporna.

An Orang Ulu baby carrier decorated with colourful beads and cowrie shells.

Conservation

Although nearly all molluscs produce many thousands of offspring, at least 90 per cent are destroyed by the vagaries of nature and by the effects of pollution or destruction of their habitats. They are also endangered by irresponsible shell collecting. Certain Malaysian species, even the more abundant and least expensive shells, such as cowries and button shells, are becoming endangered because they are over-collected. Although the *Conus ammiralis* and *C. aulicus* are not used in handicrafts because they are difficult to find in any number, they also need protection as they are in demand by collectors. Environmentalists are working hard to create a greater awareness among the Malaysian public and tourists about the importance of conservation of all marine life, including seashells.

Popular Malaysian shells

Many attractive Malaysian shells are in demand from collectors. One is the large, orange-red Indian volute (*Melo melo*). A few of these volutes have two or three wide, broken brown bands. They are mostly found on the west coast of Peninsular Malaysia. Another, much heavier shell, also popular with collectors, is the noble volute (*Cymbiola nobilis*), a colourful shell with a flaring lip. There is also a dwarf variety of *Cymbiola nobilis* which is cream coloured with two purplish-brown broken bands and brown zigzag lines. Other popular species include the less common admiral cone (*Conus ammiralis*), Aulicus cone (*C. aulicus*), punctate cowrie (*Cypraea punctata*) and Saul's cowrie (*C. saulae*), which are mostly found on the east coast of the Peninsula.

Ternate false fusus
(*Hermifusus ternatanus*)

Humpback cowrie
(*Cypraea mauritiania*)

Sunburst carrier shell
(*Stellaria solaris*)

Pen shell
(*Pinna incurva*)

Poulsen's triton
(*Cymatium poulsenii*)

Scallop
(*Pecten tranquebaricus*)

Noble volute
(*Cymbiola nobilis*)

Indian volute
(*Melo melo*)

Fringing coral reefs, such as those around Pulau Payar, Tioman, Pangkor and other islands, are common habitats for various species of molluscs.

Many molluscs live in the mud in mangroves, such as those in Matang, Perak, where they feed on decomposed mangrove leaves.

Intertidal sand and mud shores, such as at Kuala Selangor, contain much organic matter, including dead plankton, that provide food for many molluscs.

Shell collecting

Some conservationists believe that pollution and excessive commercial fishing are the major causes of mollusc reduction, and that controlled collecting of shells stimulates interest in the living molluscs and contributes towards their preservation. However, informed shell collectors collect only perfect specimens and return all damaged specimens and young ones for future propagation. They know it is vital to preserve the natural habitat where the molluscs live. In designated marine parks, it is forbidden to collect seashells and this is a vital conservation measure that collectors and the public alike should respect.

Poisonous molluscs

Some species of molluscs are dangerous. Those shells above—(1) *Conus textile*, (2) *C. aulicus*, (3) *C. marmoreus*, (4) *C. geographus* and (5) *C. striatus*—contain venom capable of delivering a very painful and serious sting.

Worms

Marine worms are among the most colourful organisms visible in tropical waters. Worldwide, there are seven phyla with the common name 'worm', of which six also have marine species. Representatives of all the phyla are found in Malaysia, as well as in other tropical Indo-Pacific coastal regions. However, the number of species in Malaysia is insignificant compared with other countries. Although most marine worms are very small in comparison with other invertebrates, they are ecologically important as their feeding activities help to aerate the sediments at the bottom of the sea.

This fan worm (*Sabellastarte* sp.) is a segmented worm living in a tube built into coral.

1. A colony of Christmas tree worms (*Spirobranchus giganteus*) share their coral habitat with a large, yellowish fan worm (*Sabellastarte* sp.). They are all so sensitive to light that the slightest movement or shadow will cause them to contract back into their tubes.

2. Like all flatworms, this one (*Pseudoceros lindae*) can move in the water by undulating its body margins.

3. Flatworms often have brilliant colours, such as this species (*Pseudoceros ferrugineus*). Bright colours indicate that the worm is poisonous.

Habitats

Tropical waters harbour a greater diversity of worms than any other aquatic environment. Some of the more conspicuous groups of marine worms found in Malaysian seas include flatworms, segmented worms and ribbon worms. The worms come in various shapes and live in a variety of places in the marine environment. Some burrow into the sediment or into living or dead corals, some hide inside crevices, while others live on other invertebrates such as sea cucumbers and sand dollars. Sometimes other organisms, such as crustaceans or crabs, are found within the tubes or burrows made by segmented worms.

Flatworms

Flatworms belong to the phylum Platyhelminthes. Usually less than 8 centimetres in length, they have a flat, oval body with a flattened head, simple organs and microscopic eye spots.

The free-living forms are the turbellarians, which have dazzling colours that often lead to them being mistaken for nudibranchs (molluscs without shells or mantles). However, unlike nudibranchs, worms lacks external gills or other projections. Flatworms glide, moving by the minute bristles on their underside and by muscle contractions over a self-secreted film of mucus. Their process of respiration is through diffusion. They feed on organic detritus, and food can be distributed to the entire body by diffusion as well. Although flatworms

usually reproduce sexually, some also reproduce asexually. In sexual reproduction, although each worm possesses both male and female reproductive organs, two individual worms are needed to procreate. One worm passes sperm to the other and receives eggs from it in return. Asexually, free-living flatworms can regenerate a new worm from a detached part. The remaining worm will also grow back to normal size after a part has been detached.

Segmented worms

Segmented worms belong to the phylum Annelida, which comprises three main classes, namely Polychaeta (marine), Oligochaeta (terrestrial and fresh water) and Hirudina (marine, fresh water and terrestrial). Although there are over 70 families and 12,000 species worldwide, their exact numbers in Malaysia are as yet unrecorded.

Polychaete worms are numerous and of different sizes. The majority are sedentary types living in or on the bottom sediment but some are pelagic (free-living types). The distinguishing characteristic of polychaetes is the division of the body into similar segments, each bearing a series of short bristles called setae, which help in sensing and movement as well as in defence.

Although some polychaetes are beautiful, they should not be handled with the bare hands. Their setae can easily penetrate the skin and break off, causing pain. Other polychaetes bite.

Sedentary worms such as Christmas tree worms (Serpulidae) and feather dusters (Sabellidae) live in tubes made out of calcium carbonate secreted from their bodies and mixed with fine sand. The tubes protect them from waves, currents and predators.

Feather duster worms

Some segmented worms do not look like worms because of their unusual body shapes. One of these is the feather duster worm (*Filogranella elatensis*) which lives in a tube built into coral.

A young worm settles on a coral head and secretes a tube to kill the underlying coral polyps. New coral grows quickly to surround the tube. However, the worm defies eviction by secreting additional tube construction material (a mixture of calcium carbonate and sand) to keep pace with the coral. Such tube worms are basically filter feeders, trapping organic debris in moving water with their fine 'nets'. Their bright colours deter predators.

Dying to survive

Some free-living segmented worms have separate sexes and produce eggs and sperm in their bodies. Regardless of how aroused they become, they have no opening in their bodies to release sperm and eggs. On a certain night of the year, sexually mature males and females gather en masse and ascend towards the surface to mate. They literally tear themselves apart in a frenzy in order to release their sperm or eggs so that the sperm and eggs can meet to reproduce. Thus, they must die to ensure the survival of their species.

An annelid worm tries to tear itself apart by stretching up to 10 times its body size.

When it contracts, like a rubber band, it falls to the ground and breaks apart.

Sperm and eggs are released into the water so that they can unite. The worm then dies.

Ecological importance

All worms play beneficial roles in one way or another within a community, especially those of mud or sand bottom areas. A considerable amount of sand is eaten by worms on sandy beaches, and later eliminated from their bodies.

This ingestion and expulsion of sediment helps in turning over and mixing the sediment. In the soft bottom environment, their filter-feeding activities help to aerate the anaerobic condition within the top layer, whilst their tentacle movements create water currents through their burrows or tubes.

Worms that bore can destroy living corals as well as reduce dead coral skeletons to fine sediment. They break the skeletons with their horny teeth or by chemically dissolving the calcium carbonate matrix. Destructive though this may be, it can help to reduce dead coral to fine sediment, which eventually becomes a foundation for continued coral growth. Thus, worms are an integral part of a coral reef ecosystem.

Species of polychaetes also serve as pollution indicators. Their larvae develop from fertilized eggs, drift along with the currents as plankton, and settle at the bottom of the sea, developing into young worms. If the environment is contaminated with pollutants, the young worms are not able to develop. Thus, the absence of the worms indicates pollution.

Reproduction is mainly sexual as most polychaetes have separate sexes. However, some, such as syllids and serpulids, are hermaphrodites. Males release sperm and females release eggs simultaneously into the sea. Fertilized eggs develop into planktonic larvae and drift along with the current, eventually settling on a suitable bottom and developing. Reproduction can be asexual, too, for many polychaetes. If certain segments of the body are lost, the missing segment can be regenerated.

Feeding habits of worms

Polychaetes can be broadly divided into two types: sedentary and free-living. Some are entirely free-swimming, whilst others are crawlers, burrowers, or temporary and permanent tube builders. Because of their different ways of living, they have different feeding habits and different diets.

The shape of this fan worm (*Bispira* sp.) (above) resembles a large flower rather than a worm. In contrast, the flatworm (left) (*Pseudoceros lindae*) has a more typical worm-shaped body.

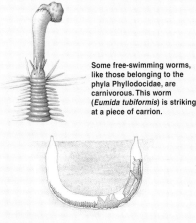

Some free-swimming worms, like those belonging to the phyla Phyllodocidae, are carnivorous. This worm (*Eumida tubiformis*) is striking at a piece of carrion.

A sedentary tube worm in its normal filter-feeding posture. By holding its funnel erect and waving its tentacles, it creates a current that draws food particles into its tube.

Sedentary tube worms like the *Chaetopterus variopedatus* are deposit feeders. As they are unable to move, they take in sediments from the surrounding environment and feed on the organic contents.

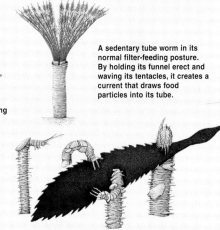

Some crawling marine worms eat plants. They can move around their environment in search of suitable marine plants to feed on. This worm (*Diopatra ornata*) is feeding on a frond of seaweed.

Ribbon worms

Ribbon worms, or nemerteans, belonging to the phylum Nemertea, are not only found in marine habitats, but also in fresh water and terrestrial habitats. Most of the 900 known species are marine dwellers. They are easily recognized by their soft, elongated, ciliated and unsegmented bodies and their retractile proboscis. The proboscis is muscular and armed with a piercing stylet which is used to capture prey. The majority of ribbon worms are small, only about 1–3 centimetres long, and feed mainly on tiny marine invertebrates.

Reproduction in ribbon worms is mainly sexual, but the worm can also reproduce asexually. If a segment is broken off, the worm can easily regenerate itself, and the broken off segment can also regenerate into a new worm.

Ribbon worms are among the less colourful marine worms.

Barnacles

Although barnacles look like molluscs because of their shell-like covering, they are in fact crustaceans. They are divided into two groups: non-stalked or 'acorn' barnacles, which are surrounded by plates, and stalked or 'goose' barnacles, which are attached to the end of a stalk. The hard, white, cone-like acorn barnacle predominates in Malaysia, attaching itself to rocks and any other hard surface that gets covered by water. Most species in Malaysia grow no more than a few millimetres tall and live in dense colonies primarily in the intertidal zone.

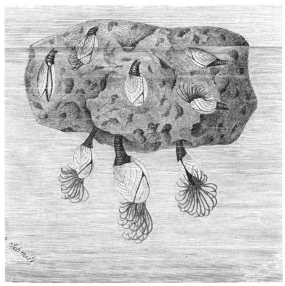

A lithograph from *The Royal Natural History*, Richard Lydekker (ed.), Vol. VI, London, 1896, showing stalked or 'goose' barnacles attached to a pumice.

The acorn barnacle

Top view of an adult acorn barnacle showing its rigid wall of calcareous plates arranged in the shape of a flat-topped cone.

Side view of an acorn barnacle showing the legs protruding from between the plates.

Local species

Only one species of stalked barnacle is found in Malaysia (*Lepas anatifera*), but there are several non-stalked species, including *Balanus amphitrite rafflesi*, *B. amaryllis*, *B. amphitrite variegatus*, *Chthamalus withersi*, *Chelonibia testudinaria* and *Tetraclita porosa viridis*. Most of the non-stalked barnacles are found in the intertidal zone where their distribution mirrors the different tidal ranges at different locations. In Penang, for example, this ranges from about 0.5 metre above the mean sea level to 0.5 metre below, whereas in the western part of the Johor Strait, it ranges from 0.9 metre above the mean sea level to 1.0 metre below. The tidal range is highest around Port Klang.

Many of the barnacles found above the mean high water level, where they are exposed to air for longer periods, are either dead or smaller than those encrusted lower down. However, perhaps the most common causes of barnacle mortality are over-crowding and smothering by other barnacles.

Physical features

Both non-stalked and stalked barnacles have a segmented body and six pairs of jointed, feather-like feeding appendages or 'legs', called cirri. The body and legs face upwards and are contained within a cavity formed of calcareous plates, which are secreted by the barnacle.

The number of plates differs for each species. The non-stalked *Balanus* and *Chthamalus* barnacles have six neatly fitting plates (called mural plates) that encircle them, plus four central plates which form a 'door' that the animal can open or close depending on the tide. Other non-stalked barnacles can have up to 12 plates. The more a barnacle eats, the more it grows, and the tighter its living

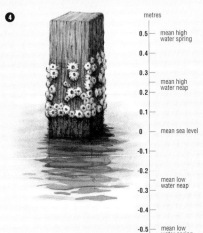

metres	
0.5	mean high water spring
0.4	
0.3	mean high water neap
0.2	
0.1	
0	mean sea level
-0.1	
-0.2	mean low water neap
-0.3	
-0.4	
-0.5	mean low water spring

Barnacle encrustation

1. A wreck off One Fathom Bank, in the Strait of Melaka, covered with barnacles.
2. Barnacles are commonly found on coral reefs off the east coast of Peninsular Malaysia.
3. Rocky surfaces are a favourite environment for barnacles.
4. Barnacles often encrust pillars of jetties or stilts of houses standing in the water.

Fouling

There are several thousand species of biofouling organisms in the marine environment, including many invertebrate species. Mingled with barnacles, periwinkles (*Littorina scabra*), mussels (*Perna viridis*), oysters (*Pinctada* sp.), grapsid crabs, tube worms (*Pomatoceros* sp.), woodborers (*Martesia striata*), bryozoa (*Bowerbankia* sp.), tunicates (*Botrylloides* sp.) and seaweeds (*Gracilaria* sp.) can often be found. The worst biofoulers, however, are barnacles. These can encrust an entire surface within weeks after submergence in water. Barnacles attach themselves to any hard surface—rocks, bridge pillars, jetties, sewage outfalls, inlet and outlet pipes of power plants, retention walls of seaside resorts and premises, bottoms of boats, fish nets, and even sea turtles or crabs.

Effects of fouling

Barnacles are among the most destructive fouling organisms on ships. Not only do they impede the speed of ships but they increase fuel consumption because of increased friction and weight. Fouling of internal submarine pipelines and fish cages clogs up these structures and prevents free exchange of water. Costly cleaning and maintenance work has to be carried out periodically on these structures.

The usual form of maintenance is to physically remove the encrusted barnacles from the surface of structures, after which they are painted with anti-fouling paint or, if pipes, flushed with biocides such as chlorine. Both methods are able to control new encrustation to a certain degree and reduce the frequency of maintenance.

Life cycle

The life cycle of a barnacle consists of three stages: a planktonic naupli larval stage, a settling cypris stage, and the adult sedentary stage. Most barnacles are hermaphrodites, meaning they have both male and female sex organs However, to create baby barnacles, they must be fertilized by a neighbour. Barnacles have proportionately probably the largest penis in the animal kingdom. This retractable tube, containing sperm, can reach outside the shell as far as several inches to fertilize a nearby barnacle. After fertilization, the barnacle broods its eggs until they hatch and are released into the sea.

Both larval forms, the nauplius and the cypris, have a single compound eye which is absent in the adult barnacle. The nauplius, the first stage that emerges from the eggs, feeds voraciously on plankton, growing and moulting into the shrimp-like larva cypris. The cypris larvae remain swimming until they are ready to settle head down on a suitable surface. They generally seek out surfaces that are well lit and concave. The presence of plenty of organic matter as well as suitable water current and direction are also important factors. Cement glands found in the antennae of the cypris secrete a substance which allows it to attach itself to a solid surface.

Attached to a suitable surface, the remaining parts of the cypris swing freely in the water current, searching for the best place to capture food particles. The cypris itself does not feed since it does not have an intestine, but uses its stored reserves to survive. Gradually the attached cypris grows into an adult barnacle and the cycle of life begins all over again.

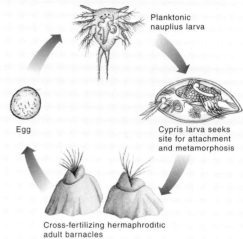

Life cycle of an acorn barnacle (*Balanus* sp.)

Planktonic nauplius larva

Egg

Cypris larva seeks site for attachment and metamorphosis

Cross-fertilizing hermaphroditic adult barnacles

environment becomes. Not only is it constrained by its own thin shell, or cuticle, but also by its surrounding plated home. Barnacles, like lobsters, shed their cuticle when it gets too small for them, at the same time enlarging their home. The barnacle secretes a chemical from its mantle which dissolves the inner layers of the plates, simultaneously adding new material to the outside.

In the adult stage, the shell plates of the non-stalked barnacles attach themselves directly to the surfaces of rocks and wooden structures, while the stalked barnacles are attached by a distinct stalk. The glue the acorn barnacles secrete for attaching themselves is so strong that the barnacle's cone base still remains long after it has died. Because of their hard outer covering, they are also highly resistant to temperature and chemical changes, wave damage, as well as exposure to air. Since banacles are sedentary and live in the intertidal zone where the tide ebbs and flows, they have evolved ways of avoiding dessication. When the tide goes out, the barnacle withdraws, tightly closing its central plates to conserve the moisture trapped during high tide. During this time it does not feed or do anything except try to keep moist. As the tide come in, a muscle opens up the four central plates and the jointed, feathery legs of the barnacle, set with sensory hairs, brush through the water sweeping plankton suspended in the water into the mouth of the barnacle (see 'Plankton'). The main predators of barnacles are snails that envelop the barnacle's cone and force the plates open.

Fishermen have to scrape barnacles off the bottoms of their boats every two or three months. Encrustation by barnacles on the bottom of boats impedes speed and increases fuel consumption.

Chemical control

Although marine anti-fouling paints are employed to control barnacle encrustation, many environmentalists object strongly to their use. The active ingredient in anti-fouling paints is tributyl tin (TBT), and studies have shown that TBT causes adverse side-effects on marine organisms, particularly molluscs. Concentrations of as low as 0.01–0.15 ug/L (parts per billion) can cause mortality of the Pacific oyster (*Crassostrea gigas*). They can also cause imposex (change in sex) or the appearance of a penis-like organ in female molluscs. The fear is that a high accumulation of TBT in molluscs may eventually be passed on to humans through the food chain. Although TBT has been banned in many places, including Europe and the United States, it is still in use in Malaysia, where the prohibition of anti-fouling chemicals is being weighed against the economic costs of fouling.

Biological control

Biological control of fouling, in which certain species 'invade' others, acting as a control on their growth, has received wide attention from the scientific community. It has been suggested, for example, that whelks (*Morula marginalba* and *Thais orbita*), the main predators of barnacles, could be introduced in barnacle zones. The whelks envelop the barnacle's hard cone and force the valves open. However, the application of such biological controls and its cost-effectiveness remain to be explored.

Crabs

Crabs belong to the group crustaceans, which are the most common creatures of the sea. Many species of crabs are found on the Malaysian seashore. They come in a variety of shapes and sizes, and range from a few millimetres to 20 centimetres in diameter. Some crabs prefer sand substrates, while others live in mud or sand-mud environments. A few species of marine crabs are adapted to dry land and may be seen in burrows well above the high tide mark.

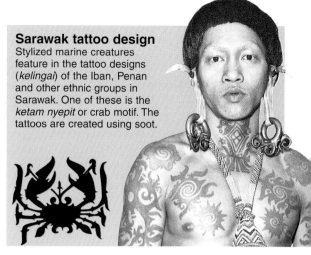

Sarawak tattoo design
Stylized marine creatures feature in the tattoo designs (*kelingai*) of the Iban, Penan and other ethnic groups in Sarawak. One of these is the *ketam nyepit* or crab motif. The tattoos are created using soot.

Sign language

The male fiddler crab has one enlarged claw which it uses to attract the female during courtship, as well as to defend its territory against other males. Shown here is the initial stage of the mating ritual. Starting with the large claw in front of its face, the crab then swings it back to an open position before rotating it up and down.

Characteristics

A variety of crabs live in the intertidal zone, the area where the land meets the sea. The largest group in this zone belongs to the Ocypodidae family and includes ghost, sand bubbler and fiddler crabs. As these crustaceans breathe air, they are well adapted to living in the intertidal zone. During high tide, they hide in their burrows and survive on oxygen from a trapped air bubble in the burrow. Tufts of fine hair on their abdomens prevent dehydration by helping them absorb water from the damp sand and keeping their gills wet. At low tide, they emerge from their burrows to forage for food.

A distinctive characteristic of crabs is that they walk sideways. This method of walking, with their four hindmost legs, is due to the flattened shape of their bodies. As the legs of one side pull and those of the other side shove, the crab walks and runs sideways with amazing speed and agility.

Crabs of sandy and sand-mud shores

Various species of crabs live on sandy and sand-mud shores in Malaysia. Inhabiting the upper parts of sandy shores, inundated only by the highest spring tides, are ghost crabs (*Ocypode ceratophthalma*). These crabs get their common name from their greyish carapace, prominent eyes set on long stalks and nocturnal habits. Since they move very fast, they are also difficult to catch. Ghost crabs are most active at night, preying on small animals or scavenging on debris at the water's edge. They also prey on turtle hatchlings as these emerge from their nests and dash for the sea, and are therefore an additional threat to endangered turtle species.

The soldier crab (*Dotilla myctiroides*) is dominant on shores where there is a mixture of mud and sand, as in Port Dickson and Morib on the west coast of Peninsular Malaysia. The movement of thousands of these tiny crabs close together, like armies, at the shore has given rise to their common name. As the tide recedes, soldier crabs emerge to feed in groups, particularly along the edges of puddles. They feed by scooping sand into their mouths with their claws, where organic matter is selected for ingestion and sand is rejected. The ejected sand—the feeding pellet—is collected by one of the claws from the mouth and discarded. Where there is a large population of soldier crabs, the exposed shore becomes covered with feeding pellets. Because they are able to breathe in air as

Crabs of sandy and sand-mud shores

The crabs living on sandy and sand-mud shores live in burrows to escape from the hot sun by day and from predators at night. Ghost crabs burrow more than a metre down in order to reach moist sand. Bubbler crabs feed on the surface of the sand, forming straight, shallow trenches radiating from the burrow opening. Feeding pellets are laid along the trenches. The burrows of fiddler crabs are L-shaped and slightly inclined. All these crabs feed on organic matter found in the sand or mud.

1. Soldier crab (*Dotilla myctiroides*)
2. Bubbler crab (*Scopimera intermedia*)
3. Ghost crab (*Ocypode ceratophthalma*)
4. Sentinel crab (*Macrophthalmus malaccensis*)
5. Fiddler crab (*Uca annulipes*)

well as in water, soldier crabs are adapted to life both in and out of water. The gill chambers located within the body are full of blood vessels, which help to increase oxygen intake. Like other crabs, the soldier crab also has gills to enable it to breathe in water. The ability to breathe air enables it to spend several hours on the surface feeding, without going into burrows to replenish water in its gill chambers. When soldier crabs are disturbed, they quickly burrow sideways and disappear beneath the sand.

The upper shores of sand flats are also home to bubbler crabs (*Scopimera intermedia*). Although these crabs resemble soldier crabs, they are smaller and their tufts of water-absorbing hair are on the thorax, not the abdomen. There have stiff black bristles on their legs. Like the other crabs, they forage close to their burrows, leaving a bubble-like pattern of sand pellets radiating from the burrow opening.

The fiddler crab (*Uca annulipes*) is also prominent on the upper shores of sand flats. The male has one enlarged claw for fighting and courtship, and one small claw for feeding. The females have two similar sized spoon-shaped claws for feeding. During low tide, fiddlers excavate their burrows and carry the sand to the surface as small balls, depositing them near the burrow entrance. As the high tide approaches, they return to their burrows and plug the entrance. Fiddler crabs come out at low tide to feed near their burrows and court on the surface. When disturbed, they rapidly return to their burrows.

The sentinel crab (*Macrophthalmus malaccensis*) is common on the lower shores of sand–mud flats, where its permanent burrows are easily visible to the discerning eye. The crab may be recognized by its rectangular shell and exceedingly long eye-stalks.

Crabs of mud flats and mangroves

A large number of crab species live in mud because it is a good medium for burrowing. There is also an abundance of organic matter, consisting of diatoms and organic detritus, on the mud surface. The habitat is thus suitable for deposit (mud) feeders.

The mud flat situated in front of mangroves and facing the sea is the home of numerous species of crabs, the most conspicuous being *Macrophthalmus teschi* and *Metaplax crenulatus*. Both species can only be observed from a distance as they quickly escape into their burrows when approached.

The mangrove shore is colonized by a large variety of fiddler and grapsid crabs. On the lower shore, the most common fiddler crab is the bright blue *Uca dussumieri*, the largest of Malaysia's fiddler crabs. On the upper mangrove shore, fiddler crabs

Crabs of the mud flats and mangroves

Like the crabs which live on the sand-mud shores, the crabs on mud flats in Malaysia do so because it is easy to burrow into the mud. As mangroves are also muddy, these crabs can live there, too, especially since there is an abundance of food. They feed on the organic matter in the mud. Some crabs, such as the grapsid crabs, even feed on fallen mangrove leaves, thus playing a major role in nutrient recycling in the area.

The fiddler crabs living in such environments are deposit feeders, scooping surface mud with their spoon-shaped claws and tipping

1. Mud crab (*Scylla serrata*)
2. Signaller crab (*Metaplax crenulatus*)
3. Grapsid crab (*Sesarma versicolor*)
4. Fiddler crab (*Uca dussumieri*)
5. Sentinel crab (*Macrophthalmus teschi*)

it into their mouths, where they sieve out the organic particles and then discard the waste as a pellet. Such pellets are usually scattered in the vicinity of the crabs' burrows.

All these crabs play an important role in the ecosystem as their constant burrowing ensures that buried nutrients are recycled.

include the distinctive *Uca rosea* and *Uca triangularis* species. The male of *Uca rosea* has bright red claws, one greatly enlarged for fighting (for both territory and females) while the male of the small *Uca triangularis* species has yellow claws.

Grapsid crabs are represented by many species, and are dominant in the high shore of mangroves. The common grapsid is *Sesarma versicolor*. It has purple claws with white margins along the inner surface. Grapsids feed on fallen mangrove leaves and hence play a major role in nutrient cycling.

The mud crab (*Scylla serrata*) is an edible crab which favours mud flats and mangroves. It is now recognized that there are four species of *Scylla* of what was originally thought to be a single species, *Scylla serrata*. The mature female migrates offshore to release its eggs, which are locally considered a delicacy, and the larvae migrate into shallow waters, including mangroves and mud flats, to feed and grow. There are commercial fisheries of the mud crab in Malaysia, where it is relished as a seafood delicacy. However, as the harvest is inadequate to meet local demand, Malaysia imports substantial quantities from Indonesia and Sri Lanka.

Crab predators

The catfish (*Arius* sp.), catfish eel (*Plotosus*), snake (*Cerebus rhyncops*) and mudskipper (*Periophthalmodon schlosseri*) are the major predators of mangrove and sand-mud flat crabs despite the speed and agility of most crab species. These predators usually live in soft bottom intertidal areas and migrate up and down the intertidal zone according to the tide. They move swiftly over the substrate to catch their prey, or pop out of burrows to strike.

Mudskipper (*Periophthalmodon schlosseri*)

Prawns

Prawns or large shrimps are decapods, crustaceans which, along with crabs, lobsters and crayfish, have five pairs of walking legs. The two main groups of prawns, the Penaeoidea and the Caridea, are both found in Malaysia, with the majority being penaeoid prawns. Around 80 000 tons of marine prawns are captured annually in Malaysian waters, making a small but significant percentage of the total fisheries catch. Both marine and freshwater prawns are cultivated commercially as well, since demand for Malaysian prawns is high, both locally and abroad.

Shrimp paste (*belacan*), made from tiny dried and pounded shrimps, adds to the pungent flavour of many Malaysian dishes.

Types and origin

Of the two main types of prawns, penaeoid prawns are all marine prawns, whereas carid prawns can be either marine or fresh water. Members of the family Penaeidae are the most abundant and well known. They have branched gills. Their first three pairs of walking legs have pincers. When they spawn, their eggs are released directly into the sea. About 53 species of penaeid prawns are recorded in Malaysia, but only 30 species are fished commercially.

Carid prawns, on the other hand, have leaf-like gills, two pairs of pincers, and the spawned eggs are carried by females below their abdomen. Penaeoid

prawns are primitive decapods that evolved during the late Triassic period about 200 million years ago. Carid prawns evolved more recently, during the Jurassic period, 180 million years ago.

The basic prawn body is elongated, segmented and compressed from the sides. The front part comprises the head and thorax, with the latter bearing five pairs of walking legs. The body is covered by an external skeleton or shell that is shed periodically to allow the animal to grow before a new skeleton hardens. The shell covering the prawn's front part often bears a long, toothed blade called the rostrum.

This poster from the Fisheries Department, often displayed at local supermarkets or outlets selling prawn products, shows the many different types of commercial prawns available in Malaysia.

Marine prawns are found mainly in tropical and subtropical waters, from shallow estuaries to deep seas, though a few species are found in cold, temperate waters. Many inhabit the shallow coastal waters close to mud flats or intertidal vegetation such as mangroves, salt marshes and seagrasses. These habitats serve as nursery areas for young prawns, providing abundant food as well as refuge from predators. Young prawns feed on living microscopic plants and animals, as well as fine particles from decomposing mangrove, seagrass and seaweed matter. Adult prawns feed on small plants and animals living at the sea bottom, such as algae, crustaceans, segmented worms and molluscs.

Migration and spawning

Most penaeoid prawns spawn in deep offshore waters. Prawn species found in the Strait of Melaka migrate offshore for distances of 5–80 kilometres to mature and spawn. Locally, banana prawns (*Penaeus merguiensis*) migrate the farthest. However, there are other species that migrate longer distances to spawn. For instance, in China, the fleshy prawn (*Penaeus chinensis*) migrates 500 kilometres offshore to the Yellow Sea in winter.

Prawns have separate sexes. The male has a reproductive organ called the petasma, found between the first pair of swimming legs, whilst the female has a seminal receptacle called the thelycum, found between the last pair of walking legs. During mating, sperm packets are inserted into the thelycum with the petasma. Sperms within their packets are viable for several weeks. When the female spawns, the stored sperms are released along with her eggs, and hence fertilization of eggs is external. A female prawn, depending on the species, can release between 50,000 and over a million tiny eggs at a single spawning.

Life cycle of the banana prawn, a penaeoid prawn

The adult banana prawn migrates long distances to mature and spawn.

1 The tiny spawned eggs sink to the sea bottom, whilst larger eggs spawned by other species are buoyant and classed as plankton.

2 The nauplius larva has a pear-shaped body and only three pairs of limbs, used for swimming. It does not feed but subsists on its internal yolk supply.

3 The protozoea has an oval-shaped shell, an elongated region forked at the end, and compound eyes. It swims by paddling its front two antennae, and feeds on microscopic plants and animals.

4 The mysis looks more adult. It swims by rotating the outer branches of its legs in a circular motion. It filter feeds initially, but as it grows larger it also seizes planktonic animals.

5 The post-larva swims using its now fully developed swimming legs. It swims in the water column, but after four or five days settles down on the sea bottom. Initially, it feeds on plankton, but in time on other plant and animal matter.

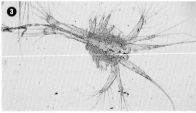

6 After the post-larva loses its tail spines, when it is about 3.5 cm long, it is considered a juvenile. Juvenile prawns develop in shallow coastal waters, initially in estuarine mangrove swamps, then in more saline offshore waters.

Commercial prawns of Malaysia

The annual catch of marine prawns in Malaysian waters is about 80 000 tons, or 8 per cent of the total fisheries catch, and is valued at about RM900 million (US$237 million). The bulk of the catch (more than 99 per cent) comprises penaeoid prawns. Penaeoid prawns are also cultured in brackish water ponds which produces another 9500 tons annually. Only about 1 per cent of the total prawns landed are sold as dried prawns.

The largest prawn landings by four states, in order of importance, come from Perak, Sarawak, Selangor and Sabah. In all areas, the prawns are caught together with fish, but by using fishing nets of smaller mesh sizes. These include trawl nets (*pukat tunda*), bag nets (*pukat bakul*), drift or trammel nets (*pukat hanyut*), seine nets (*pukat tarik*), scoop nets (*pukat surung*) and barrier nets (*pukat rentang*) (see 'Fishing methods').

Of the total prawns landed in Malaysia, about 15 per cent, including frozen as well as preserved or dried prawns, are exported to Japan, the United States and Europe. This demand from overseas, coupled with equally high local demand, has resulted in a considerable rise in the price of prawns in recent years.

PRAWN LANDINGS IN MALAYSIA BY STATE 1997

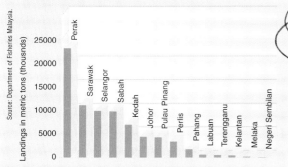

PROPORTION OF PRAWN LANDINGS TO OTHER FISHERIES IN MALAYSIA

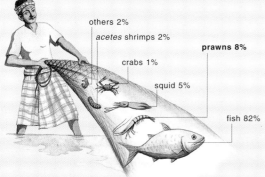

others 2%
acetes shrimps 2%
prawns 8%
crabs 1%
squid 5%
fish 82%

Source: Department of Fisheries Malaysia.

Main species in Malaysia

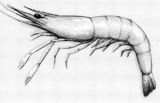

The **Roshna prawn** (*Exopalaemon styliferus*), known locally as *udang gantung*, is one of two important species of carid prawns exploited commercially. The other species is the giant freshwater prawn, *Macrobrachium rosenbergii*. Roshna prawns grow to a maximum length of 9 centimetres. They are fished seasonally in estuaries and in coastal mud flats.

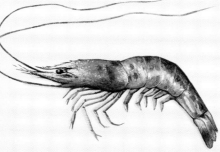

The **giant tiger prawn** (*Penaeus monodon*), known locally as *udang harimau*, is the largest known penaeoid species, reaching a length of 35 centimetres. The prawn is widely distributed, but because it is mainly fished in deep, offshore waters is of minor fishery importance to Malaysia. It is, however, the main species cultured commercially. The young are found in estuarine waters.

The **fiddler prawn** (*Metapenaeopsis stridulans*), known locally as *udang pasir*, gets its name from the ridges on the shell covering its head and fore-body. Together with other species of its genus, and of the genus *Trachypenaeus*, it is commonly called the 'sand prawn', because it lives on coarse sandy or coralline bottoms. The fiddler prawn can grow up to 10 centimetres in length, but is of minor commercial importance.

The **pink prawn** (*Metapenaeus affinis*), known locally as *udang merah ros*, is a widely distributed penaeoid species, reaching a maximum length of 22 centimetres. Juveniles are found in mangrove waters and coastal mud flats. This species is the major fishery species on the west coast of Peninsular Malaysia.

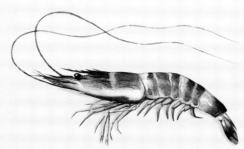

The **rainbow prawn** (*Parapenaeopsis sculptilis*), known locally as *udang kulit keras*, is widely distributed in Malaysia. It can grow up to 17 centimetres in length. It is mainly fished in shallow inshore waters where spawning adults are often found. The young live mainly in coastal mud flats or sand flats near to mangroves.

Local prawn products

Malaysian food products derived from prawns or shrimps include (clockwise) *cincaluk*, *otak udang*, prawn crackers, dried prawns, *belacan* and prawn balls. *Otak udang* is a thick, black prawn paste used as a salad dressing or flavouring for a spicy noodle soup called Assam Laksa. *Cincaluk* is a fermented mixture of shrimps, rice and salt, eaten with fried fish or used as a seasoning in omelettes. *Belacan*, also made from shrimps, is a pungent dried paste used to add flavour to spicy local dishes. The *grago* or shrimps used for making *cincaluk* and *belacan* are known as *Acetes* shrimps (*udang baring*) and belong to a different family from the usual prawns. Their catch is seasonal. Prawn balls are often added to noodle soups and fried noodles, or are deep-fried and eaten with rice.

Traditional dowry

A popular old Malay wedding custom is the presentation of a dowry (*wang hantaran*) to the bride from the groom. Money always makes up part of the dowry and it is usually creatively presented, folded into floral, animal or other shapes. The RM10 notes shown here take the form of a prawn.

Fish

A great number and variety (about 20,000 species) of fish live in the world's seas and oceans. Of these, 4,000 species are found in Malaysia. Although different species of fish are found throughout the water column and at varying distances from the coastline, it is coral reefs that harbour the greatest diversity. Fish are the most primitive of the vertebrates (animals with backbones). Although most fish have the same basic body plan, they vary greatly in size, shape and colour and have adopted ingenious methods for survival.

A sleeping yellow-faced parrot fish (*Scarus* sp.) found near Pulau Tioman. Its beak-like jaws of fused teeth give this fish its name.

Coral reef fish

Pipe fishes	2%
Parrot fishes	2.5%
Snappers	2.5%
Butterfly fishes	3%
Surgeon fishes	3%
Blennies	3.5%
Groupers	5.5%
Cardinal fishes	6%
Damsel fishes	9%
Wrasses	10%
Gobies	13%
Others	40%

Source: Department of Fisheries Malaysia

Groupers, such as the red-barred grouper (*Epinephelus fasciatus*), are classified under the genus *Epinephelus* which comprises more than 150 species. Some species can grow to 2 metres in length.

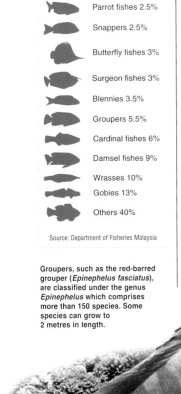

Great diversity

Malaysia's warm tropical seas and coral reefs support an abundant fish biodiversity. Most of the commercial food fish caught are non-coral reef fish (see 'Commercial fish'). However, demand for live coral fish in restaurants is growing, and is an increasing threat to the survival of certain species.

The less commercially important non-reef species are demersal fish (those dwelling nearer the sea bed), which are usually caught by trawlers. They include the glass fish (*Ambassis* sp.), the common pony fish (*Leiognathus* sp.) and the greater lizard fish (*Saurida tumbil*), which are considered trash fish because they are very small or very bony. They are sold as feed for caged fish or as animal feed.

In addition to the bony fishes, Malaysia also has a number of species of cartilaginous fishes, among them sharks and rays. Common sharks include the hammerhead shark (*Sphyrna lewini*), the dog shark (*Scoliodon sorrakowah*) and the cat shark (*Schiloscyllium indicum*). The many species of rays include the spotted stingray (*Dasyatis kuhli*).

Symbiotic relationships exist between certain fish, for example, between remoras (*Remora* sp.) or shark suckerfish and their hosts, which can be sharks, swordfishes or manta rays. A remora is a slender fish with a slatted organ on top of its head. This organ is an efficient suction disc that it uses to attach itself to its host. Remoras act as cleaner fish, removing parasites from the skin of their hosts.

Klein's butterfly fish (*Chaetodon kleinii*) feeding among the corals at Pulau Sipadan. Their small, flattened bodies enable them to hide in crevices.

Coral reef fish

In Malaysia, many families of fish live among the coral reefs, which provide food and shelter as well as act as breeding and nursery grounds.

Gobies (family Gobiidae) This is the largest group, with over 300 species. Gobies are small fish which dwell on sandy sea bottoms.

Wrasses (family Labridae) This is the next largest group. Wrasses live on sandy bottoms and among seaweeds.

Damsel fish (family Pomacentridae) Mostly found in shallow waters, damsel fish are active during the day. Like gobies and blennies, the males guard the eggs during spawning.

Cardinal fish (family Apogonidae) These small nocturnal fish are large in number and variety. Most have large, silvery or translucent scales. They also have large mouths for sheltering their young.

Groupers (family Serranidae) Their distinguishing features are large, torpedo-shaped bodies with mottled patterns, continuous dorsal fins with spines, prominent jaws and canine teeth. A growing taste for live coral fish in Malaysian restaurants is threatening groupers.

Basslets (family Serranidae) These small fish have a forked tail, a long continuous dorsal fin and long, delicate pelvic fins. They can change sex, starting life as females before changing into males.

Blennies (family Blennidae) Among the smallest reef fishes, most blennies are herbivorous bottom dwellers. They are distinguished by their puffy cheeks, bulbous eyes and scaleless bodies.

Surgeon fish (family Acanthuridae) They are so-called because they have a sharp, retractable spine on both sides of the base section of their tails. These medium to large-sized fish also have continuous dorsal and anal fins.

Butterfly fish (family Chaetodontidae) These are small and delicate fish with distinctive

Survival tactics

The clown trigger fish (*Balistoides conspicullum*) has so many patterns and colours on its body that it is difficult for predators to spot it. It gets its name from its patterns.

The longnose butterfly fish (*Forcipiger longirostris*) has a false eyespot near its tail. This deceives a predator into thinking that it is attacking the fish's head.

The regal angelfish (*Pygoplites diacanthus*) has brilliant stripes which advertise its territory and send signals to other members of the same species.

The rockmover wrasse (*Novaculichthys taeniourus*) has many lines and spots on its body that help to disguise its fish shape and provide camouflage.

The bronze trumpet fish (*Aulostomus* sp.) has the same orange colour as the corals among which it lives. This similarity of colours serves as good camouflage.

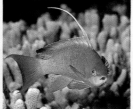

The scalefin basslet (*Pseudanthias squamipinnis*) is so colourful that it is difficult to distinguish it from the equally colourful corals among which it lives.

Many fish have evolved myriad colours and patterns in order to survive. In particular, coral reef fishes, such as those found in Malaysia, are highly colourful to provide camouflage amidst the brilliant corals (see 'Coral reefs'). These fish have hues similar to that of the particular corals among which they live, making it difficult to see them. Some colours indicate that a fish owns a particular territory while others indicate a fish is ready to mate and help to attract the opposite sex.

Stripes, spots or patches on a fish's body help to break up the fish's usual outline. In many cases, the spots comprise false eyespots near the tail, which make predators think that they are the fish's actual eyes. This further confuses most predators.

There are also fish which use electricity from natural batteries, that have evolved from their nerves or muscles, as a means of defence or attack. These include electric eels, skates and rays.

colour patterns. They have a compressed disc shape, a scaly dorsal fin and sometimes an elongated snout.

Snappers (family Lutjanidae) Medium to large sized, these fish have an elongated profile, single dorsal fin and canine teeth. Their long, pointed faces are their outstanding feature.

Parrot fish (family Scaridae) Although they look like wrasses, they have heavier bodies and beaks with fused teeth which they use to scrape algae off dead corals and rocks.

Pipe fish (family Syngathidae) Their long, slender bodies with elongated snouts make them look different from most fish.

Poisonous fish

Certain fish found in Malaysian waters are dangerous to humans because they possess poisonous organs or flesh. Such venomous fish cause pain or death by injecting a toxin into their prey. The extent of the venom ranges from mild, like that inflicted by the spikes of the dorsal and pectoral fins of the sea catfish (*Plotosus lineatus*), to serious, like that from the spines of the toad fish (*Synanceia verrucosa*), known locally as *lepu*, which causes severe pain and even death.

Other venomous fish found in the seas around Malaysia include the stingray (*Dasyatis* sp.), which possesses a barbed spine near the base of its tail containing a potent poison, and the lion fish (*Pterois antennata*), which has venomous spines. The rabbit fish (*Siganus javus*), known locally as *dengkis*, also has poison glands connected to its fin spines.

Malaysians have been known to be poisoned from eating the flesh of certain fish. Some reef fishes, like the trigger fish and the wrasse, become toxic after feeding on the microplankton known as dinoflagellates, which contains toxin (see 'Plankton').

Puffer fishes possess internal organs that contain the dangerous poison tetradotoxin. These organs must be removed from the fish immediately after death or else the poison may permeate the flesh. In Japan, some puffers, known as *fugu*, are eaten after preparation by special chefs who have been trained for years to clean all the toxic parts from the muscles.

Spotfin lion fish (*Pterois antennata*)

Rabbit fish (*Siganus javus*)

Seal puffer fish (*Arothron nigropunctatus*)

Fatal incident

Fisherman killed by flying fish

By THOMAS SOON

On 17 March 1999, *The Star* reported that a fisherman in Kelantan had been killed by a garfish. The garfish (*Tylosurus leiurus*), known locally as *todak*, has an elongated body and sharp jaw. When alarmed, the fish leaps up from the water and travels long distances over the surface, propelled by its tail. In this instance, the fish killed a fisherman who was unfortunately in its way.

Fish motifs in Malaysian crafts

Fauna-based motifs are commonly incorporated in Malay and Iban crafts, particularly on silverware or pandanus mats. Patterns include fish motifs such as fish fry, scales and the eye of the anchovy.

1. A silver waist buckle (*pending*), shaped like an eye and decorated with a motif of fish scales (*sisik kelah*).

2. A silver kris sheath decorated in repoussé work with vegetable and fish scale motifs.

3. A silver tobacco box decorated in repoussé work with floral motifs on its surface and fish scales on the hinges.

4. A pandanus mat pattern from Rusila, Terengganu, featuring fish scales.

Sea snakes

Sea snakes belong to the family Hydrophiidae. Except for the yellow-bellied sea snake (Pelamis platurus), found only in the warmer parts of the Indo-Pacific region, sea snakes occur in coastal waters from the Persian Gulf eastward to Japan, Australia and Polynesia. Of the 50 species worldwide, 22 are found in Malaysia. All sea snakes are poisonous and some are deadly.

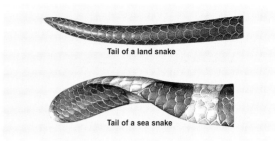

Tail of a land snake

Tail of a sea snake

Unlike the tail of a land snake, the tail of a sea snake is flattened at the tip. This paddle-shaped tail is an adaptation for swimming.

A sea krait (*Laticauda* sp.) slithering across a rock on Kalampunian Damit, an island off Sabah which is a breeding ground for these sea snakes.

Habitats

Sea snakes prefer sheltered coastal waters, and are usually found around the mouths of rivers. Along the shore, they may inhabit rock crevices, tree roots, coral boulders or pilings. A factor governing the distribution of most sea snakes seems to be the depth of water in which they feed as it has to be shallow enough for them to reach the bottom to feed and then rise to the surface. They feed on fish, eels and crustaceans.

Sea snakes are able to float, lying motionless for long periods of time, because they have large, flat bodies. They can also remain submerged for hours. However, they need to come up to the water surface to breathe once in a while.

Characteristics

Sea snakes usually have small heads and slender necks and bodies. The average length of a sea snake is around 1.3 metres, but some are known to grow up to 3 metres. They shed their skins quite frequently, at 2–6 week intervals. Like sea turtles and some sea birds, sea snakes possess a special means of excreting excess salt from sea water by squirting it out through salt glands located under their tongues.

Except for those snakes from the subfamily Laticaudinae, which lay eggs in crevices on rocks, all other species give birth to their young, like mammals. A female snake can give birth to 20–40 offspring at a time, in shallow coastal waters.

Sea snakes are usually found swimming alone or in small numbers. However, there have been occasional reports of large numbers, such as a large group of sea snakes (*Astrokia stokesii*) seen moving in a 10-foot-wide line parallel to a ship for about 60 miles in the Strait of Melaka in 1932.

Differences between land and sea snakes

Sea snakes can be easily distinguished from land snakes by the shape of their tail, which is flatter and broader and looks like the blade of an oar. This is an adaptation for swimming. The colour patterns of the body are also distinctive. Most sea snakes are marked with alternate light and dark bands of various colours, usually black or shades of brown, grey or blue. The bands may go completely or partially round the body. Only two species of land snakes, the common and banded kraits (*Bungarus candidus* and *B. fasciatus*), which have similar body colour patterns, can be confused with sea snakes. However, their tails are generally pointed.

Sea snakes generally have smaller fangs, which are fixed, compared with certain land snakes, such as pit vipers, which have long

COMMON MALAYSIAN SPECIES

NAME	LENGTH	COLOUR	DIET	LOCATION
1. *Enhydrina schistosa*	1–1.3 m	Grey on top and white below, with dark grey or black crossbars.	Fish, eels	Peninsular Malaysia, Sabah, Sarawak
2. *Hydrophis cyanocinctus*	Maximum 2 m	Olive or yellowish with black bands. Yellowish belly.	Fish	Peninsular Malaysia, Sabah
3. *Hydrophis melanosoma*	Maximum 1.6 m	Greenish-yellow dorsal scales with black margins and broad, black bands. Black head with yellowish mottling at the snout.	Fish	Peninsular Malaysia, Sabah, Sarawak
4. *Laticauda colubrina*	1.3–1.6 m	Light or dark bluish-grey on top, with black bands round the body. Yellowish belly between the bands. Black and yellow head.	Fish, crustaceans	Peninsular Malaysia, Sabah
5. *Lapemis hardwickii*	Maximum 0.8m	Greenish or yellowish-olive on top, whitish below.	Fish, eels	Peninsular Malaysia, Sabah
6. *Hydrophis caerulescens*	Maximum 0.6 m	Bluish-grey on top, yellowish-white below, with broad bands. Dark grey head.	Fish	Peninsular Malaysia, Sabah, Sarawak
7. *Hydrophis ornata*	Maximum 1 m	Greyish on top, whitish below, with the two colours meeting on the flank. Grey or olive head. Tail banded with white.	Fish	Peninsular Malaysia, Sabah
8. *Hydrophis spiralis*	2–3 m	Yellowish-green on top. Dorsal scales with black edges. Black rings. Yellow head.	Fish	Peninsular Malaysia, Sabah, Sarawak

Sea snake bites and poisoning

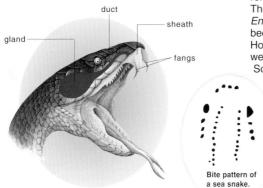

The venom apparatus of sea snakes consists of venom glands and a duct connecting the glands with the fangs. Although some species have only one fang on each side, most sea snakes have two.

Bite pattern of a sea snake.

Sea snake bites
It is important to differentiate between a snake bite and snake poisoning. A bite from a venomous snake may not necessarily be followed by poisoning because, at the time of the bite, the snake may have already exhausted its supply of venom because of previous bites. Obstructions like clothing and shoes may prevent the penetration of the fangs, or the snake may not have had enough time or sufficient grasp of the victim's body to inject its venom. Snake poisoning occurs only when venom is injected into the victim during the bite.

Effects of venom
When a snake bites, its fangs penetrate the flesh of the victim and venom is forced down the groove or hollow of the fangs into the wound by special muscles which compress the gland at the time of biting. The snake can control the amount of venom it injects, rarely injecting the full content of its glands. Its venom is neurotoxic, that is, it acts on the nervous system of the prey's body, causing paralysis and cardiac arrest.

After the initial attack, sea snake bites are painless. There is a short time lapse between the bite and the onset of creeping paralysis of the body. The venom is used to kill or paralyse the prey and to serve as a digestive agent. It is of little value as a defensive weapon, except as a threat, since large animals as well as human beings seldom die within a short period of time, unless they are injected with a lethal dose of venom. The only remedy for sea snake poisoning is antivenin, which is specific for each species.

Sea snake poisoning
Sea snake poisoning is most commonly encountered by fishermen handling their nets and sorting fish. Occasionally swimmers are also bitten. About two-thirds of sea snake bites occur on the lower limbs—feet and legs—with the

remainder usually on the fingers, hands and forearms. The species known to cause the most fatal bites are *Enhydrina schistosa* and *Hydrophis cyanocinctus*, mainly because they are so commonly found in coastal waters. However, bites by other species have been recorded as well. Sea snake bites are highest along the coasts of Southeast Asia and the Persian Gulf. Although sea snakes are generally considered docile and at times reluctant to bite, some species are aggressive and have no biting inhibitions. The most dangerous areas in which to swim are river mouths, where sea snakes are numerous and, as the waters are more turbid, more difficult to see.

First aid treatment
A person bitten by a snake initially suffers from shock. Thus, reassuring the victim and keeping him or her warm is advised. Do not give them any alcohol. Immobilize them immediately after the bite and do not allow them to walk or exert themselves in any way. The bitten area, in particular, must be kept still. In the case of a bitten limb, this can be achieved by splinting. The immobilized limb should be kept below the level of the heart. Gently clean the site of the bite, but do not attempt to cut the wound and suck out the poison. This will only introduce infection and cause excessive bleeding.

Apply a tourniquet to the upper leg for foot, ankle or leg bites, and to the upper arm for hand, wrist or arm bites. To apply a tourniquet, wrap a cloth or bandage around the limb several times and tie. Then insert a stick and twist so that the tourniquet is firm but does not cut off the flow of arterial blood. The tourniquet should be left in place until the antivenin is administered. However, the tourniquet should be released for 90 seconds every 10 minutes and should not be used for more than eight hours. A tourniquet is useless if applied later than 30 minutes after the bite.

Take the patient to the nearest doctor or hospital. If possible, kill the snake and take it to the hospital. This is very important for the identification of the snake in order to select the most suitable antivenin.

Symptoms of sea snake bite
- The victim feels muscle aches and pain and stiffness when attempting to move. These symptoms develop within half to one hour after the bite.
- Mild to acute pain upon gentle movement of the limbs, neck or main body muscles is felt. This develops within 1–2 hours after the bite.
- The victim's urine turns a deep red-brown colour within 3–6 hours of the bite.
- If local pain follows immediately after a bite, it is not a sea snake bite.
- If no general muscle movement pain is present one hour or more after the bite, the poisoning has not been significant. This is the case in two-thirds of sea snake bites.

Predators of sea snakes
The white-bellied sea eagle (*Haliaeetus leucogaster*) is one of the main predators of sea snakes. It catches snakes quite easily from the surface of the water when they come up to breathe. Other predators include sharks and moray eels. All these animals have some means of protecting themselves against the sea snake's venomous bite.

and movable fangs. With the exception of those from the Laticauda subfamily, sea snakes have nostrils on the upper surface of their snouts and watertight valve-like closures for keeping water out. Unlike most land snakes, sea snakes do not hiss when confronted.

❽

❻

❼

Sea turtles

Malaysian beaches provide nesting habitats for four of the seven species of sea turtles in the world. Although sea turtles have existed for over 100 million years, their existence today is seriously threatened because of decades of egg exploitation, incidental capture in fishing gear, coastal and tourism development on nesting beaches, marine pollution, and from the direct hunting of turtles for their meat and other products such as shells. Conservation measures have been intensified, but much more needs to be done to prevent sea turtles from becoming extinct.

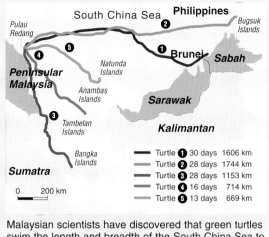

Long-distance migration

Turtle ❶	30 days	1606 km
Turtle ❷	28 days	1744 km
Turtle ❸	28 days	1153 km
Turtle ❹	16 days	714 km
Turtle ❺	13 days	669 km

Malaysian scientists have discovered that green turtles swim the length and breadth of the South China Sea to return home to their feeding grounds after nesting on Pulau Redang off the east coast of the Peninsula. Applying the latest satellite tracking technology, scientists have been able to follow the day-to-day long-distance travel of five female green turtles.

The map above shows the routes taken by the five turtles in 1993 and 1994. One of the turtles travelled 1744 kilometres straight across the South China Sea to reach Bugsuk Island in the Philippines in 28 days. Another journeyed 1153 kilometres south to Bangka Island in Indonesia in 28 days. The third turtle completed her travels off the southwest coast of Sabah, not far from Kuala Penyu, after a 30-day journey of 1606 kilometres. The remaining two turtles travelled in a southeast direction from Pulau Redang, with one ending up near the Natuna Islands of Indonesia after travelling 669 kilometres in 13 days. The final turtle was not tracked to her final destination due to transmission failure after 16 days.

Species in Malaysia

The species found in Malaysia are:
1. The olive Ridley (*Lepidochelys olivacea*), the smallest of the sea turtles.

2. The hawksbill turtle (*Eretmochelys imbricata*) which has a beautiful shell, unfortunately in great demand for ornaments.

3. The green turtle (*Chelonia mydas*), by far the most common species found in Malaysia.

4. The large leatherback turtle (*Dermochelys coriacea*), which is covered with leathery skin and has seven ridges on its shell.

General characteristics

Sea turtles are reptiles whose streamlined bodies are protected by a shell, with their limbs modified into flippers. Unlike their terrestrial and freshwater counterparts, sea turtles have lost the ability to retract their heads and limbs into their shells. Being reptiles, they have lungs and need to surface regularly for air. Although sea turtles spend most of their lives at sea, the adult females must return to the land to lay eggs. The choice of nesting beach is not random. Female turtles return to nest on the same beach on which they were born.

The life cycle of sea turtles

Although sea turtles occupy different niches in the marine environment, and each turtle has its specialized feeding habits, they share remarkably similar life cycles. After a long maturation period of 20–50 years, adults migrate from feeding grounds to nesting beaches. The males return to their feeding grounds after mating, while the females remain to complete nesting before migrating home.

Green turtles mating.

Females lay an average of 4–6 clutches of eggs per season, with each laying separated by an internesting period of 9–11 days. Individuals do not nest every year; instead, nesting cycles are separated by an interval of 2–8 years.

Nesting takes place under cover of darkness. As the female is extremely sensitive, any light or disturbance on the beach scares her back into the water. About 100 eggs are laid per nesting. No parental care is exercised and the eggs are left to incubate in the sand nest unguarded for the next 45–60 days. Nest temperatures vary, depending on where the female has selected her nest site. In the shade, cool temperatures mean the eggs require a longer incubation period. This also produces more males.

Nests in more open areas are subject to higher sand temperatures which shortern the incubation period and result in mostly female hatchings.

When the hatchlings emerge, usually at night, they head instinctively towards the water, unless disoriented by artificial lighting. Since only one in a thousand hatchlings will survive to adulthood, turtles must produce hundreds of eggs per nesting cycle.

Hatchlings which survive their first perilous hours in the water engage in a swimming 'frenzy' for a period of a few days. Feeding does not occur during this time since all energy requirements are derived from the re-absorbed yolk at hatching. The hatchlings head for the open ocean currents where they drift for the next few years. Upon reaching a shell length of 35–40 centimetres, the young turtles settle into shallow water feeding areas, and slowly mature into breeding adults.

Conservation

Turtle conservation programmes in Malaysia are undertaken by various government agencies, including the Department of Fisheries, Sabah Parks, the Wildlife Department of Sabah, the Forestry Department of Sarawak, the Sarawak Museum and the Sea Turtle Research Unit (SEATRU) of Kolej Universiti Terengganu (KUT).

GENERAL FEATURES OF MALAYSIAN SPECIES

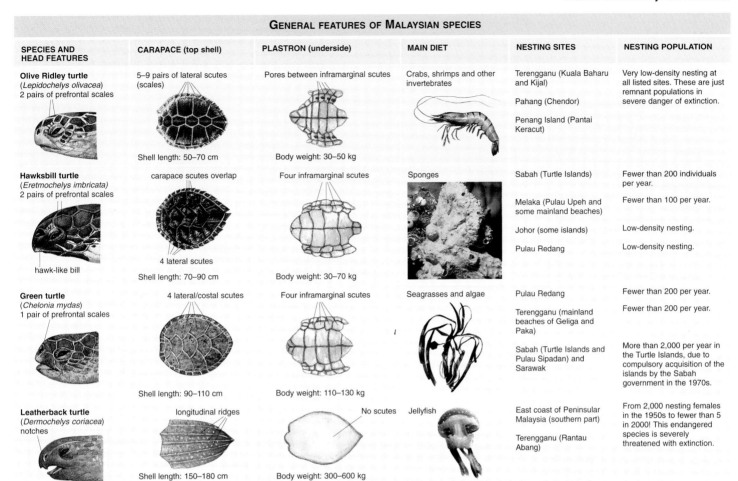

SPECIES AND HEAD FEATURES	CARAPACE (top shell)	PLASTRON (underside)	MAIN DIET	NESTING SITES	NESTING POPULATION
Olive Ridley turtle (*Lepidochelys olivacea*) 2 pairs of prefrontal scales	5–9 pairs of lateral scutes (scales) Shell length: 50–70 cm	Pores between inframarginal scutes Body weight: 30–50 kg	Crabs, shrimps and other invertebrates	Terengganu (Kuala Baharu and Kijal) Pahang (Chendor) Penang Island (Pantai Keracut)	Very low-density nesting at all listed sites. These are just remnant populations in severe danger of extinction.
Hawksbill turtle (*Eretmochelys imbricata*) 2 pairs of prefrontal scales hawk-like bill	carapace scutes overlap 4 lateral scutes Shell length: 70–90 cm	Four inframarginal scutes Body weight: 30–70 kg	Sponges	Sabah (Turtle Islands) Melaka (Pulau Upeh and some mainland beaches) Johor (some islands) Pulau Redang	Fewer than 200 individuals per year. Fewer than 100 per year. Low-density nesting. Low-density nesting.
Green turtle (*Chelonia mydas*) 1 pair of prefrontal scales	4 lateral/costal scutes Shell length: 90–110 cm	Four inframarginal scutes Body weight: 110–130 kg	Seagrasses and algae	Pulau Redang Terengganu (mainland beaches of Geliga and Paka) Sabah (Turtle Islands and Pulau Sipadan) and Sarawak	Fewer than 200 per year. Fewer than 200 per year. More than 2,000 per year in the Turtle Islands, due to compulsory acquisition of the islands by the Sabah government in the 1970s.
Leatherback turtle (*Dermochelys coriacea*) notches	longitudinal ridges Shell length: 150–180 cm	No scutes Body weight: 300–600 kg	Jellyfish	East coast of Peninsular Malaysia (southern part) Terengganu (Rantau Abang)	From 2,000 nesting females in the 1950s to fewer than 5 in 2000! This endangered species is severely threatened with extinction.

Non-governmental agencies such as WWF Malaysia, the Malaysian Society of Marine Sciences and the Malaysian Nature Society also contribute by conducting awareness campaigns. The various conservation programmes concentrate on protecting the nesting females and their eggs, although some measures have been implemented to provide protection to turtles out at sea. Key nesting sites, such as Sabah's Turtle Islands, Sarawak's Turtle Islands, Rantau Abang and nesting beaches on Pulau Redang, have been, or are being, established as state parks or turtle sanctuaries.

Turtle eggs are protected through egg incubation programmes in beach hatcheries or by allowing the eggs to develop in their natural nests. Where commercial egg harvesting has been banned, such as in the Turtle Islands of Sabah and Sarawak, Pulau Sipadan and Rantau Abang, all of the eggs laid are conserved. However, many nesting populations are still subjected to egg exploitation. In some programmes, eggs for conservation have to be purchased from licensed egg collectors. A national ban on the sale of turtle eggs in Malaysia is advocated by many conservation organizations to ensure that 100 per cent of the eggs laid are protected.

As fishing accounts for numerous turtle mortalities at sea, several fisheries regulations have been promulgated to protect turtles, such as the establishment of the restricted fishing zone in

A turtle watch signboard at a Kuala Terengganu beach shows what turtle observers should not do.

Rantau Abang to protect leatherbacks. Trawling is prohibited within 5 nautical miles of the coastline. Sunken gill nets, such as the *pukat pari*, which is used for catching stingray, have been banned since 1989. The Department of Fisheries has also initiated the use of devices which allow the escape of turtles caught in trawl nets.

The marine environment has become increasingly polluted, and turtles often mistake tar and plastic materials, which are fatal to them, for food. Both public education and government intervention through legislation can help to combat marine pollution.

Turtles undertake long-distance migrations between feeding and nesting grounds, often in different countries. Thus, regional collaborative efforts are essential to ensure that the turtles are protected throughout their range. To this end, the Turtle Islands Heritage Protected Area has been established between Malaysia and the Philippines to develop uniform conservation measures. ASEAN is now developing more of such regional conservation programmes.

The egg incubation programme at Pulau Redang

An average of 100 eggs are laid at each nesting. The turtles are allowed to complete the nesting process without any disturbance.

The eggs are left in their natural nests to incubate. Each nest is marked by a labelled wooden stake.

After egg-laying, each turtle is tagged to monitor its nesting activity for the season and its returns in subsequent seasons.

Turtle hatchlings emerge after an incubation period of 45–60 days and are allowed to crawl to the sea to replenish the population.

After the hatchlings emerge, the nest is excavated to determine hatch rates and the condition of unhatched eggs.

Sea birds

Sea birds can be divided into two groups: oceanic birds and shore birds. Oceanic birds are truly birds of the open seas and oceans, while shore birds inhabit coastal waters. There are very few species of oceanic birds in Malaysia, but birds that frequent the rich Malaysian coastal waters, estuaries and coastal mangrove mud flats are numerous.

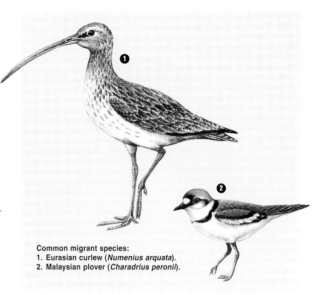

Common migrant species:
1. Eurasian curlew (*Numenius arquata*).
2. Malaysian plover (*Charadrius peronii*).

A little heron (*Butorides striatus*) hunting for fish in a mangrove mud flat.

Beaks and feet

Different birds have differently shaped beaks to help them catch their food. They also have different types of feet, depending upon where they need to land or what they need to grip.

Whimbrel

Great crested tern

Brown booby

Pacific reef egret

Common sandpiper

Wader's foot

Bird of prey's foot

Webbed foot

The white-bellied sea eagle, standing around 70 centimetres high, feeds on fish and snakes.

Shore birds

Shore birds are not truly sea birds, but may be considered such when describing the biodiversity of the seas. Often called waders, they are not confined to the seashore but forage and breed inland. One resident wader found on the sandy beaches of the east coast of Peninsular Malaysia is the Malaysian plover (*Charadrius peronii*). Most of the waders in Malaysia are migrants. Forty-one species come to mangrove coastal areas and mud flats, such as at Kuala Selangor, to escape northern winters. They range from the small, 15-centimetre-high little stint (*Calidris minuta*) to the 58-centimetre-long Eurasian curlew (*Numenius arquata*). This habitat is all-important for these birds. Without it they would perish, as it is their source of food and shelter.

The resident little heron (*Butorides striatus*) and great egret (*Egretta alba*) are two shore birds that inhabit both the inland marshes and the mangrove mud flats. Three other egrets—the little egret (*E. garzetta*), the Chinese egret (*E. eulophotes*) and the plumed egret (*E. intermedia*)—are all migrants sharing the same habitat.

Two common birds of prey can be found in the coastal waters of Malaysia: the white-bellied sea eagle (*Haliaeetus leucogaster*) and the brahminy kite (*Haliastur indus*). The white-bellied sea-eagle ventures 2–3 kilometres out to sea, but both also fly far inland searching for prey.

Oceanic birds

Oceanic birds spend most of their time at sea, coming to land only to breed. Some species, which have evolved for prolonged flights, even sleep on the wing and can glide effortlessly for long periods of time over the oceans. Many have webbed feet for diving and swimming, with the frigate bird being an exception. It does not swim. Fish, shrimps and other small marine life which float near to or on the surface of the sea make up its diet.

These sea birds breed in colonies on small islands and islets, which are often little more than bare rocks. Their nests vary from a few scraps of vegetation and small pebbles, and depressions in shallow soil, to bare rock ledges and burrows. Their egg clutch is small,

only 1 or 2 eggs. The nesting cycle is fairly long, ranging from 3–5 months from incubation to when the fledglings appear.

Migrants

Seven families of oceanic birds, including the tern family Laridae (included here as oceanic birds, as some species of terns can be found far out at sea), are found in the seas around Malaysia. Most of these birds do not breed locally but are migrants.

There are 14 species of terns in Malaysian waters, but only five breed locally. Except for the noddy tern (*Anous stolidus*), also known as the brown noddy, the four other species of resident terns that breed in Malaysia are not truly pelagic. The brown

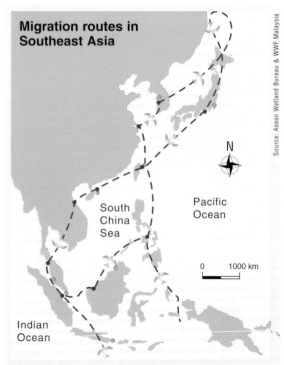

Migration routes in Southeast Asia

South China Sea

Pacific Ocean

Indian Ocean

N

0   1000 km

Source: Asean Wetland Bureau & WWF Malaysia

Bird migration routes often follow coastlines. The estuaries and mud flats found along them provide rich feeding grounds and rest stops. The flyways of migrant birds of prey are dependent on thermal currents, called updrafts, which the birds ride to gain altitude. After gaining height, they soar at these high altitudes.

Malaysian breeding colonies

Only two species of oceanic birds nest in Malaysian waters in large enough numbers to be considered as having Malaysian breeding colonies. These are the brown booby (*Sula leucogaster*) and the brown noddy (*Anous stolidus*).

Closely related to the western gannet, the brown booby is found throughout tropical seas. As it is the size of a goose, it is called locally *angsa laut* or sea goose. It breeds on Pulau Perak, a rocky outcrop about 114 kilometres north of Penang in the northern part of the Strait of Melaka. The booby can dive from a height of 120–180 metres into the sea to catch fish.

Brown noddies sit facing the wind.

It can also pursue fish under water. It hunts for fish while flying low above the waves. Although it is a protected bird, its nesting site is subject to poaching by both local fishermen and those from neighbouring countries.

The brown noddy breeds on Pulau Perak, too, usually laying a single egg on bare rock. Also known as the noddy tern, it is one of the five species of tern which breed locally. It is truly pelagic, usually staying well out to sea. It is known to float on the waters while feeding, just as gulls do.

A brown booby sits in its rocky nest far out at sea.

noddy not only nests on islands like Pulau Perak in the middle of the sea, but also on small islands close to the mainland and on coastal sandbanks.

The little tern (*Sterna albifrons*), the black-naped tern (*S. sumatrana*), the roseate tern (*S. dougallii*) and the bridled tern (*S. anaethetus*) breed on offshore islands and sandbanks on the east and west coasts of Peninsular Malaysia, Sabah and Sarawak. Other main islands where terns breed in Malaysia are the Tioman group of islands, the Layang-Layang group, Labuan Island, the Talang-Talang islands and small islands and islets off the east coast of Peninsular Malaysia, Sabah and Sarawak. The rest of the terns are migrants visiting the seas around Malaysia to escape harsh northern winters. These wintering terns arrive in September and depart for the summer in April and early May. The white-winged tern (*Chlidonias leucopterus*) is a common migrant to Malaysian coastal waters, estuaries and coastal rice fields. It arrives in its white winter plumage, with black on its crown. When it departs for the summer, it will have moulted its winter plumage. Its summer plumage comprises a black head, body and forewing, while the rest of the wings and body retain the white coloration. There are also some other species which are non-migrant visitors to Malaysia's coastal wetlands.

Except for the terns, all the oceanic birds recorded around Malaysia are birds of the high seas and are seldom seen near the coast. Some of them

The common tern, a migrant, often perches on driftwood or follows small boats, fishing in their wake.

are exotic, like the red-billed tropicbird (*Phaeton aethereus*), which can be encountered even in the middle of the ocean where no other bird would venture. It is a tern-like white bird with very long, double tail streamers. On rare occasions, the white-tailed tropicbird (*Phaeton lepturus*) appears in the seas off the Sabah coast. The nearest breeding grounds of these birds are well away from Malaysian waters in the Indian and Pacific oceans. Another Malaysian exotic, the tube-nosed streaked shearwater (*Calonectris leucomelas*), which breeds in the waters of Japan, North China and Korea, is a long-distance flyer journeying as far south as New Guinea.

The lesser frigate bird (*Fregata ariel*), standing half a metre high and with very long wings, is also a common visitor, especially off the coasts of Sabah and Sarawak. An occasional visitor is the Christmas frigate bird (*Fregata andrewsi*), which breeds on Christmas Island. The most interesting physical characteristic of the male frigate bird is its inflatable red throat membrane, called a gular pouch, that it inflates like a balloon to attract the female during courtship. Sometimes called 'man-o-war' birds, frigate birds attack other birds carrying food and rob them of the food while in flight. They often take unguarded chicks from the nests of other oceanic birds as well. However, they can catch fish while flying very low over the water. This method is used more frequently than robbing.

Another sea bird, Wilson's storm petrel (*Oceanites oceanicus*), can be seen following in the wake of ships plying the Strait of Melaka and the South China Sea. Storm petrels are tube-nosed and hook-billed birds which range worldwide. They get their name from the myth that they appear whenever a storm is brewing. There are two species of gulls, the common black-headed gull (*Larus ridibundus*) and the brown-headed gull (*Larus brunnicephalus*), which also visit Malaysian waters, but they do so in very small numbers.

Nesting grounds of terns on the Layang-Layang islands, located off the northwest coast of Sabah.

Hunting techniques of sea birds

Surface plunging tern

Dipping brown noddy

Dipping gull

Dipping frigate bird

Pattering storm petrel

The male frigate bird at its most alluring.

A frigate bird flies off with a fish it has robbed from a common tern. It attacks the other bird, making it drop the fish, and then swiftly snatches the falling fish.

Sea mammals

Almost 20 species of sea mammals have been recorded in Malaysian waters to date. The main species are dolphins, whales and the dugong. Until recently there has been very little research into this group of creatures, and detailed population numbers and up-to-date habitat surveys are not yet available. Some species have been hunted for centuries, others are considered dangerous by local populations and, despite international bans on their killing, many species, having been severely affected by modern fishing techniques and pollution in recent decades, are on the endangered list.

Bottlenose dolphins in Cowie Bay, Tawau, Sabah.

Malaysia's sea mammal inhabitants

Malaysian waters historically had a rich sea mammal population. Despite modern pressures, it is still possible to find a number of species. The ten most commonly spotted are six species of dolphin—the Irrawaddy, Indo-Pacific humpback, bottlenose, long-snouted spinner, pantropical spotted and Fraser's; the short-finned pilot whale and the false killer whale; the finless porpoise, and the dugong. Some of Malaysia's estuaries, mangroves and inshore islands also support populations of otters, though these are river otters, adapted to coastal environments, and therefore not classified as sea mammals.

Habitats

There are no official counts of sea mammal populations in Malaysia but surveys have been conducted by the Malaysian Marine Mammals and Whale Shark Working Group which works with the

Malaysia's ten most common species

Indo-Pacific humpback dolphin (*Sousa chinensis*)

N P H

Short-finned pilot whale (*Globicephala macrorhynchus*)

N

Department of Fisheries and WWF Malaysia. Much of the research has centred on the coasts of Sabah and Sarawak, and consequently the pattern of recordings of whales, dolphins and dugongs is high there, with few official recordings from around the coast of Peninsular Malaysia. However, inshore dolphins and porpoises, such as the Irrawaddy dolphin and the finless porpoise, are known to inhabit shallow waters in the bays and estuaries of the main river systems in both the Peninsula and Sabah and Sarawak. Distinct dugong populations are found in various locations in Sabah—Kudat, Sandakan and Semporna—and in the Teberau Strait and along the southeast coast of Johor.

Offshore species, such as the short-finned pilot whale and pantropical spotted and long-snouted spinner dolphins, are frequently spotted near the Layang-Layang archipelago off the northwest coast of Sabah, and near Sipadan and Ligatan islands on the east coast, often swimming together. Three pods of about 70 killer whales were sighted in May 1996 passing Layang-Layang Island, and there have been other sightings at Sipadan.

The endangered dugong

The dugong is a large, slow-moving sea mammal which can grow to about 3.2 metres in length and weigh as much as 400 kilograms. It has a blunt, whiskered head, thick body, small flippers and whale-like tail. Its common name—the sea cow—refers to the fact that the dugong, unlike other sea mammals which feed on marine animals, grazes on vegetation, primarily seagrasses, which form 'meadows' on the sea floor.

Until the mid-20th century, dugongs were sufficiently numerous in coastal areas off Sabah and Johor to be harpooned for profit: the meat was said to resemble beef when cooked; the oil was used as a substitute for cod liver oil; the hide was dried and made into walking sticks, while the tusks were fashioned into elegant smoking pipes. When captured, the eye of the dugong exuded a clear mucous resembling tears, which was much valued as a love potion by Malays. Today, much publicity is given to strandings of the endangered dugong and to their accidental capture in fish nets and *kelong*. A spate of dugong deaths has raised the issue of the degradation of dugong habitats and the importance of arresting the decline in the dugong population.

Fisheries Department officers examining a dugong carcass washed up along the Strait of Melaka.

Newspaper articles frequently highlight problems facing the elusive sea cow.

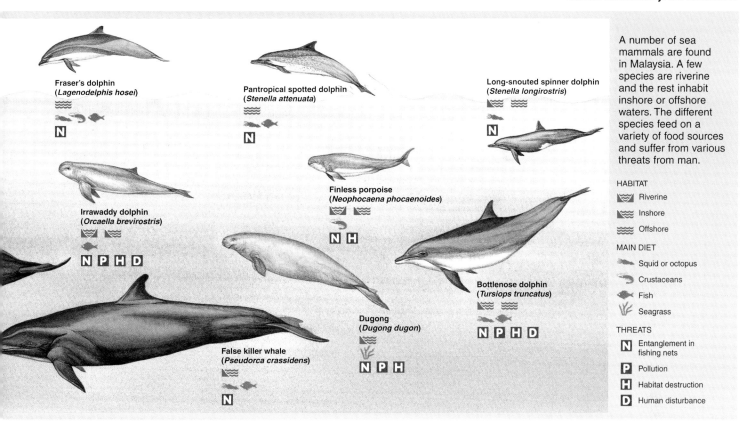

Fraser's dolphin
(*Lagenodelphis hosei*)

Pantropical spotted dolphin
(*Stenella attenuata*)

Long-snouted spinner dolphin
(*Stenella longirostris*)

Finless porpoise
(*Neophocaena phocaenoides*)

Irrawaddy dolphin
(*Orcaella brevirostris*)

Bottlenose dolphin
(*Tursiops truncatus*)

Dugong
(*Dugong dugon*)

False killer whale
(*Pseudorca crassidens*)

A number of sea mammals are found in Malaysia. A few species are riverine and the rest inhabit inshore or offshore waters. The different species feed on a variety of food sources and suffer from various threats from man.

HABITAT

Riverine

Inshore

Offshore

MAIN DIET

Squid or octopus

Crustaceans

Fish

Seagrass

THREATS

N Entanglement in fishing nets

P Pollution

H Habitat destruction

D Human disturbance

Unlike some baleen whales (those which use plates hanging from the upper jaw instead of teeth to capture prey), long-distance migration is not a regular feature of Malaysia's two baleen species—Bryde's and minke whales. Bryde's whales are non-migratory but minke whales are known to make infrequent small-scale migrations to colder waters to take advantage of the plankton blooms there, before returning to the tropics to breed and calve.

Endangered species

All of Malaysia's sea mammals are endangered or vulnerable according to the World Conservation Union (IUCN) classification. The dugong has one of the highest profiles among Malaysia's endangered species and there are frequent reports in the media of trappings and deaths. Historically, the dugong was hunted for its meat, which was regarded as a delicacy. In more recent times, it has suffered from being accidentally trapped and suffocated in fishing nets and *kelong*, and from the destruction of its favoured habitat (seagrass beds), as well as from pollution and severe floodings. Fishermen do not always pass up the opportunity to catch a dugong.

Dolphins and porpoises are also frequently caught accidentally in fishing gear, particularly gill and trawl nets. They are also badly affected by habitat loss caused by pollution from sewage discharge, logging and the run-off of agricultural and industrial wastes, particularly chemicals, as well as from damming. This is evident, for example, in the Kinabatangan River and Sandakan and Cowei bays. The Irrawaddy dolphin, in particular, with its riverine habit, is under great threat from the pollution resulting from various human activities.

Conservation measures

Few specific conservation projects have been set up for endangered and vulnerable sea mammal species, and detailed information and research on many of the species and their habitats is only now being collected. In 1996, the Marine Mammals and Whale Shark Research and Conservation Programme of the Universiti Malaysia Sabah (UMS) was initiated, drawing on the help and expertise of a number of agencies, including universities, fisheries departments and Borneo Divers and Sea Sports (Sabah) Sdn Bhd. A major integrated study is now under way and its findings, due to be released in 2001, should act as a strong basis on which to plan and implement specific conservation projects. One of the participating research bodies, the Borneo Marine Research Institute of UMS, runs a Stranding Programme to rescue accidentally caught marine mammals in Sabah.

SEA MAMMAL SPECIES FOUND IN MALAYSIA

1. Bottlenose dolphin (*Tursiops truncatus*)
2. Fraser's dolphin (*Lagenodelphis hosei*)
3. Indo-Pacific humpback dolphin (*Sousa chinensis*)
4. Irrawaddy dolphin (*Orcaella brevirostris*)
5. Long-snouted spinner dolphin (*Stenella longirostris*)
6. Pantropical spotted dolphin (*Stenella attenuata*)
7. Risso's dolphin (*Grampus griseus*)

8. Bryde's whale (*Balaenoptera edeni*)
9. Cuvier's beaked whale (*Ziphius cavirostris*)
10. False killer whale (*Pseudorca crassidens*)
11. Killer whale (*Orcinus orca*)
12. Melon-headed whale (*Peponocephala electra*)
13. Minke whale (*Balaenoptera acutorostrata*)
14. Short-finned pilot whale (*Globicephala macrorhynchus*)
15. Sperm whale (*Physeter catodon*)

16. Finless porpoise (*Neophocaena phocaenoides*)

17. Whale shark (*Rhincodon typus*)

18. Dugong (*Dugong dugon*)

A marine mammal and whale shark sighting survey of the seas between Kota Kinabalu and Kudat, conducted from the research vessel UMS *Galaxea*. During the survey, 18 sightings of sea mammals were recorded.

Staff of the Borneo Marine Research Institute Museum in Universiti Malaysia Sabah preserving the skeleton of a 6-metre female Cuvier's beaked whale (*Ziphius cavirostris*), found stranded at Mimpian Jadi beach, Tuaran, Sabah.

A long stretch of the Malaysian coastline can support a number of different ecosystems. These include sandy beaches and rocky shores, mangroves, hard bottoms, and sand or mud flats. Offshore, there are coral reefs, and under the sea is a soft bottom ecosystem.

1. Coral reefs, the most beautiful of all ecosystems, are also the most fragile.

2. Although mangroves constitute only 2 per cent of Malaysia's total land area, they are important nurseries for fish and prawns.

3. Sandy beaches often give way to sand flats, another important ecosystem.

4. The purple heron (*Ardea purpurea*) is a waterbird often seen on Malaysian mangrove shores.

MARINE AND COASTAL ECOSYSTEMS

An ecosystem is an organized group of organisms living at a particular place and time, interacting with one another as well as with their environment. Malaysia's seas and coasts contain a number of distinct and globally significant ecosystems. Of these, the zones of mangroves and coral reefs are the most important.

The grapsid crab (*Sesarma* sp.) lives in mud flats or mangroves, forming part of the food chain there.

Mangroves and coral reefs are the signature systems of Malaysia's marine environment. They not only harbour a great range and number of species, but also act as nursery areas for many vital fish and mollusc species. They are economically important as they support, through being nursery and feeding grounds, a large percentage of the commercial fish caught in Malaysia. Both ecosystems have been, and continue to be, under great pressure from modern development and fishing methods. Mangroves, which line estuaries and sheltered stretches of coastline, are a key Malaysian ecosystem, also providing breeding and nursery grounds for fish and prawns. Today, they make up around 2 per cent of the country's land area. Aquaculture and other coastal developments have taken their toll on the country's stretches of mangrove, with half of their extent having been lost in recent decades. Encouragingly, recognition of the importance of mangroves is increasing, and much of what is left stands a better chance of being safeguarded. In areas such as the Matang mangrove in Perak, sound sustainable forest management is being practised to promote the well-being of this ecosystem. Corals grow best in clear waters and thus the country's coral reef communities are mainly found off the east coast of Peninsular Malaysia and Sabah where the waters of the South China Sea are clear. Although there is one oceanic reef system off the coast of Sabah, the majority of the country's reefs are fringing reefs, lying in the shallow waters just off the beach. Fish, crustaceans and nudibranches all live in and off these reefs, contributing to their amazing biodiversity.

Estuaries, with their importance to human and bird communities, among others, are a key feature of Malaysia's coastline, particularly on the west coast of Peninsular Malaysia. Sand and mud flats, a distinct enough ecosystem to be considered separately, are also found in some estuaries. Here huge communities of molluscs and worms congregate, providing, among other uses, great feeding grounds for birds. Associated with the estuaries, there are many areas of mud flats along the west coast of the Peninsula.

Sandy beaches and rocky shores are two other ecosystems found in Malaysia, particularly on the east coast of the Peninsula. Here the environment changes daily, from one extreme to the other, submerging and exposing the ecosystems at least once, sometimes twice, a day. Besides supporting a variety of organisms, including an array of crustaceans and molluscs, which have adapted to the harsh environment, sandy beaches and rocky shores act as natural breakwaters, thus playing a vital role in protecting the hinterland.

5. The hermit crab (*Dardanus megistos*) lives on intertidal sand flats. It makes an empty seashell its home.

6. The false skunk striped anemone fish (*Amphiprion perideraion*) lives in an anemone coral. It is immune to the anemone's stinging cells, the slightest touch of which paralyses other fish.

7. Christmas tree worms (*Spirobranchus giganteus*) live in tubes in corals. They are very sensitive to light and movement.

Estuaries

An estuary is where a river meets the sea. As it is an interface system, many biological, chemical and physical phenomena occur and interact here. The circulation pattern of water in estuaries is complex, affecting the distribution and growth of fish and other fauna. Estuaries form important breeding and nursery grounds for fish, prawns and birds. In wet tropical climates such as Malaysia, most of the estuaries are lined by mangroves and settled and exploited by humans.

Fish and prawns are cultivated in ponds set up close to many Malaysian estuaries (see 'Aquaculture').

Definitions

An estuary is defined as a 'semi-enclosed mass of water where sea water is measurably diluted by riverine fresh water' or 'a semi-enclosed mass of tidal water'. Estuaries—and their boundaries—vary enormously. Large expanses of diluted water surrounding the unenclosed mouths of rivers, such as the Amazon in South America, are often not considered estuaries. Those divided into distributaries by sediments are called deltas.

A mangrove-fringed estuary in the Sungai Bujang, a tributary of the Sungai Merbok in Kedah.

All rivers have estuaries but these vary in their length and nature. In Peninsular Malaysia, the major Sungai Perak, with its high water flow during most of the year, has only a short estuary with a tiny mangrove fringe at its mouth. In contrast, a smaller river like the Sungai Merbok in Kedah is fringed with mangroves for about three-quarters of its length. These are the extremes. More typical estuaries in Malaysia are seen at the mouths of the Johor, Klang, Merbok, Sarawak, Rajang, Maruap and Kinabatangan rivers.

Interactions

Numerous physical and chemical interactions occur when fresh water meets salt water in estuaries. Where the salinity of the estuarine water is about one-tenth the concentration of oceanic waters, many substances settle out, creating a region of maximum turbidity. As a result, light penetration drops, lowering the photosynthetic activity of photoplankton. The fresh water and sea water organisms carried into the estuary by river flows and tides are also affected. Some, especially fresh water organisms, are unable to tolerate the change in salinity and eventually die. Certain chemicals and other pollutants in estuaries, such as heavy metals, will move from a soluble state at the zone of maximum turbidity and settle at the bottom of the estuary, which becomes a 'sink' for these pollutants.

The zone of maximum turbidity fluctuates throughout the year, moving upstream or downstream depending on the phase of the tidal cycle and the volume of fresh water flow. Thus, estuarine hydrodynamics—the flow of water—is important for determining biological, chemical and other processes in the area.

Floating fish cages for aquaculture are found at the mouth of many estuaries.

Mangroves are found along most estuaries in Malaysia, such as at the Merbok estuary in Kedah.

Estuarine circulation

Stratification and mixing

Measuring the salinity of water at different depths of an estuary indicates whether the water in the estuary is well mixed or stratified. If the water is well mixed, the difference in salinity between the surface and bottom waters is very small; if the water is stratified, the difference in salinity is large.

An estuary may be well mixed for most of the year, or only for a particular period. For instance, the Merbok estuary on the west coast of Peninsular Malaysia goes through a cycle of being well mixed during the spring tide, when tidal currents are strong, to being stratified during the neap tide, when tidal currents are weak.

Stratification occurs because water with a higher salinity contains more salt, and the heavier, saltier water sinks to the bottom of the estuary. Water coming in from the sea stays at the bottom, while river water flowing into the estuary floats on top. This type of flow, a key feature of estuaries, is known as gravitational circulation. In most estuaries, the circulation is more complex, sometimes with different patterns occurring simultaneously. In wider estuaries, for example, two or more channels may be seen; if current measurements are taken across a section, they will show that not only does water flow in at the bottom and out at the top, but it can also flow in via one channel and out by the other at the same time.

Features and uses of a typical estuary

A number of features are typically found in Malaysian estuaries. They include natural features, such as mangroves, as well as human usage of the surroundings, such as rice fields, aquaculture farms and fishing villages.

The availability of flat land and river water for irrigation makes rice growing viable near estuaries.

A fisherman using a bag net (known locally as *pompang*) to fish in an estuary. The strong spring ebb tides sweep fish and prawns into the net.

Fishing villages—and their fleet of ocean-going fishing boats—are commonly located along esturaies in Malaysia.

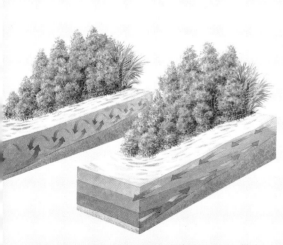

An estuary under well mixed conditions (left) and under stratified conditions (right). Arrows show the pattern of water circulation in the estuary. The darkest blue indicates sea water which grades into brackish and fresh water (increasingly lighter shades of blue).

Significance of estuarine circulation

Understanding how water circulates in an estuary is essential to understanding other marine processes. For example, with gravitational circulation, plankton are able to maintain themselves in estuaries rather than being washed out into the sea. They move down the estuary only to be carried back by the incoming tide.

In many mangrove estuaries, the water currents entering the estuary during flood tides are weaker than the currents flowing out during ebb tides. This is because the mangrove roots and stems offer more resistance to waters flowing in during flood tides. The ebb tides actually help to flush the estuarine channels and keep them clear. Widespread destruction of mangroves causes channels to silt up, with the sediments brought down by the river waters leading to navigation problems.

Most local bag net and other fishermen have this knowledge, so they only set their nets for ebbing tides. They also know where fish and other fauna are to be found in abundance in estuaries, including fish and prawns which grow faster in brackish water than in salt water. For example, the tiger prawn (*Penaeus monodon*) grows very slowly in full-strength salt water because it has to exert a lot of energy expelling excess salt from its body. Although the adult prawn lives in the sea, its young return to mangrove estuaries to feed and grow.

Some fish need to lay their eggs in estuarine conditions because their eggs or their young cannot survive either in full-strength sea water or fresh water. The giant freshwater prawn (*Macrobrachium rosenbergii*) also has to move from its normal freshwater habitats upstream into estuaries to lay eggs.

Understanding estuarine hydro-dynamics is also important in order to understand how pollutants are transported by the water and how long they may stay in an estuary before being washed out to sea. Such circulation and mixing processes in estuaries are complex, but attempts are being made to model these processes mathematically, to be better able to predict what happens under changing conditions.

Sandy beaches and rocky shores

Sandy beaches and rocky shores are two common ecosystems found along Malaysia's extensive coastline. In these harsh habitats, the environmental forces fluctuate from one extreme to another, submerging and exposing the ecosystems once, and sometimes twice, daily. Besides supporting a variety of animals and plants which have adapted to the forces of nature, beaches and shores also play a vital role in protecting the hinterland from flooding and wind erosion.

A sandy beach at Pulau Perhentian Besar, off Terengganu on the east coast of Peninsular Malaysia. There are more sandy beaches than rocky shores in Malaysia.

ABOVE: A watercolour of the sea lettuce (*Scaevola sericea*), known locally as *ambong ambong*. This vegetation is found at the upper limits of the sandy beach, at a cape or near a coastal forest.

ABOVE TOP: A watercolour of the sea hibiscus (*Hibiscus tiliaceus*), known locally as *bebaru*. It also grows at the upper limits of the sandy beach or near a cape.

Sandy beaches

Picture postcard sandy beaches are common along the east coast of Kelantan, Terengganu, Pahang and Johor, bordering the South China Sea. Despite their usually serene appearance, all is change and movement. The unconsolidated sand particles are unstable, constantly moved by tides, currents and wind. The beach has different zones, from the upper beach, which is comparatively dry and dominated by beach vegetation, to the front part of the beach, which is comparatively wet, being the area inundated by tidal waters.

Fewer animals are found on sandy beaches than in other marine environments, primarily because of the unstable coarse substrate, wave action and low organic content of the beach. Most creatures who do survive here burrow in the sand.

At the water's edge, seashells (bivalves of *Mactra* and *Donax* sp.) and tiny shrimp-like crustaceans of *Gammarus*, *Hippa* and *Emerita* sp. can be seen temporarily exposed before they quickly bury themselves in the sand. Bivalves are also common at the water's edge, as are the hermit crab of *Diogenes* sp. and the sand dollar (*Arachnoides placenta*), a type of sea urchin which moves with the tides and is usually found in the water or at the water's edge, but not in the sand itself.

In the drier middle part of the beach, ghost crabs of *Ocypode* sp. are common on clean beaches. They leave their burrows to foray for food and to occasionally wet their buccal cavities (mouth parts) in order to moisten their gills.

Adaptation to tides and dryness of sandy beaches

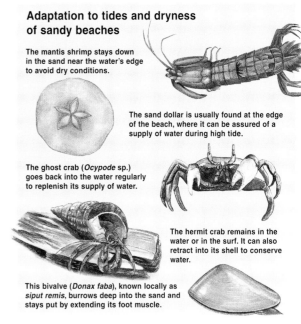

The mantis shrimp stays down in the sand near the water's edge to avoid dry conditions.

The sand dollar is usually found at the edge of the beach, where it can be assured of a supply of water during high tide.

The ghost crab (*Ocypode* sp.) goes back into the water regularly to replenish its supply of water.

The hermit crab remains in the water or in the surf. It can also retract into its shell to conserve water.

This bivalve (*Donax faba*), known locally as *siput remis*, burrows deep into the sand and stays put by extending its foot muscle.

The upper beach is dry and supports little animal life. It is normally dominated by trees such as casuarinas and coconut palms, as well as creepers such as *Ipomoea* sp. While the function of the larger trees is to lessen the force of the strong monsoon winds, the main role of the creepers is to stabilize the beach by trapping and storing wind-blown sediments. The trapped sediments are stored as a sandbank on the upper beach, to be used in repairing the eroded areas of the beach during the monsoon. Destruction of the vegetation makes the beach unstable. There will be less trapped sand to repair damage during storms and erosion will persist.

Rocky shores

In Malaysia, rocky shores are found in places such as Port Dickson in Negeri Sembilan, the Chendering, Bari and Kuala Abang beaches in Terengganu, as well as the various offshore islands around the Peninsula. Rocky shores support a diverse array of marine plants and animals. At low tide, a variety of these can be observed in between crevices and holes and in small tidal pools.

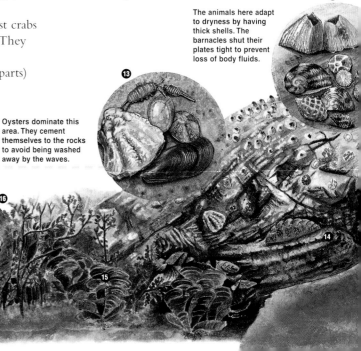

The animals here adapt to dryness by having thick shells. The barnacles shut their plates tight to prevent loss of body fluids.

Oysters dominate this area. They cement themselves to the rocks to avoid being washed away by the waves.

Small algae (seaweeds) are susceptible to desiccation, and are therefore found in the wettest part of the shore.

LOW TIDE LEVEL

The organisms of the rocky shore compete for food and space. Smaller creatures, such as bivalves of *Septifer* sp. (a seashell) and barnacles, commonly attach themselves to oysters, and may be as abundant as their host. The gastropod (*Thais* sp.), another seashell, feeds on oysters while other seashells and limpets feed by grazing on algal mats (tiny seaweeds). Barnacles, oysters and mussels feed by filtering small, edible portions of organic matter from sea water. Barnacles cement themselves to the rock and extend their long, feathery limbs to gather food particles as the water comes in.

For protection from predators, seashells use colour as a camouflage. Their colours range from shades of dull grey to bright shades of yellow or orange depending on the species and the colour of the background rocks.

The living conditions of animals and plants on rocky shores range from being submerged most of the time at the low tide level to being exposed to the air most of the time at the high tide level. Thus, the animal and plant populations are distributed in horizontal zones up the rock face, their distribution clearly related to the various adaptations to the forces of nature, such as wind, waves and sunlight, they have evolved over the generations.

In the tide pools, fish such as skippers (*Abudefduf* sp.) and mullets, as well as crabs, come in with the tide and are trapped in the pools when the tide runs out. Hermit crabs and sea anemones are common, as is the odd sea cucumber. Adaptation to constantly changing environmental conditions, involving salinity, temperature and oxygen levels, is important for their survival in the tide pools. Marine vegetation, especially red, green and filamentous algae, is abundant and provides the main source of food.

Natural protectors

Besides supporting a wide range of animals and vegetation, beaches and shores also play a very important, though less well known, physical role. They are the natural protectors of the hinterland. Stable rocky shores act as natural breakwaters, while sandy beaches absorb wave energy via moving sands and by changing their shape in relation to the strength of the waves.

Having a self-repairing mechanism, beaches quickly recover during non-monsoon seasons. Without beaches and rocky shores, millions of Malaysian ringgit would have to be spent annually to protect the hinterland or to build hard structures to simulate the efficiency of these natural protectors in breaking and absorbing wave energy.

Animals and plants on the rocky shore

A UPPER ZONE (above high tide level)
1. Lichens (Species unknown)
2. Snails (*Nodilittorina* sp.)

B TIDE POOL
3. Sea anemone (*Anthopleura* sp.)
4. Hermit crab (*Eupagarus* sp.)
5. Fish (*Abudefduf* sp.)
6. Crab (*Grapsus* sp.)
7. Brittle star (*Ophiarachnella gorgonia*)
8. Red algae (*Laurencia* sp.)
9. Sea cucumber (*Holothuria* sp.)
10. Green algae (*Chlorodesmis* sp.)

C MIDDLE ZONE (between low and high tide levels)
11. Crab (*Grapsus* sp.)
12. CLOCKWISE: Barnacles (*Tetraclita* sp.), Snails (*Littorina* sp.), Limpets (*Patellidae* sp.), Gastropod (*Thais* sp.), Gastropod (*Nerita* sp.)
13. CLOCKWISE: Isopods. Limpets (*Patellidae* sp.), Green-lipped mussels (*Perna viridis*), Oysters (*Saccostrea* sp.)
14. Chiton (*Lepidochitona* sp.)

D LOWER ZONE (below low tide level)
15. Algae (*Padina* sp.)
16. CLOCKWISE: Bivalve (*Isognomon* sp.), Rock oysters (*Saccostrea* sp.), Gammaridae (*Gammarus* sp.), Gastropod (*Trochus* sp.)
17. Algae (*Sargassum* sp.)

Lichens grow very high up where almost no sea water reaches and conditions are very dry.

Some small snails are usually found high up here where it is dry most of the time, as they have thick, impervious shells.

HIGH TIDE LEVEL

Some crabs, for example, *Grapsus* sp., adapt to dry intertidal conditions by staying in crevices or under boulders.

Sand and mud flats

The basic nature of a shore is determined by the geology and shape of its adjacent coastline and by various physical processes, particularly the action of rivers and waves which supply sediments. Thus, depending on location, there can be sand or mud flats on a shore, or a mixture of both. There is a wealth of life on intertidal sand and mud flats. As they receive organic matter consisting of plankton, and detritus consisting of decomposed mangrove and algal matter, these flats are inhabited by marine worms, molluscs and crustaceans, which in turn provide food for birds at low tide, and fish, crabs and prawns at high tide.

Collecting razor shells

Collecting razor shells on the sand flat at Morib.

The razor shell is one type of seafood consumed in Malaysia.

Razor shells (*Solen* sp.), known locally as *pahat*, are collected at low tide on sand-mud shores, such as at Morib in Selangor, on the west coast of Peninsular Malaysia. To collect the shells, a stick laced with calcium hydroxide (slaked lime) is plunged into the burrow of a razor shell. Stunned by the alkaline solution, the bivalve escapes to the surface where it is easily collected.

The shells are sold to local seafood restaurants which often serve them stir fried with chillies. Although razor shells can grow up to 12 centimetres, the population at Morib, because of over-exploitation, now consists of mainly smaller bivalves.

Location

Beaches of coarse sand are normally found on open ocean coasts, such as along the east coast of Peninsular Malaysia, where granite or similar rocks are exposed and eroded. On such beaches, the water drains away rapidly at low tide. Because of the dry conditions, these beaches support few organisms. In contrast, shores of fine sand in sheltered bays on open coasts, or along coasts where the prevailing winds do not blow onshore, support more species.

Sandy shores grade into muddy shores where there is increased shelter from waves, and where there is also a steady supply of fine clay and silt brought down by rivers. Mud shores are confined to shores with reduced wave action, such as at the mouths of rivers or estuaries.

Sand and mud flats are dotted all along Malaysia's 4800-kilometre-long coastline. Mud flats are dominant on the west coast of Peninsular Malaysia as the coast is sheltered by the large island of Sumatra. Tin-mining activities and land development in the hinterland since the beginning of the 1900s have also assisted the growth of muddy shores by supplying copious amounts of fine sediments to the coast. Sand flats are more common on the east coast of the Peninsula, which is more exposed.

Open coastlines—those not sheltered by estuaries or enclosed bays—in Sabah and Sarawak are typically sand or sand-mud, except in and near estuaries where mud flats predominate.

A sand flat at Morib in Selangor. The most common organism found here is the razor shell.

A mud flat in Johor. Cockles are commonly found on mud flats.

Vertical zones

In Malaysia, it is possible to observe two vertical zones in fine sediment shores: an oxygenated layer at the surface, and a grey or black layer below it where there is a total absence of oxygen. This layer occurs because the oxygen supply is too low to oxidize the organic matter.

In the absence of oxygen, bacteria break down organic material by fermentation and give rise to hydrogen sulphide. Much of this compound becomes fixed as iron sulphides, such as pyrite, which gives deeper layers of the substrate a grey colour, in contrast to the surface yellow sand where ferric oxide predominates.

Ecological importance

Intertidal sand and mud flats are ecologically very important coastal ecosystems. These habitats receive organic matter consisting of plankton as well as larger inputs of detritus comprising decomposed mangrove and algal matter. The surface of the substrate supports abundant growth of diatoms—microalgae which are able to photosynthesize.

Thus, a large variety of organisms, such as polychaete worms, molluscs and crustaceans (mainly crabs) live in these flats and feed on the algae. In turn, this rich community forms the feeding grounds of resident and migrant birds at low tide, and of fish, crabs and prawns at high tide.

Impact of reclamation

Reclamation destroys important habitats of the permanent and temporary organisms living there. Reclamatiom of sand or mud flats also has serious effects on adjoining coastal systems, especially if it deflects long-shore currents (see 'Moving sands'). When longshore currents are deflected, erosion and deposition of sediments can occur elsewhere along the coast, leading to costly erosion control.

vegetation (strand)

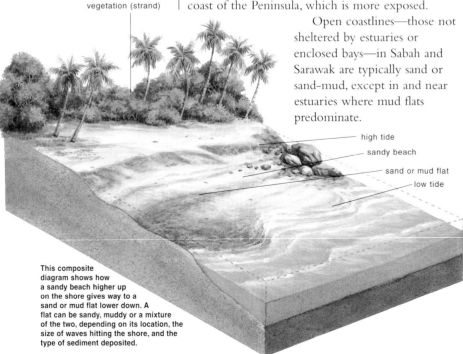

high tide
sandy beach
sand or mud flat
low tide

This composite diagram shows how a sandy beach higher up on the shore gives way to a sand or mud flat lower down. A flat can be sandy, muddy or a mixture of the two, depending on its location, the size of waves hitting the shore, and the type of sediment deposited.

The varied world of soft bottom communities

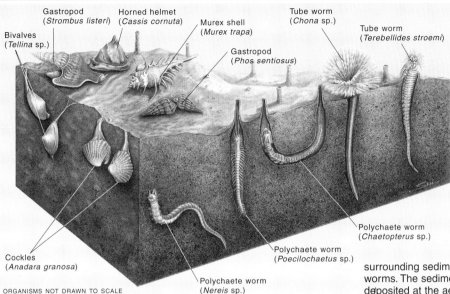

Gastropod
(*Strombus listeri*)

Horned helmet
(*Cassis cornuta*)

Murex shell
(*Murex trapa*)

Tube worm
(*Chona* sp.)

Tube worm
(*Terebellides stroemi*)

Bivalves
(*Tellina* sp.)

Gastropod
(*Phos sentiosus*)

Cockles
(*Anadara granosa*)

Polychaete worm
(*Chaetopterus* sp.)

Polychaete worm
(*Poecilochaetus* sp.)

Polychaete worm
(*Nereis* sp.)

ORGANISMS NOT DRAWN TO SCALE

Activities affecting the presence of oxygen

The organisms of soft bottom communities interact with their substrate and over time and space both the composition of species and the characteristics of the sediment change. The soft bottom substrate usually contains high levels of organic matter. This affects the rate of oxygen depletion in the sediment. Large numbers of bacteria decompose the organic matter, depleting the dissolved oxygen. This reduction of oxygen at the surface of the sediment affects the distribution of organisms.

Other organisms also interact with the environment to change the condition of the sediment. Most of the polychaetes found in soft bottom communities are deposit-feeding organisms as opposed to suspension-

feeding organisms found in greater abundance on sandy substrates. Furthermore, the fauna which inhabit such an environment are mostly burrowing types, whose activities help in mixing the sediment and allowing dissolved oxygen to penetrate the deeper parts.

Polychaete worms, such as those belonging to the families Spionidae and Maldanidae, and some bacteria produce mucopolysaccharides (sticky substances). They use this mucus to fuse particles together, making them larger and more resistant to erosion. In this way, they help to stabilize the sediment.

Mixing and recycling of sediments

Some polychaetes use their ability to produce mucus to build tubes in which to live. The tubes can be some distance down in the sediment. These tube-building worms are generally deposit feeders. Within and at the lower end of the tube, the worms take in sediments, creating an empty space which the surrounding sediment fills, bringing more sediments to the feeding worms. The sediment passes through the worm's intestine and is deposited at the aerobic opening of the tube. These activities help in the oxygenation of the anaerobic sediment below, creating the resuspension of finer particles. Although these are an important source of food for suspension-feeding organisms, this activity tends to destabilize the immediate environment. Some molluscs also suspend sediments through feeding activities.

The high organic content and the fine silt and clay particle components of the soft bottom sediment are important to many deposit feeders which are not tube dwellers. Many gastropods and polychaetes take in organic sediments for nourishment, eliminating what they do not need. Other organisms then take in what they eliminate. This ingestion and egestion plays an important role in the active mixing and recycling of the various components of the soft bottom sediment.

Life in the sand and mud flats

Sand flat organisms

The appearance of a sandy shore changes with ebbing tides. After a while, the smooth surface of the sand becomes broken with worm casts and the feeding pellets of crabs. Many inhabitants of the shore have adopted the habit of burrowing, not only to escape the effects of desiccation of the hot sun but also to escape from predators such as birds and fishes. Clean, sandy beaches like those at Batu Ferringhi in Penang, Langkawi in Kedah, and Pangkor in Perak are highly valued as prime natural resources for the tourist industry.

The small whelk (*Nassarius* sp.) is a gastropod which is found in large numbers on sand flats. It is a scavenger which feeds on carrion—dead fish, crabs and other organisms.

Pea crabs are so-called because of their extremely tiny size. Hundreds of them are usually found massed together.

The button shell (*Umbonium vestarium*) is the most common organism on some low shore, fine sand flats on Malaysian coasts, such as at Teluk Aling in Penang. It is a small, multicoloured gastropod only about 1 centimetre in diameter. Button shells usually occur in great abundance, exceeding 10,000 individuals in 1 square metre.

Mud flat organisms

Wherever the force of the waves on a shore is reduced because of its sheltered nature, fine sediments accumulate to form muddy shores, particularly in or near estuaries. With their rich organic matter, these mud flats on the west coast of Peninsular Malaysia—in Penang, Perak and Selangor—are prime areas for the aquaculture of the blood cockle (*Anadara granosa*) (see 'Cockles and mussels').

Young cockles, called spats, settle down at high densities on specific mud flats on the coast after a short period of planktonic

life in the water column. The spats are collected and cultured at lower densities on estuarine mud flats. Studies at the Kuala Selangor mud flats indicate that two predatory gastropods (*Thais carinifera* and *Natica maculosa*) consume about 40 per cent of the *in situ* cockle production.

Other common organisms found on mud flats include the gastropod (*Cerithidea cingulata*), the polychaete (*Pectinaria*), the carpet clam (*Paphia undulata*) and the brachiopod (*Lingula*) or lamp shell.

The carpet clam (*Paphia undulata*) occurs in great abundance on mud flats, especially on the coast of Kedah. Known locally as *lalah*, it is a Malaysian seafood delicacy.

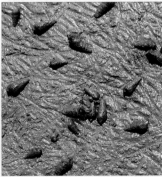

The gastropod *Cerithidea cingulata* is about 3 centimetres long. It feeds on the mud surface, deriving nutrition from decomposed plant fragments and other microorganisms.

Mangroves

The mangrove ecosystem is the dominant estuarine vegetation in the tropics. In Malaysia, mangroves cover some 600 000 hectares—around 2 per cent of the total land area. Conservation is important because mangroves form the base of a complex food web, act as nursery areas for many fish and prawn species, provide fuel wood, stabilize the coast, and act as stores of carbon dioxide. Malaysian mangroves exhibit high biodiversity and have a great potential for ecotourism development.

Distribution of mangroves

Despite the federal government's policy of protecting mangrove areas, mangroves are still being decimated in some states. Land matters come under the jurisdiction of the regional states rather than the federal government.

Propogules on a mangrove tree. These long, hanging seedlings are ready to drop into the mud below where they grow into new trees.

Plant and animal adaptations

The mangrove ecosystem—a combination of terrestrial and aquatic ecosystems—is an interface between the land and the sea. Mangroves develop on coastal plains where rivers bring down sediments which the prevailing sea conditions do not wash away. The presence of plants with the necessary adaptations to live in the intertidal zone defines this ecosystem.

These plants have special roots that help to anchor them in the mud, or aid respiration in the low oxygen or anaerobic conditions. They can withstand sea water by being able to prevent salt from getting into the roots. Species of *Rhizophora*, known locally as *bakau*, do this. Another species, *Avicennia*, known locally as *api-api*, excretes excess salt through salt glands in its leaves. Seedlings grow rapidly so that they are not easily swept away by the tides. Many species are viviparous, that is, the seeds germinate while still attached to the parent tree. The nipah palm (*Nypa fruticans*) is another characteristic mangrove tree species with economic uses—thatch from its leaves and sugar and alcohol from its flowers.

Aquatic animals living in mangroves often have adaptations to withstand the unique environment. For example, mudskippers are fish which can live

The fruit of the mangrove tree *Heritiera littoralis*, known locally as *dungun*, is adapted for dispersal by water. It is smooth and light and floats easily.

out of water for a period of time by filling their gills with oxygenated water. They can also breathe through their skins. The mud lobster lives in mounds and digs its burrow, which reaches down to the water table. Many mangrove crabs are able to tolerate long periods out of water as they have special respiratory mechanisms to allow them to breathe in air. For example, in *Sesarma* crabs, when water is scarce, the water that has been passed over the gills is not expelled but is channelled back along grooves under the edges of the shell, allowing reoxygenation before it re-enters the gills.

Productive trees

Despite having to adapt to various environmental stresses, especially saline water and the soft, anaerobic substrate, mangroves grow surprisingly fast in areas with a high and evenly distributed rainfall. In Malaysia, total biomass production is 20–30 tons per hectare per year, placing mangroves amongst the most productive of ecosytems. This is one reason why the use of mangrove forests for pole and charcoal production has been so successful in the country (see 'The Matang mangroves').

Mangrove trees also produce a lot of leaf litter, somewhere around 8–10 tons per hectare per annum. The mangrove ecosystem has evolved to take advantage of this high litter production (see box on 'The mangrove food chain').

Store of carbon dioxide

The high production of 20–30 tons of biomass per hectare per year makes mangroves an important sink (store) of atmospheric carbon dioxide. The amount of carbon absorbed from the atmosphere is 10–15 tons per hectare of mangroves per year. Part of this carbon is returned to the atmosphere when the mangrove is harvested and the wood used for fuel. Another part forms the base of the food chain in the mangrove ecosystem and the fixed carbon is taken up by various organisms. Yet another part of this carbon, which is fixed in the plant biomass, remains trapped in the mangrove forest—for example, the burial of leaf litter in the mud. In this case, the mangrove ecosytem truly functions as a long-term sink of atmospheric carbon.

Some dominant types of mangrove roots

Stilt roots, such as those of *Rhizophora*, are roots that rise from the trunk, form branches and then grow down into the substrate. These roots provide additional mechanical support to trees growing in the soft, muddy substrate.

Pneumatophores or breathing roots, such as those of *Sonneratia*, rise from the laterally spreading underground cable root system. Extending upwards into the air as small conical projections, they are used in respiration.

Buttress roots, such as those of *Bruguiera*, rise from the base of the trunk and expand into flattened blade-like structures. Buttress roots help to provide mechanical support for the tree growing in the soft, unstable substrate.

People of the mangrove

Few groups of people live in mangrove forests today. However, one unique group, fully adapted to their habitat, are the Mah Meri, also known as Ma' Betise', which means 'people with fish scales'. They are Orang Asli and live on the mangrove islands off Port Klang and Pulau Carey. This population of 2,600 people have lived in these forests for 100 years. Their belief system and way of life stresses maintaining harmony between man and nature. Their livelihoods are dependent on fishing and growing fruit but also importantly on carving. Traditionally, they have carved masks of ancestral spirits from mangrove wood such as *nyireh batu* (*Xylocarpus moluccensis*), which provides an ideal wood for carving. With reductions in the mangrove area, these trees are becoming scarce.

Specially carved masks are used by dancers during the harvest celebration.

Fewer and fewer Ma' Betise' men are carving wood sculptures for a living because the type of wood needed is becoming scarce.

Impact of global change

Mangroves form the 'forefront' vegetation zone in coastal areas. Thus, when the sea level rises, the mangroves are likely to retreat landwards, that is, the outer fringe of the land becomes mangroves, and the former mangrove area becomes sea. Palaeontological evidence from the Seberang Perai coastal plain proves that mangroves once existed 6–15 kilometres inland of the present shoreline, indicating that the sea level was once higher than it is today (see 'Sea level change').

Human pressures from population increase and development continue to exert a disastrous impact on mangroves. In Malaysia, mangroves have been converted to housing estates and to airports. For example, the Bayan Lepas International Airport in Penang is built on mangroves. Around 20 per cent of the Merbok mangroves in Kedah have been converted to aquaculture ponds. Other areas have been converted to rice fields, though often not very successfully in the long term as mangrove soils are potentially acid sulphate.

The mangrove food chain

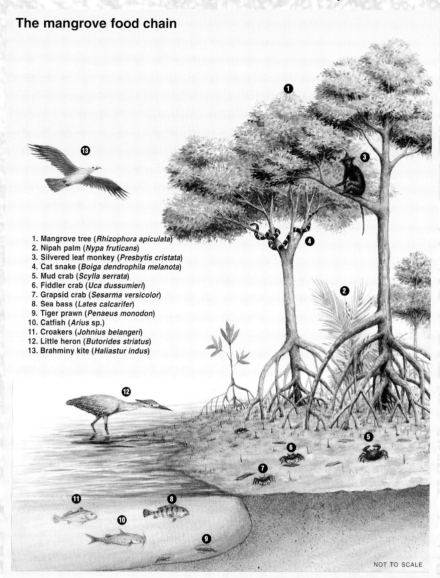

1. Mangrove tree (*Rhizophora apiculata*)
2. Nipah palm (*Nypa fruticans*)
3. Silvered leaf monkey (*Presbytis cristata*)
4. Cat snake (*Boiga dendrophila melanota*)
5. Mud crab (*Scylla serrata*)
6. Fiddler crab (*Uca dussumieri*)
7. Grapsid crab (*Sesarma versicolor*)
8. Sea bass (*Lates calcarifer*)
9. Tiger prawn (*Penaeus monodon*)
10. Catfish (*Arius* sp.)
11. Croakers (*Johnius belangeri*)
12. Little heron (*Butorides striatus*)
13. Brahminy kite (*Haliastur indus*)

NOT TO SCALE

The food web in the mangrove ecosystem is largely detritus-based, with dead leaves from the mangrove trees forming the primary food source. The organisms which feed directly on this decaying organic material are called detritovores. Some crabs, for example grapsid crabs such as *Sesarma versicolor*, are detritivores as they feed directly on newly fallen leaves. In some mangroves, these crabs consume most of the leaf fall.

In other areas where detritivorous crabs are absent or uncommon, micro-organisms such as bacteria, fungi and protozoa feed on the detritus. They break it down into smaller pieces, and as they attach themselves to the detritus their own tissues add to its nutritional value. These nutritionally packed parcels are eaten by crabs, including the mud crab and other crustaceans and smaller organisms (microdetritivores), which are in turn grazed upon by molluscs.

Some of the detritus gets transported from the forest floor to the tidal body of the estuary and is consumed by fish and prawns, which themselves are eaten by other predators, such as fish and birds.

The need for conservation

Conservation of Malaysia's mangroves is essential for a number of reasons. Mangroves cover only 2 per cent of the land area of Malaysia, making them a very precious commodity. Yet their biodiversity is very high—there are over 30 species of mangrove trees compared with only four species in the Florida mangroves—and it is important to sustain this. Importantly, mangroves provide protection on the coast where they occur, form the base of a complex food web, and are an important sink for atmospheric carbon dioxide. They also act as nursery grounds for commercial fish and prawn species. In addition, they provide wood for charcoal, firewood and poles on a sustainable basis in certain locations, such as the Matang mangroves in Perak. Mangroves are also potential sites for ecotourism. One such site is the Kuala Selangor Nature Park.

The lesser adjutant stork can be seen at the Kuala Selangor Nature Park, a popular area for ecotourism.

Coral reefs

Coral reefs are structures made up of a complex association of marine organisms, the main ones being the corals themselves, cemented by the growth of coralline algae. They are mainly restricted to the tropical and subtropical seas, between about 30 degrees north and 30 degrees south of the equator. Malaysia's reefs are modest in size compared with the Great Barrier Reef of Australia, which is the world's largest reef and stretches for more than 2000 kilometres, but they are equally spectacular, with their biodiversity ranking amongst the highest in the world.

The 'Hanging Garden' off Pulau Sipadan, Sabah, displays a large variety of beautiful soft corals (*Siphonogorgia* sp.).

Location of coral reef islands

1. Pulau Timbun Mata
2. Pulau Sibuan
3. Pulau Mantabuan
4. Pulau Bodgaya
5. Pulau Sebangkat
6. Pulau Maiga
7. Pulau Tetegan
8. Pulau Bohey Dulang
9. Pulau Pom Pom
10. Pulau Selakan
11. Pulau Puan
12. Pulau Bumbun
13. Pulau Mabul
14. Pulau Kapalai
15. Pulau Danawan
16. Pulau Si Amil
17. Pulau Sipadan
18. Pulau Ligitan

Location

Many Malaysian coral reefs are found in the South China and Sulawesi seas, where they lie around various island groups off the coasts of Terengganu and southeast Johor, and around the Semporna group in Sabah and the Labuan islands. Some reefs are also found in the Strait of Melaka, around Pulau Langkawi and Pulau Pangkor. Smaller reefs occur around Tanjung Tuan in Melaka.

Types of corals

There are two main types of corals: zooxanthellate, which have unicellular algae living symbiotically within their tissues, and azooxanthellate, which do not. The former require sunlight for the algae to photosynthesize. Mineral waste products from the algae supply most of the food needs of these corals, enabling them to grow at a rapid rate and form the spectacular structures known as reefs. Azooxanthellate corals live in deeper waters and depend on capturing plankton as their main food source. They are often slow growing and do not form reefs.

Because they live under the water, corals are vulnerable to changes in water clarity, which affects the amount of sunlight penetrating the water. The clear seas around coral reefs are a reflection of the low amount of suspended particles found in these waters. Concentrations of nutrients, such as nitrates and phosphates, are minimal compared with other coastal marine systems. This means that the reef ecosystems have to be super efficient in recycling materials to survive and grow. Such a finely tuned and delicate ecosystem is fragile and its balance easily upset by changes in conditions such as temperature change, pollution and excess sediments.

Types of reefs

Those corals that form reefs produce two different types in Malaysia: fringing reefs and oceanic reefs. Fringing reefs lie adjacent to a landmass, such as an island, and extend down into the water as far as sufficient light penetrates—the lack of light and suitable substrate for coral growth being the main limiting growth factors. All but one of the reefs in Malaysia are fringing reefs and typically they extend to a depth of between 2 and 20 metres.

The only oceanic reef in Malaysia is the coral reef at Sipadan, off the coast of Sabah. Pulau Sipadan is a pinnacle which rises more than 610 metres from the sea floor. Where this pinnacle breaks the surface of the water, it forms a vegetated cay—a small, low island composed of sand and coral fragments. The cay is surrounded by coral reefs which form one of the most diverse marine areas of the world. The reef is a world famous dive site with hard coral species colonizing down to 40 metres and soft corals found as deep as 80 metres.

Life on the reefs

There is a great diversity of animal life on Malaysian reefs. Apart from the corals, there are colourful reef fishes, sea turtles and mammals, including dolphins and dugongs. However, the most diverse groups are the invertebrates.

Parrot fish (*Scarus* sp.)

Diadem basslet (*Pseudochromis diadema*)

Porcupine fish (*Diodon liturosus*)

Blue damsel fish (*Pomacentrus coelistis*)

Spotted garden eel (*Heteroconga hassi*)

A boulder-like coral (*Porites* sp.) from the family Poritidae.

A brain-shaped coral (*Outophyllia crispa*) from the family Favidae.

A cabbage-shaped coral (*Montipora* sp.) from the family Acroporidae.

high water mark

mean water mark

low water mark

UPPER REEF FLAT   LOWER REEF FLAT   REEF SLOPE soft corals

Coral reefs fringe the steep and rocky eastern coastline of Pulau Tenggul, off the coast of Terengganu (top). The diagram (bottom) shows a typical cross-section of a Malaysian fringing reef.

The fringing reef

In a typical Malaysian fringing reef, the reef flat forms the bulk of the coral system. It is characterized by colonies of hard corals which are tolerant of the harsh and changing intertidal environment. Species of *Porites*, *Favida* and *Favites* predominate as they can withstand the relatively high amount of sediment in the water.

At the extreme end of the reef flat is the reef slope, a sharp drop-off in the reef structure. This area is not exposed to the air, even at the lowest tide. It is here that the highest diversity of corals is usually found. The slope then extends down to the sea floor, where the reef ends. The extent and depth of the slope is a reflection of the water turbidity experienced by the reef. Coral reefs in the Strait of Melaka, such as at Tanjung Tuan in Melaka and Teluk Datai in Pulau Langkawi, have poorly developed slopes that only extend 2–4 metres in depth. On the reefs of the South China Sea, where the waters are clearer, such as at Pulau Redang, the slope can extend to more than 20 metres.

Fringing reefs can be damaged by runoff from coastal activities such as the building of island resorts and the application of excessive fertilizer which pollutes the waters. Excess nutrients, such as nitrates and phosphates in the water, favour the growth of algae, but if this pollution is stopped, the algae will die and the corals will revive and grow again.

The importance of reefs

Coral reefs are of great ecological importance. The diversity of life they contain is considered to rival that of rainforests. Both the biological and chemical diversity in coral reefs point to a large, untapped potential (see 'Pharmaceuticals'). Traditionally, reefs have also been the fishing grounds of local fishermen. They are feeding and breeding grounds of many commercial fishes. The problem of overfishing is now severe on some reefs and conservation projects such as placing artificial reefs to attract coral and fish species are being established. The reefs of Malaysia also attract many tourists and divers. To ensure sustainable tourism development and conserve the reefs, marine parks have been established (see 'Marine parks and reserves').

Nudibranch (*Chromodoris* sp.)

Sea urchin (*Echinothrix mathael*)

Pacific lobster (*Panulirus versicolor*)

Reef crab (*Carpilius convexus*)

Crown-of-thorns starfish (*Acanthaster planci*)

Red-lipped starfish (*Fromia monilis*)

91

1. A cultured pearl farm on Pulau Bohey Dulang in Sabah. The filigree-like grid is a raft set on white flotation tanks, which holds cages containing oysters.

2. On Redang Island, Terengganau (shown here) and in Sabah there are communities, such as the Bajau Laut, who live in villages on stilts built out into the sea. The villagers catch fish for food.

3. A woman spreading out sea cucumbers to dry. These are used for medicinal purposes.

4. Squid being dried on a jetty at Pulau Redang. The squid will later be made into snacks.

5. Most fishermen in Kelantan and Terengganu continue to use traditional boats. These are light but robust enough to weather rough seas during the northeast monsoon.

6. Carpet clams, known locally as *lalah*, are harvested from the sea, mainly off Kuala Kedah. They are sold fresh or shelled and also sent to factories for canning.

FISHERIES RESOURCES

Over many centuries the communities who live along Malaysia's long coastline have developed a great expertise in and reliance on living off the rich harvest of the sea. Fish is the cheapest and most easily attained source of protein for Malaysians and demand for it is great. Malays, predominantly on the east coast, and Chinese, mainly on the west coast, make up most of the fishermen of the Peninsula. Earning a living can be a struggle and many are forced to diversify into boat repairing and building and fish processing, especially when the weather is bad during the north-east monsoon. There are other small communities in the Peninsula, such as the Ma' Betise', who have lived in the mangroves of Selangor for over a century, making a living by fishing, growing fruit, and carving the wood of one of the country's mangrove species. Most of Sabah and Sarawak's coastline, consisting of either sandy beaches or muddy swamps, is inhabited by isolated communities who earn their livelihood by fishing around offshore islands.

Modern commercial boats, such as trawlers, operate throughout Malaysia but many fishermen prefer to rely on the traditional boats and fishing gear which have been used for centuries. Variations in the size, design and decoration of these boats can be seen throughout the country. Boats on the east coast of the Peninsula are the most colourful and intricately decorated while those in Sabah and Sarawak, where the coasts are more sheltered from the monsoons, are usually smaller and lighter.

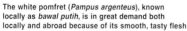

Malaysia has a wealth of fisheries resources, including fish, prawns, squid, cuttlefish, jellyfish, octopuses, cockles and mussels. A significant quantity of high-quality fish, such as pomfret (*bawal putih*), is

The white pomfret (*Pampus argenteus*), known locally as *bawal putih*, is in great demand both locally and abroad because of its smooth, tasty flesh.

exported since it fetches higher prices abroad than at home, whilst a small quantity of low-grade fish, such as the Indian mackerel (*kembung*), is imported to meet local requirements. Demand and requirements change over time. In recent years, anchovies (*bilis*), once the fish of the poor, have become an increasingly sought after catch for the markets of the wider Southeast Asia region.

Aquaculture—the farming of fish, prawns and oysters—which now contributes about 10 per cent to total fish production in Malaysia, has also grown in importance over the last couple of decades. Once seen as the answer to diminishing inshore stocks, it is now realized that only very carefully sited and managed systems are sustainable over the longer term, and the government is not promoting an increase in the current levels of production.

Fishing has traditionally been concentrated on inshore areas, but with depleting stocks and increasing demand since the mid-1980s, the government has been trying to develop offshore fisheries. Government bodies such as the Department of Fisheries Malaysia and the Fisheries Development Authority of Malaysia (LKIM) have also implemented various measures to promote improved management of resources and sustain yields. At the same time, they have worked to help raise the living standards of fishing communities by modernizing boats and gear. The multi-species nature of Malaysia's fisheries makes this a far from easy task.

Fishing communities

As Malaysia is almost totally surrounded by seas, fishing provides a livelihood for many people living along the coast, as it has done for many centuries. Most Malaysian fishermen still use traditional gear, though some have already modernized their operations and use trawlers and other commercial boats. Life is hard; fishermen are affected by changing weather conditions, the monsoons and declining fish stocks. However, as fish is one of the cheapest sources of protein for Malaysians, the high demand ensures a ready market for their landings.

Kampung Kuala Besut, in Terengganu, is a Malay fishing village where many fishermen still go out to fish in small, traditional wooden boats.

Fish trawlers, often used on the west coast of Peninsular Malaysia, are simple to operate, requiring a crew of only three or four people. They are now the most important type of fishing craft in Malaysia.

Fishing villages

There are a few areas in Sabah where fishermen, such as the Bajau Laut, still live on boats, but most Malaysian fishermen now live in modern houses, mainly made of wood with zinc roofs, and these houses are built on land. In sheltered areas in Penang and most other states in the country, a small number of fishermen still live in houses constructed on stilts over the water. In Peninsular Malaysia, such houses are usually located upstream, a little way up from river mouths. Almost all the houses in the fishing villages on the west coast have electricity and clean piped water, but a small percentage of those on the east coast and in Sabah and Sarawak have yet to enjoy such amenities.

Local fishermen, especially those on the east coast who are forced to suspend fishing activities during the northeast monsoon which occurs between November and February, are less affluent than other communities. There is a high school drop-out rate in these villages as children have to find work to supplement the family income. The government has therefore implemented a number of projects to raise the living standards of such fishing communities, such as supporting diversification into food processing and improving the standard of boats.

Main activities

The pattern of fishing activities in Malaysia, especially in the South China Sea, is dictated by the monsoons (see 'Monsoons and the seas'). As the west coast of Peninsular Malaysia is sheltered from the strong monsoon winds by the mountains of the Main Range and the island of Sumatra across the Strait of Melaka, the effects of the monsoons there are greatly reduced.

The northeast monsoon (locally referred to as *musim tengkujuh*) affects the country at the end of each year, beginning in November and lasting till the following March. The exposed east coast of the Peninsula is more badly affected than the west coast. Bringing strong winds, heavy rains, floods and rough seas, the northeast monsoon limits fishing in the South China Sea to large fishing vessels. On the west coast, however, fishing is still possible, even though rough weather sometimes prevents small vessels from going out to sea. There are times, however, during the five-month period of the northeast monsoon when it is impossible for even the largest vessels to go out to sea. Nevertheless, the fish landings during this period are relatively high because some fishermen double their fishing efforts knowing that their catch can fetch a higher price.

A typical fisherman's house in Marang, Terengganu, is made of wood and stands on stilts to avoid flooding during the northeast monsoon at the end of the year.

MAIN FISHING COMMUNITIES				
ETHNIC GROUP % PLACE	BUMIPUTRA	CHINESE	THAI	OTHER ETHNIC GROUPS
Peninsular Malaysia (East coast)	74	9	17	–
Peninsular Malaysia (West coast)	40	50	9	1
Sabah and Sarawak	78	3	–	19

In Malaysia, the more prominent fishing communities are the Bumiputra (Malays and other indigenous groups), Chinese, and those of Thai and Filipino descent, although there are also those of Indian, Portuguese or Indonesian origins. There are large fishing communities on the east coast as well as the west coast of Peninsular Malaysia. Bumiputra, especially Malay fishermen form the largest group in every state except Selangor, Perak and Penang, where there are more Chinese.

During the southwest monsoon between April and October, the seas are calmer. Fishing peaks within this period. As much as 70 per cent of the total marine fish landings on the east coast, 60 per cent on the west coast and slightly less in Sabah and Sarawak, occur during this time.

A variety of fishing gear is used by Malaysian fishermen and can be categorized into commercial and traditional gear (see 'Fishing methods'). Commercial gear includes trawls and purse seines, while traditional gear includes gill nets, traps and handlines. The majority of fishermen in Malaysia use traditional gear, though generally boats on the west coast are more mechanized than those on the east coast (see 'Trawlers and traditional boats'). Fishing boats of equal categories nationwide are basically similar in design.

The operation of different gear requires varying lengths of time at sea. Commercial trawlers and fish purse seiners spend different numbers of days per trip at sea, depending on the size of the vessels. Fishing vessels of 70 GRT (gross registered tonnage) usually stay up to seven days at sea, while small vessels of less than 10 GRT come back to port daily. Commercial anchovy purse seiners of all sizes, however, return daily.

With the exception of trap fishermen, all other traditional gear operators have a routine of going out to sea in the morning and coming back to port in the afternoon. Purse seiner fishermen usually go out to sea at 5.00 pm and return at dawn, about 12 hours later. They go out to their purse seiners by speedboat. The purse seiners make several stops throughout the night and early morning, stopping at each location for one or two hours. To attract the fish, the fishermen float two or three oil lamps. Most fishermen on the east coast work continuously for a month, then take a week's rest.

Off-season activities

During the northeast monsoon, fishermen who depend on smaller traditional boats resort to land-based fishery related activities, such as mending nets, repairing boats or building boats. When they are unable to put out to sea, the fishermen of the east coast also make fish crackers (*keropok*), fish sauce (*budu*), shrimp paste (*belacan*) and other fish products from their catch to supplement their income. Some of them take up other non-fisheries jobs, including working as labourers and construction workers.

Boat building in Malaysia is a lucrative business. The shipyards are categorized into traditional and modern. Most traditional shipyards, scattered throughout the country, deal with boat repairing. Some also build new, mostly traditional boats. The more modern shipyards are capable of building wooden, fibreglass and steel boats of any size, and work on Malaysian ships as well as contracts for overseas markets. There are relatively few of these, and most are located in Penang, Johor and Sarawak.

Processing anchovy sauce (*budu*) in Geting, Kelantan, is an off-season activity for east coast fishermen.

Fishermen mend their nets during the northeast monsoon when they cannot go out to sea.

Fish is salted and dried under the sun. Many fishermen earn extra income from selling salted fish.

Many traditional shipyards in Kelantan and other east coast states concentrate on repairing fishing boats. Some also build new traditional boats.

Boat festivals continue to be celebrated by indigenous communities in Sabah.

Cultural beliefs and practices

All fishing communities in Malaysia, regardless of ethnic origin, have beliefs and practices related to fishing, although many practices are dying out. For example, Malay fishermen on the east coast of the Peninsula used to celebrate a festival known as Puja Pantai, at which a buffalo or cow was slaughtered as an offering to the sea in anticipation of a good harvest. Some Chinese fishermen still offer prayers to the god of the sea for a more bountiful catch. The coastal Melanau from Sarawak carry small fishing fetishes, carved in bone or horn, as a good luck charm. Today, however, most fishermen tend to rely more on good boats, modern machinery and efficient fishing gear than on cultural practices for successful fishing operations.

Project for fishermen's wives

KUNITA (Kumpulan Wanita Nelayan) is a project under the Fisheries Development Authority of Malaysia (LKIM). The project aims to raise the living standards of fishing communities by equipping the womenfolk with various cottage industry skills, such as batik printing, handicrafts, making fish products and snacks like *keropok*, and sewing school uniforms. The women also run small food businesses. For example, the KUNITA group in Port Dickson supplies local cakes (*kueh*) to hotels in the area. LKIM provides financial aid, training, equipment, and help with marketing. There are about 80 KUNITA groups in the country.

One of the many KUNITA projects includes teaching basket weaving to fishermen's wives, to help them supplement the family income.

Fishing methods

Fisheries play an important role in the Malaysian economy by providing two-thirds of the animal protein requirement of the population. Many types of fishing gear are used. The two main gear groups are trawl nets, which contribute about 55 per cent of the total marine fish landings, and purse seines, which contribute about 18 per cent. The more powerful fishing boats, such as trawlers and purse seiners, operate large nets offshore, while traps and other smaller nets are normally used inshore.

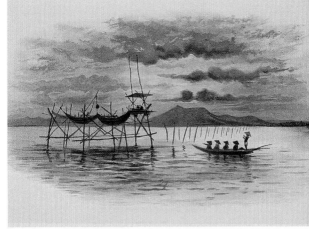

An early engraving showing traditional fishing stakes at the mouth of the Sarawak River. The stakes support large, fixed traps in shallow waters.

Fish bait device

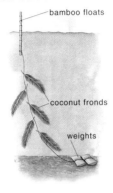

The *unjang* is made up of a rope, with coconut fronds attached at 1–2 metre intervals. Fish are attracted to baits swaying in the water. Such baits are set in groups in the fishing grounds.

Fish sources

The Malaysian fishing industry is divided into three distinct sectors: marine fisheries, coastal aquaculture and inland freshwater fisheries. Of the three, the marine fisheries sector contributes more than 90 per cent of the total fishery production. Aquaculture produces about 9.5 per cent, with the remaining small amount coming from freshwater fisheries.

The marine fisheries sector can be further classified into inshore and offshore fisheries. Differentiation between the two is based on the tonnage of the vessel used and the area of operation. Inshore fishing vessels are those below 70 GRT (gross registered tonnage) which operate in waters less than 30 nautical miles from the coastline. The inshore fisheries sector, with a fishing fleet numbering nearly 31,000 fishing vessels, contributes around 90 per cent of the total marine catch.

The licensed offshore fishing fleet operates trawl nets, purse seines, hooks and lines and drift gill nets. In accordance with new agricultural policies, offshore fisheries are being developed with the introduction of new technology to meet future demand for fishery products.

Selective fishing

About 65 per cent of the trawl catch in Malaysia consists of trash fish, 69 per cent of which is made up of the young of commercially important species. Selective fishing is, therefore, a very common practice. (Selective fishing is the ability of a particular type of gear to select fish of a certain size or shape, through specifying the mesh size or size and type of hook.)

Over-exploitation

In many countries, the intense competition for fisheries resources and the shortsighted belief that the seas can provide unlimited fish resources have resulted in overfishing. Research and development in the field of fishing boats and their equipment have led to very efficient vessels with highly sophisticated equipment for navigation and fish finding.

In Malaysia, while fisheries resources in the Strait of Melaka have been exploited to the maximum sustainable limit, there is considered to be good potential for the expansion of offshore fish catches in the South China Sea and Sulu Sea.

How Malaysian fishing nets work

1. The **push net** (known locally as *sondong*) is a triangular net used in shallow waters. When the net is full, the fisherman empties the catch by turning over the net. During certain seasons, the push net is used to catch mysids, small, prawn-like organisms which are dried and then pounded into a paste.

2. The *bubu* is a small, portable fish trap made from a wood or bamboo frame covered with fine wire netting. It allows fish to come in but does not allow them to escape. This is achieved through a one-way valve-like feature in the opening. The net is placed near coral reefs or other fish habitats and retrieved daily or weekly.

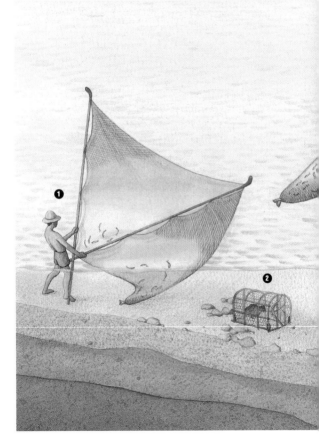

Source: Annual Fisheries Statistics 1996.

MARINE FISH LANDINGS BY GEAR GROUPS, 1996

GEAR GROUP	CATCH (TONS)	PERCENTAGE OF TOTAL	ESTIMATED NUMBERS OF GEAR
Trawl nets	601 980	53	62 337
Purse seines	214 444	19	13 717
Gill or drift nets	144 040	13	142 472
Hooks and lines	44 341	4	21 977
Bag nets	33 015	3	8 507
Lift nets	31 947	3	687
Traps	12 616	1	8 230
Shellfish collection	17 989	2	1 504
Push or scoop nets	16 568	1	9 045
Barrier nets	4 832	0.5	3 402
Miscellaneous gear	4 917	0.5	9 521
Total	**1 126 689**	**100**	**281 399**

More than 80 types of fishing gear are used in the Malaysian fisheries, classified by method of operation.

Fishing gear needs to be maintained in good condition to be able to function well. Nets which are torn have to be mended in preparation for the next fishing trip. Mending nets is often done during the monsoon months when the fisherrmen are unable to go out to sea.

3. The **trawl net** is a triangular net towed by a boat. The mouth of the trawl net is opened by means of floats and sinkers. The horizontal opening of the net mouth is achieved by otterboards. All organisms in front of the open trawl net are caught and the catch collected at the back of the net, called the cod end.

4. A **gill net** is strung in the water over long distances, like an extended badminton net. When fish swim into the net, their gills get entangled. The size of the net is selected to match the target species of fish. Variants include the trammel net and the entangling net, which are set anchored to the ground or as floating gill nets.

5. The **purse seine** is a large, rectangular net, which takes on a rounded shape when in use. Measuring up to 800 metres wide and 80 metres deep, it is set around a school of fish before the base is closed by a purse line. Once closed, it is hauled on board the vessel and the catch emptied.

6. The **longline** is a variety of hook and line gear. It consists of a main line carrying smaller branch lines, each bearing a baited hook. Another variation of the hook and line gear is the vertical handline, which uses up to 10 hooks per main line. When in operation, it is usually set over long distances.

7. The **lift net** is set in the water beneath a fish-attracting device such as coconut fronds. An experienced diver has to determine which species and size of fish will gather around the device. Lift nets such as the *pukat tangkul* are slowly dying out due to their size and complicated method of operation.

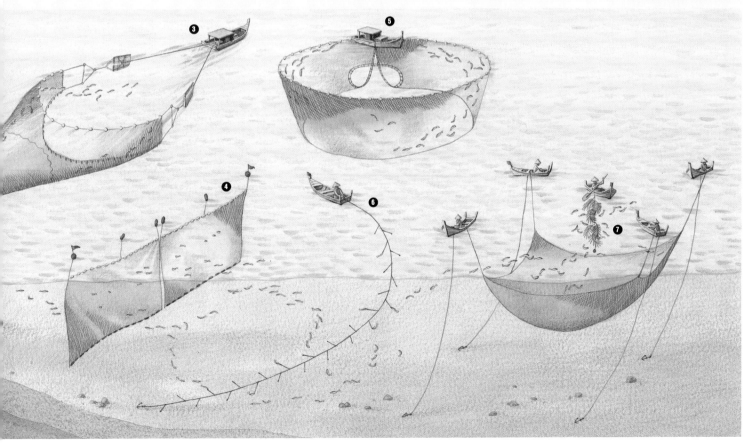

Trawlers and traditional boats

There are many types of fishing vessels in Malaysia, ranging from large, well-equipped modern boats such as trawlers to smaller traditional craft such as sampans. The largest group of fishing vessels are the gill net boats which account for 54 per cent of licensed fishing vessels. Trawlers represent the second largest group, accounting for about 17 per cent. In order to separate commercial operators from traditional fishermen, and safeguard the livelihoods of traditional fishermen, fishing vessels in Malaysia are licensed under four categories (see 'Sustaining yields').

Fish trawlers and prawn trawlers look similar. Even the nets are the same shape. The only difference is that prawn trawl nets are smaller, with smaller mesh sizes for catching prawns.

A fishing village at Marang, Terengganu, built near a lagoon. The wooden houses are built on stilts to avoid monsoon tides and are shaded by coconut palms.

Trawlers

A trawler is a boat equipped to tow a wide-mouthed net through the water in order to trap any fish it encounters into the path of the main bag and then into the main collecting part of the net known as the cod end, located at the back of the trawl net.

As trawlers are simple to operate and require a crew of only three or four people, they are now the most common method of fishing in terms of catch, both for inshore and deep sea fisheries. In 1996, trawlers represented 54 per cent of licensed deep sea fishing vessels, which are 70 GRT (gross registered tonnage) and above, in Malaysia.

There are basically three types of trawlers operating in the country: bottom trawlers (the most common), which tow their nets on the sea bed, pair trawlers (where a large single net is towed between two boats) and mid-water trawlers. The last type is less popular as the boats are complicated to operate and mid-water species are not very abundant in Malaysian waters. Boats are further classified into fish and prawn trawlers. Fish trawlers use larger nets of a bigger mesh size in order to catch larger fish. Some examples of fish caught by Malaysian trawl nets are Spanish mackerel (*tenggiri*), yellow-striped trevally (*selar kuning*), golden striped snapper (*jenahak*), red snapper (*merah*), coral cod (*kerapu*), sharp-toothed bass (*kerisi*) and scad (*selar*).

As fish and prawns are usually found in the same fishing grounds, there is little differentiation in the catch of fish and prawns in trawl nets. However, prawn trawlers use smaller nets with smaller mesh openings because their target species is smaller. The catch usually contains a higher percentage of by-catch of other species, including the young of commercially important species.

As laid down in the Fisheries Act 1985, the cod end mesh size for prawn trawls must not be less than 38 millimetres while that of the fish trawl should not be under 50 millimetres. This selective fishing, to control the size of the catch, is necessary to sustain yields (see 'Sustaining yields') and ensure that trawling does not become destructive—wiping out fish stocks of particular species altogether.

How a trawler operates

Most Malaysian trawlers are now equipped with sophisticated navigational aids as well as an array of deck equipment and other gear. For example, a computerized Global Positioning System (GPS) and a plotter show the exact position of the vessel at sea.

1. A fish trawler from Sungai Besar, near Kuala Selangor, on the west coast of Peninsular Malaysia, going out to sea.

2. Two fishermen winching up the net after the fish are caught in it.

3. The trawl net being opened to release the fish.

4. A fisherman sorting out the fish before storing them in drums.

5. Pouring water into the refrigerated sea water system (RSW) which cools the sea water in the drums to preserve the fish.

6. Putting fish into the RSW drums.

7. Lifting an RSW drum of chilled fish.

8. Storing the fish in plastic boxes before transporting them.

9. Loading boxes of fish onto a lorry to transport them to a wholesale wet market.

Traditional Malay fishing boats

Traditional Malay fishing boats moored at Kuala Terengganu are typical of those found on the east coast of Peninsular Malaysia. They are colourfully decorated and have mast guards.

Although early Malay fishing boats relied on sails which were augmented or replaced by oars when necessary, today there are also power-driven boats which can be classified as fish carriers (boats which only carry fish but do not catch them), launches with inboard motors, and small or medium-sized canoes (*kolek*).

Three terms, *kolek*, *perahu* and *sampan*, are used to distinguish between the relative sizes and designs of the various traditional boats used. The terms are not restricted to specific boats or even to fishing boats in general. *Kolek* is best translated as 'canoe' and usually refers to any small, open boat, but it may also refer to larger boats up to 9–10 metres long. *Perahu* indicates a larger boat, some 6–9 metres or more in length, but still without a deck. Chinese in origin, *sampan* refers to a small or medium-sized boat, again without a deck, which is flat bottomed and more stable than a true *kolek*.

Most of the boats are steered with a paddle. None have fixed decks. Instead, loose deck boards provide a dry, level base on which the fisherman can squat. The space beneath the boards is divided into compartments and is used for stowing the catch.

East coast boats
On the east coast of Peninsular Malaysia, there are many terms for Malay fishing boats, with some boats having several names. The boats are light but more robust than most boats found elsewhere in the country because they have to weather the rough northeast monsoon seas and the strong breakers which place a considerable strain on the boats during launching and landing.

They vary in length from 3–14 metres. All of them have a pointed bow (front) and stern

The traditional Malay fishermen's lunch box (left) is intricately carved with plant motifs and Jawi calligraphy, translated as 'This is a fisherman's lunch box.' The traditional tackle box (right), also carved with plant motifs and calligraphy, has compartments at each end for tackle.

(back). Built locally, they follow about 10 easily distinguished basic patterns. The boats generally used with nets in deeper water are the *perahu payang*, *perahu buatan barat* and *kolek lichang*, all of which are fairly broad.

The three most popular boats on the coast are the *gelibat*, the *kueh* and the *sekochi*. All three are quite large and use nets. Of these, the *kueh* is the most variable in both size and finish. All three types are similar in outline but the *sekochi* is less expensive to produce because of its plain finish. The *gelibat* has a characteristic finish, with a long, almost straight keel that is sharply angled. *Gelibat* vary a lot in size. Of the three, the *kueh* is the most variable in both size and finish. The fastest boat is the *jalorar*, which is 9 metres long and has a long, straight keel. It is used solely for line fishing at some distance from the shore.

Terengganu is the main centre of the traditional boat building industry in Peninsular Malaysia. Though the majority of boats are built according to the same plan, there is considerable variation in their finish and design which reflects Malay artistry and traditions.

1. and 2. Traditional east coast boats often have decorative guards to provide support for the mast when it is not in use. These intricately carved guards, called *bangau*, are usually shaped like a dragon's head or bird, surrounded by plant motifs.

3. Several distinct local patterns of tradtional boat designs can be discerned. The boats, particularly in Kelantan and Terengganu, are usually painted in brightly coloured stripes.

South and west coast boats
Smaller and lighter fishing boats, including smaller *kolek* and *perahu*, are used on the south and west coasts of Peninsular Malaysia. These coastlines are more sheltered than the east coast and much of the fishing is carried out inshore, mainly with cast nets and traps. Chinese-built boats, particularly *sampan*, are widely used on the west coast where many of the fishermen are Chinese.

A group of small, shoe-shaped *sampan* at the river mouth in Kuala Selangor on the west coast of Peninsular Malaysia. These *sampan* are built by Chinese fishermen, who mainly live along the west coast. Unlike traditional Malay east coast boats, *sampan* are plain in finish.

Commercial fish

Of the 4,000 species of fish found in Malaysian seas, about 500 are commercially important. Fish is a healthy and relatively cheap source of protein and an important part of the Malaysian diet. Malaysia has a great diversity of fish. The species are classified into two broad categories—pelagic (fish dwelling nearer the surface of the sea) and demersal (bottom-dwelling) fish—according to their distribution. The industry has a long tradition and is the livelihood of many Malaysians.

Fish stalls abound, not only in wet markets but also in supermarkets throughout the country.

Malay embroidery motifs

Malay embroidery motifs are generally inspired by nature, particularly flora, but fauna, such as fish and birds, are popular motifs among the womenfolk in fishing communities. The fish motifs on these pillow ends, produced by binding shaped cards onto velvet with gold thread, are a visible symbol of the links between Malay culture and the sea.

Pelagic fish

Pelagic fish can be grouped into three main categories: small pelagics, tuna and anchovies. The small pelagics comprise mainly mackerels, of which *Rastrelliger* is the mainstay. Other small pelagic species include *Decapterus, Selaroides, Atule, Alepes, Sardinella* and *Dussumieria,* the white pomfret (*Pampus argenteus*), the black pomfret (*Formio niger*), threadfins (*Eleutheronema tetradactylum*) and the hardtail trevally (*Megalaspis cordyla*). The small tuna species fished in Malaysia include *Euthynnus affinis, Auxis thazard* and *Thunnus tonggol.* The skipjack (*Katsuwonus pelamis*) and the yellowfin tuna (*Thunnus albacares*) are the main species of oceanic tuna caught. The key anchovy species fished is the *Stolephorus,* which is a very valuable fishery resource.

In Malaysia, pelagic fish exhibit a seasonal inshore–offshore migration pattern in relation to the northeast monsoon. During the calm off-monsoon season, there is an inshore movement of pelagic fish. During the monsoons, an offshore migration and dispersion occurs. Concentrations of pelagic fish are higher in coastal waters compared with offshore waters. Large numbers of pelagic fish are caught using a purse seine and a modified trawl called the high-opening trawl. Fish-aggregating devices are sometimes used together with purse seines to increase the catch. Traditional gear is also employed, such as push, lift and bag nets.

Demersal fish

The dominant and more valuable commercial bottom-dwelling fish harvested by Malaysian trawlers include threadfin breams (*Nemipterus* sp.) or *kerisi,* snappers (*Lutjanus* sp.), locally called *jenahak, merah, tanda* or *kunyit-kunyit,* and groupers (*Epinephelus* and *Plectropomus* sp.) or *kerapu.* The lower-value fish consist mainly of jewfish (*Sciaena, Johnius, Otolithus* and *Otolithoides* sp.) or *gelama,* lizard fish (*Saurida* sp.) or *mengkarong,* and catfish (*Trachysurus, Arius* and *Osteogeneiosus* sp.) or *duri.*

Trawl survey results conducted by the Fisheries Research Institute indicate that the highest concentrations of demersal fish are to be found on muddy sea bottoms rather than sandy sea floors. Depth of water also appears to be significant. For example, the commercially important mullids, nemipterids and lutjanids are more abundant in deeper waters.

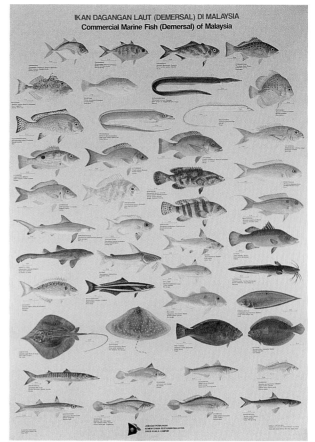

A poster from the Department of Fisheries Malaysia showing the large variety of commercial demersal fish landed in Malaysia.

Economic importance

Malaysia exports its best quality catch (grade A fish), such as white pomfret (*Pampus argenteus*) or *bawal putih,* for higher prices and imports mostly lower grade fish—grades B and C, such as Indian mackerel (*Rastrelliger kanagurta*) or *kembung*—at lower prices. The local demand for grade A fish is limited, while lower grade fish is required in large amounts. The current per capita consumption of fish is about 40 kilograms. To ensure a sustainable supply of fish, the Department of Fisheries Malaysia manages and protects and conserves fisheries resources (see 'Sustaining yields').

Around 20 per cent of local fish production is exported to Japan, Singapore, China and Europe. In 1997, fish exports totalled 108 000 metric tons (with a value of RM940 million) compared with 164 000 metric tons in 1990. At the same time, fish imports increased from 229 000 metric tons in 1990 to 298 000 metric tons in 1997. Imported fish, which makes up about 25 per cent of Malaysia's fish supply, is the raw material for local fish and food processing industries.

Malaysia imports fish from neighbouring countries, such as Indonesia and Thailand, which are able to sell cheaper fish because of a larger supply. This helps to stabilize prices and provides a greater variety of fish for Malaysians. Despite the imports, the current local demand for fish is still outpacing supply as both population and demand grows. Therefore, there is ongoing pressure on both imports and the Malaysian fish catch.

Marine fish landings

Main species caught
Of the estimated 500 species with commercial value, about 100 species are listed in the Annual Fisheries Statistics as the more commonly caught species. In 1996, 1 126 689 metric tons of marine fish were landed with a variety of gear. Besides the main species caught (a selection of which is illustrated below), other important species in demand include the white pomfret (*Pampus argenteus*) or *bawal putih*, the Indian threadfin (*Polynemus indicus*) or *kurau* and the sea bass (*Lates calcarifer*) or *siakap*.

NOT TO SCALE

Indian mackerel (*Rastrellinger kanagurta*) or *kembung*

Round scad (*Decapterus maruadsi*) or *selayang/curut*

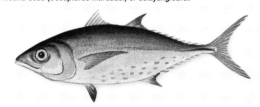

Long-tailed tuna (*Thunnus tonggol*) or *aya hitam/tongkol*

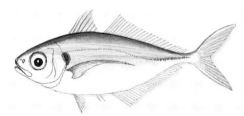

Yellow-striped trevally (*Selaroides leptolepis*) or *selar kuning*

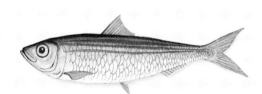

Fringescale sardinella (*Sardinella fimbriata*) or *tamban sisik*

PROPORTION OF FISH LANDINGS TO OTHER FISHERIES IN MALAYSIA

others 2%
acetes shrimps 2%
crabs 1%
squid 5%
prawns 8%
fish 82%

Trash fish
Trash fish are defined as those fish which are low in commercial value, not normally marketed for consumption. They are often small or have a bony structure. About 20–30 per cent of fish landed are the young of commercial species. These are included within trash statistics. Trawlers land a high percentage of trash fish—as much as 30–50 per cent of the catch. It is used for fish meal and for food in aquaculture.

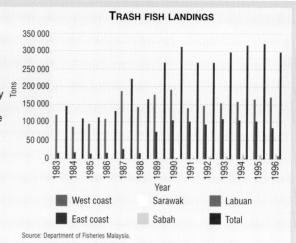

TRASH FISH LANDINGS

Tons

350 000
300 000
250 000
200 000
150 000
100 000
50 000
0

1983 1984 1985 1986 1987 1988 1989 1990 1991 1992 1993 1994 1995 1996

Year

West coast   Sarawak   Labuan
East coast   Sabah   Total

Source: Department of Fisheries Malaysia.

The decline of certain species
Trawl surveys carried out by the Department of Fisheries Malaysia have shown that some food fish, such as the false trevally (*Lactarius lactarius*) or *shrumbu* and the long-tailed shad (*Hilsa toli*) or *terubuk*, commonly caught in Peninsular Malaysia in the mid-1900s, had virtually disappeared by the 1990s. In recent years, surveys also indicate a decline in landings of croakers (*Johnius belangeri*) or *gelama*. Over-exploitation is the main reason for their decline.

To counter this decline, the Malaysian National Policy on Biological Diversity was launched in 1998 to implement strategies and projects not only to conserve the nation's biological diversity but also to promote the sustainable utilization of its resources.

The *terubuk* has reappeared in small numbers in Perak and Selangor and it is still found in fair abundance in Sarawak. The salted roe of this fish, a local delicacy, sells for more than RM100 per kilogram. Recognizing the seriousness of the continued decline of the *terubuk* in Sarawak, the state government initiated a project in 1993 to arrest the decline. This project has shown some success.

Long-tailed shad or *terubuk*

Malaysian fish products
A number of species of fish are used to make various fish products, including *surimi*, fish crackers, fish balls and fish cakes. Such products are the base for many local food industries.

Salt fish
Some of the fish caught is salted and dried. Popular varieties of salt fish include anchovies (*Stolephorus* sp.) or *bilis* and Indian threadfin (*Polynemus indicus*) or *kurau*, which fetch high prices.

Fish placed on wooden racks dries in the sun.

Fish balls and fish cakes
Fish balls and fish cakes are made from various species of fish. One is the fusilier (*Caesio caerulaureus*), known locally as *pisang-pisang* or *delah*. The Chinese call this fish *tau foo yee* ('beancurd' fish) because of the smooth texture of its flesh. It is used for making fish balls as it has few bones. Fish balls can also be made from more bony fish, such as the wolf herring (*Chirocentrus dorab*) or *parang-parang* and Spanish mackerel (*Scomberomorus guttatus*) or *tenggiri*.

Surimi
Surimi is a fish product used to make 'crab' sticks and other imitation seafood. It is imported from Thailand and other countries, or produced locally from species such as the yellow-striped trevally (*Selaroides leptolepis*) or *selar kuning*. The fish is scaled, beheaded, gutted and filleted. The fish fillet is then minced, after which it is mechanically leached in fresh water to remove the water-soluble proteins, blood and fat, leaving a whiter product. Crude fat is also removed. Leaching is usually repeated at least once. To thicken the paste, water is removed, after which the product is referred to as *surimi*.

Keropok
Making fish crackers (*keropok ikan*) is an important local industry. The fish is first pounded, mixed with sago flour, formed into 'sausages' and then boiled. The rolls are sliced thinly and dried in the sun. The *keropok* has to be deep-fried before eating. It is usually eaten as a snack.

Keropok are now made mechanically.

Anchovies

Anchovies, locally known as ikan bilis, *are a popular fish with Malaysians. They form a small but significant percentage of the total marine catch in Malaysia. Anchovy fishing is most highly developed on the west coast of Peninsular Malaysia, where it is done by purse seine boats. Almost all anchovies in Malaysia are sold in a salted and dried form. Dried anchovy fillets have become popular abroad and demand is expected to increase in the future.*

Main anchovy landing centres

N

Pulau Langkawi
Tanjung Dawai

Paka
Kemaman

Pulau Pangkor

South China Sea

Strait of Melaka

Endau

◆ Main landing centres

0   200 km

Most of the main anchovy landing centres in Peninsular Malaysia are located on the northwest coast.

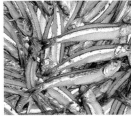

Boiled *ikan bilis* waiting to be dried.

Anchovies are caught with anchovy purse seiners. These boats use round nets called purse seines that, unlike trawl nets, are not dragged across the ocean damaging the catch. A purse seiner usually has a watch tower from where the fishermen can look out for schools of anchovies swimming close to the surface.

Malaysian species

Anchovies refer to a group of fish of the genera *Stolephorus* and *Encrasicholina*. The dominant species caught in Malaysia is *Encrasicholina heterolobus*. Two other common species are *S. andhraensis* and *E. punctifer*. Most local anchovy species are small, no longer than 10 centimetres, with the exception of *Stolephorus indicus*, which can grow up to 15 centimetres. Anchovies are pelagic in nature and feed mainly on plankton. They are generally distributed very close to the shore. Small fish are found just off islands where the more productive water provides food for the young fish. As they grow, they move slightly further away from the shore. The popular fishing grounds for anchovies are generally located between shore and the 20-metre depth contour.

Small but important

The anchovy fishery has always been a very important coastal fishery in Malaysia, generally contributing between 2 and 10 per cent of the total annual marine landings in the country. In 1996, a total of 24 000 metric tons of anchovies worth RM60 million in wholesale value were landed in Malaysia. Today anchovies are fished very efficiently by anchovy purse seine boats. These boats are manned by anything up to 20 men and the nets can be 550 metres long by 55 metres deep.

The main landing centres for anchovy purse seiners are at Pulau Langkawi, Tanjung Dawai in Kedah, and Pulau Pangkor in Perak on the west coast of Peninsular Malaysia. On the east coast, the main landing centres are located at Paka and Kemaman in Terengganu, and Endau in Johor. The anchovy fishery is more developed on the west coast of Peninsular Malaysia than in other parts of the country because of better infrastructure and marketing support facilities. The west coast is also more sheltered, which allows fishing throughout the year, compared with the east coast states which are affected by the northeast monsoon. On the west coast most anchovies are caught in the months

Anchovies usually move around in large schools.

between January and March. Catches of anchovies appear to be slightly lower during the middle of the year. Smaller quantities are caught off the east coast states, as well as off Sarawak and Sabah. Both Pulau Langkawi and Pulau Pangkor produce high-quality dried anchovies, which are both sold locally and exported. In the period from 1991 to 1994, between 500 and 1000 tons of dried anchovies were exported to Singapore annually. Anchovies are also sold to the Philippines and the United States of America.

Anchovies are popular because of their high nutritional value. Dried anchovies, whether whole or with heads and intestines removed, contain around 60 per cent protein. They also provide a good source of calcium, and vitamins A and B.

Fishermen mending anchovy nets. It is important that nets for catching such small fish are kept in good condition.

LANDINGS OF MARINE FISH BY MAIN SPECIES 1997

Source: Department of Fisheries Malaysia.

- kerisi (threadfin bream) 3%
- bilis (anchovies) 2%
- sotong (squid) 5%
- selar kuning (yellow-striped trevally) 3%
- ikan baja (trash fish) 24%
- others 35%
- tenggiri (Spanish mackerel) 1%
- udang (prawn) 7%
- selayang (round scad) 7%
- kembung (Indian mackerel) 8%
- aya/tongkol (tuna) 5%

Anchovies form a small but significant percentage of the total marine catch.

Main threats

The main threats to the anchovy fishing industry in Malaysia, particularly on the west coast, are over-exploitation of fish stocks and destruction of fishing grounds through environmental degradation. If too many young fish are caught, insufficient numbers of the next generation of fish to support the fishery will be reproduced, and if fish are caught at a rate faster than the rate at which new fish are born, the size of the stock will decrease very quickly. With careful control over harvesting through strict licensing of anchovy purse seiners and checking of nets, coupled with constant monitoring of the performance of these vessels, this valuable fishery should be able to sustain yields.

Unfortunately, this fishery is also subject to environmental damage and pollution. Thus, any measures to improve coastal pollution levels also contribute to the health and size of anchovy shoals.

A Malaysian favourite

The anchovy or *ikan bilis* is a highly popular food item in the Malaysian diet. In fact, the favourite breakfast of many Malaysians, *nasi lemak* (fragrant rice cooked in coconut milk), is traditionally served with *sambal belacan* (a hot and spicy sauce), fried *ikan bilis*, slices of cucumber, and a boiled or fried egg. Besides being served with *nasi lemak* and with plain rice, *sambal ikan bilis* is now used as a savoury filling for buns, sandwiches, doughnuts and even croissants!

As *ikan bilis* becomes very crunchy when fried, it is used in crisps as well, often with peanuts, to make tasty snacks. The salty fried *ikan bilis* is frequently served with rice porridge, too. Another popular use is to boil the fish to make a nutritious stock for soups.

A fish sauce called *budu* is made mainly from fermented second-grade anchovies, although other low-value fish may also be used. A substantial amount of salt is added to the fish in the tank before water is added and the fish left to ferment for up to six months. The fermented solution is then filtered and sold to food processors. Tamarind juice, brown sugar, and other ingredients that remain trade secrets, are added. The mixture is boiled, cooled and bottled for retail sale. Producing *budu* is a cottage industry on the east coast of the Peninsula.

Fishing for anchovies—from sea to shore

A normal trip of an anchovy purse seiner trawler from Pulau Langkawi begins early in the morning. The boat leaves port with the crew scouting for shoals of anchovies. The fish betray their presence by breaking through the water surface in patches of water. The purse seine net is shot to surround the school and then drawn or 'pursed'. A power block is used to haul in the net and its catch.

The fish are scooped into large baskets and immediately boiled in brine.

In the 1970s and 1980s, anchovy purse seiners operated in pairs, one boat catching the fish while another boat, called the 'cook boat', boiled the fish out at sea. With increasing costs, a single boat is now being used for both the fishing and cooking processes.

The purse seiner usually comes back in the evening with its trays of boiled anchovies. The catch is unloaded at the jetty, to be taken away and dried.

The size of the anchovy purse seine net has increased in length and depth in tandem with the introduction of the use of colour echo-sounders to detect fish. Most boats now use geographic positioning systems as well to aid in navigation.

Drying the fish is still dependent on sunlight although the use of steam dryers is a recent innovation.

To obtain high quality anchovies, they have to be handled carefully, boiled as soon as they are caught and stored in cold rooms if they cannot be dried immediately. Failure to observe these stages will yield low-grade dried anchovies with yellow discoloration and with heads broken off.

The dried anchovies need to be sorted out, as they are graded and marketed according to size. This tedious work is usually done manually by women who work in wooden sheds adjacent to the jetty.

Although most anchovies are sold in dried form, they are also fermented to yield *budu*, a popular condiment in Malay cuisine. With its strong fishy smell and taste, *budu* is an acquired taste.

Various grades of anchovies are sold. The largest fish (approximately 6–7 centimetres) are the least valuable; the medium-sized fish (approximately 4–5 centimetres) are of medium value, while the smallest fish (less than 3 centimetres) are the most expensive as they generally have the best taste. This grading system applies to all species of anchovy.

Aquaculture

Aquaculture is the farming of aquatic organisms, such as fish, prawns, shellfish and algae, in fresh water, sea water or brackish water. In Malaysia, aquaculture contributes about 10 per cent of the current total fish production, with culture from marine waters (mariculture) making up the vast majority of the total production. Among the main species cultivated are sea bass, groupers, tiger prawns, cockles and mussels. The main producing states are Perak, Penang, Kedah, Selangor and Johor on the west coast of the peninsula, and Sabah.

Fish are cultured in net cages (3 x 3 x 2 m) suspended from rafts. Most farmers still feed carnivorous fish (sea bass, grouper and snapper) with trash fish. A few more progressive farmers—only about 1 per cent—have advanced to the use of pellet feeds.

Feeding pellets to red tilapia.

The importance of aquaculture

Landings from Malaysian coastal fisheries have already reached the maximum sustainable yield of 900 000 metric tons. Therefore, any increase in production will have to depend on the offshore fisheries which are not yet fully exploited, as well as aquaculture. The National Agricultural Policy (1992–2010) targets a production of 600 000 metric tons from aquaculture and 400 000 metric tons from offshore fisheries by the year 2010, while sustaining the coastal fisheries production at 900 000 metric tons. When landings from capture fisheries have reached their limits, further increases in fish production will have to come from aquaculture.

Aquaculture has developed because farming aquatic species has certain advantages over farming domestic livestock. For instance, farmers can get more meat from aquatic species than from livestock for the same amount of feed given. This is because, being cold-blooded, fish and shellfish do not need to expend energy on regulating their body temperatures. Being buoyant, they also do not need to support their weight, and therefore they convert energy from food into growth more efficiently.

Effects on the environment

If practised in the traditional way, with low stocking densities and an integrated farming approach, aquaculture can be environmentally sound. However, modern aquaculture, especially on a large scale, is often polluting and can bring about environmental degradation if not managed sustainably. When developed in coastal areas, it contributes to the loss of critical habitats, such as mangroves, which are important nursery and feeding grounds for the larval and young stages of many commercial fish and shellfish species. The loss of mangroves can also cause soil erosion and flooding.

Aquaculture effluents may increase the suspended solids and nutrients and cause a fall in the oxygen content of the coastal waters. The effluents may also contain the residues of chemicals used to disinfect

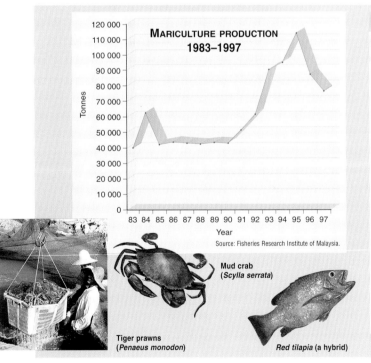

MARICULTURE PRODUCTION 1983–1997

y-axis: Tonnes (0 to 120 000)
x-axis: Year (83 84 85 86 87 88 89 90 91 92 93 94 95 96 97)

Source: Fisheries Research Institute of Malaysia.

Tiger prawns
(*Penaeus monodon*)

Mud crab
(*Scylla serrata*)

Red tilapia (a hybrid)

MARICULTURE PRODUCTION 1997

SPECIES CULTIVATED	PRODUCTION (metric tons)	% OF TOTAL PRODUCTION	MAIN PRODUCING STATES
Cockles (*Anadara granosa*)	58 400	76	Perak, Penang, Selangor
Prawns			
Tiger prawn (*Penaeus monodon*)	9375	12	Sabah, Johor, Perak, Kedah
Banana prawn (*Penaeus merguiensis*)	140	0.3	Johor
Total prawns	9515		
Fish			
Sea bass (*Lates calcarifer*)	3485	5	Perak, Penang, Johor, Selangor
Mangrove snapper (*Lutjanus* sp.)	1369	2	
Grouper (*Epinephelus* sp.)	799	1	
Red tilapia (a hybrid)	22	0.1	
Total fish	5675		
Mussels	1779	2	Johor, Melaka, Selangor
Mangrove crabs	277	0.5	Johor, Sarawak, Perak
Oysters	127	0.3	Sabah, Kedah, Terengganu
Miscellaneous	515	0.8	
GRAND TOTAL	76 288		

Source: Fisheries Research Institute of Malaysia.

farms, control pests and predators or treat diseases, as well as hormones used to induce breeding, and anaesthesia used for the transportation of fish. Concern has also been expressed over the use of antibiotics and other chemicals which not only contaminate the coastal waters but the cultivated creatures as well. Proper planning and management is, therefore, essential.

Of the adverse environmental effects brought about through unsustainably managed aqua-culture, loss of mangroves is probably the most serious concern in Malaysia. Mangroves are utilized partly because farmers are easily able to procure a temporary occupation licence (TOL) for their use. Under the guidelines provided by the Malaysian National Mangrove Committee (NATMANCOM), it has now been recommended that only unproductive hinterland be utilized, and

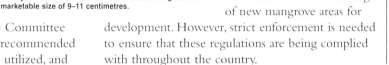

The long-line method of oyster culture involves suspending collectors made of netlon (nylon netting materials) and oyster shells from a horizontal rope held afloat by buoys. The oyster seeds take around 10–12 months to grow to a marketable size of 9–11 centimetres.

that a buffer zone of at least 100 metres be retained between the aquaculture farm and the coastline.

Owing to the environmental impact of aquaculture, the Department of Fisheries Malaysia has formulated guidelines and regulations to control aquaculture. It is now necessary for an environmental impact assessment (EIA) to be conducted for projects of more than 50 hectares. In 1996, the Malaysian government, concerned over the loss of mangrove habitats for agricultural, housing, industrial and aquaculture purposes, imposed a moratorium on the clearing of new mangrove areas for development. However, strict enforcement is needed to ensure that these regulations are being complied with throughout the country.

The grouper (top), known locally as *kerapu,* and the sea bass or *siakap* (above) are two of the main species of fish cultivated in aquaculture.

Marine prawn culture in Malaysia

Although freshwater fish culture originated in China around 2000 BCE, cultivating fish in marine waters has its origin in Indonesia in the 15th century. The first known brackish water culture was introduced into Malaysia to the state of Johor in the early 1900s, when Chinese immigrants brought with them the technique of marine prawn culture in trapping ponds. Prawn fry and natural foods were brought into the ponds with the incoming tides. Production from these ponds was unpredictable.

Marine prawn culture has grown in importance over the years, from a production of only 60 metric tons in 1984 to 9514 metric tons in 1997. Its rapid growth was first experienced in the late 1970s, fuelled mainly by the many success stories on marine prawn culture in neighbouring countries such as Thailand. The extensive culture system, dating back to

the early days of aquaculture in Malaysia, involved huge ponds and did not require aeration. The more recent phase has seen the growth of semi-intensive and intensive cultures. In semi-intensive cultures, hatchery-produced post-larvae, mainly of the tiger prawn (*Penaeus monodon*), are stocked at 10–20 per square metre, while in intensive cultures, 20–30 prawn post-larvae are stocked per square metre. Aeration, pumping of water and artificial feeding are required for both types of culture. Two crops are harvested per year. Unfortunately, some of these farms have proven to be unsustainable, and resulted in disease and death of the prawns. Some farms utilize huge tracts of mangroves and use highly intensive culture methods that do not conform to the Malaysian National Mangrove Committee (NATMANCOM) guidelines.

1. Prawn ponds are usually sited in mangrove areas along the coast, often without the provision of a buffer zone. To prevent soil erosion and contamination of coastal waters by chemicals used in prawn culture, it is essential to have a buffer zone of at least 100 metres.

2. Post-larvae at 15–20 days old are ready for stocking into ponds. In extensive pond culture, the stocking density is less than 10 post-larvae per square metre of pond. Stocking in semi-intensive culture is 10–20 post-larvae per square metre, whilst in intensive culture it is 20–30 per square metre.

3. The extensive culture system dates back to the 1900s when traditional prawn culture relied on wild fry and natural food. Pond size ranges from 2 to 20 hectares. No aeration to the pond is used and water exchange is through tidal flow.

4. Prawns are fed with pellets in the semi-intensive and intensive culture systems. Aeration is switched off and the feed scattered into the pond. Overfeeding is avoided since leftover feed may cause pollution.

5. In the semi-intensive and intensive culture systems, aeration is required to maintain the level of oxygen and to increase pond production. Pond size is usually around 0.2–1 hectare, and pumps are required for water exchange.

6. The prawns reach a marketable size of 20–25 grams after 3–5 months. Harvests from the extensive culture system are less than 1 ton per hectare, 1–2.5 tons for the semi-intensive system and 3–6.5 tons per hectare for the intensive system.

Cockles and mussels

Cockles have been cultured in Malaysia for almost five decades. From the 1960s onwards, the production of cockles increased substantially through the introduction of aquaculture until, in the 1980s and early 1990s, Malaysia became the world's largest producer. Commercial mussel culture in Malaysia was introduced during the late 1970s in Johor, which is the country's main producing region. Like cockles, these molluscs are also cultured in brackish water.

Cockle spats or larvae are collected from their natural beds to be cultured.

The ark shell or blood cockle (*Anadara granosa*) is cultured extensively in Malaysia.

The green mussel (*Perna viridis*) is cultured on a small scale in Malaysia.

Location

In Malaysia, the term cockle usually refers to the ark shell (*Anadara granosa*). Known locally as *kerang*, it is also called the blood cockle because, unlike most molluscs, its blood contains the red respiratory pigment haemoglobin instead of the more common bluish haemocyanin. The mussels cultivated in Malaysia are green mussels (*Perna viridis*).

Cockles are commonly found along the mud flats lining the west coast of Peninsular Malaysia, Sarawak and parts of Sabah. They occur beyond the river mouth, in the lower intertidal zone and are dwellers of soft, muddy substrates with high organic content. Green mussels thrive in Malaysian coastal waters where the warm temperatures are ideal for their rapid growth. The mussels filter feed on plankton and organic detritus.

Cockle culture

Like mussels and other bivalves, cockles have traditionally been harvested for food by coastal villagers. The main producing states are Perak, Penang and Selangor, all on the west coast of Peninsular Malaysia. The local cockle industry is based entirely on the collection of young cockles, also known as seeds or spats, and their subsequent culture. This means that variations in the natural spatfall or seed supply can affect the annual production. As the acreage under culture increases, seed supply has become limiting in certain years when natural spatfalls are low.

In response to a serious shortage of seed supply during the 1980s, scientists at Universiti Sains Malaysia and the Fisheries Research Institute experimented with the artificial production of cockle seeds. Although they succeeded, this did not lead to large-scale commercial production. The process is not economically viable, given the low market price of cockles and the usually adequate supply of seed in most years.

In Malaysia, progress in the development of cockle culture has occurred through the introduction of various management practices. These include regulation and licensing of spat collection at a number of natural spatfall sites in Penang, Perak and Selangor, licensing the use of cockle culture beds, and regulating the minimum size (31.2 millimetres) at which cockles can be harvested. Cultured cockles can be harvested after 10–12 months once they reach a length of approximately 30–35 millimetres. Post-harvest improvements include cleaning and storage under cool conditions at the landing sites and during transportation. The use of purifying plants has reduced bacterial levels, while chilled storage in supermarkets has increased the shelf-life of cockles.

Marketing

Bivalves are highly perishable, particularly in high temperatures. Both cockles and mussels are usually sold fresh and the product quality deteriorates rapidly unless great care is employed in storage. Under ambient temperatures, fresh mussels die within a day while cockles last a couple of days if kept moist. Bacteria within the bivalves can build up rapidly but refrigeration can prolong shelf-life for up to four days. The meat is also sold as frozen blocks or as canned products preserved in brine.

Production

Although the number of areas and culturists did not fall (see table on the right), cockle production in Malaysia declined by a significant 19 per cent, from 71 795 metric tons in 1996 to 58 400 metric tons in 1997. This was mainly due to poor spatfall—the decreasing numbers of young cockles from natural beds. The decline was highest in Perak. The production in Selangor, however, increased slightly.

STATE	COCKLE CULTURE 1997		NUMBER OF CULTURISTS
	FARMS	AREA (sq. m)	
Perlis	0	0	0
Kedah	1	18	1
Pulau Pinang	63	770	51
Perak	216	2890	214
Selangor	18	710	18
Negeri Sembilan	0	0	0
Melaka	1	4	7
Johor	3	50	2
Pahang	0	0	0
Terengganu	0	0	0
Kelantan	0	0	0
Sarawak	0	0	0
Sabah	0	0	0
Total	**302**	**4442**	**293**

Source: *Annual Fisheries Statistics 1997.*

Cockles are sold at most wet markets and supermarkets in Malaysia. They are often cooked with noodles.

At hawker stalls cockles are often skewered before they are boiled and then eaten with chilli sauce.

Mussel culture

Commercial culture of green mussels, locally known as *siput sudu*, is practised extensively in the southern states of Peninsular Malaysia, particularly Johor, Melaka and Selangor. From the late 1980s onwards, production was increased through commercial culture.

Local mussel culture consists of two processes: spat (larvae) collection and grow-out (allowing the young to grow). The main method of culture involves the use of ropes suspended from floating rafts. As the mussels are fully immersed in water they can feed continuously, resulting in faster and more even growth.

Unlike cockles, for which little can be done to increase spatfall, mussel spat collection can be enhanced by placing collectors—ropes of natural or synthetic materials—in the water when the mussel larvae are ready to settle.

The timing of placement of the collectors is very important since settlement peaks only last for 2–3 weeks. Collectors placed in the water too early (or too late) will soon be covered by sediment and other settling organisms such as barnacles or oysters which crowd out the mussel spats. Accurate forecasting of the spatfall peak is therefore crucial.

If too many spats settle on the ropes, then 'reseeding' (thinning) is necessary. This is done 2–3 months later when the mussels are 1–2 centimetres long. During reseeding, the original collector is stripped of its attached spats. The detached spats are then distributed evenly on cotton netting material, wrapped and bound to the rope used for grow-out. Reseeding is usually completed within 1–2 days after stripping and the prepared ropes returned to the water. The cotton netting usually disintegrates within a couple of weeks, by which time new seeds have attached themselves to the ropes. Cultured mussels can be harvested when they reach a shell length of 7–8 centimetres.

Advantages of suspended culture

Although the use of suspended culture involves greater initial outlay for the construction of rafts as well as the purchase of ropes, it has certain advantages. Suspended culture taps the nutrient-rich upper layers of the sea water, allowing the submerged mussels to feed almost continuously. The type of substrate is not important, and being suspended, the mussels are not exposed to bottom-dwelling predators. As aspects of the system can be mechanized, large-scale operations can also be carried out.

In Malaysia, the culture of mussels is often a small family enterprise, such as this one in Muar, Johor.

1. The rope used for the mussel larvae to settle on can be natural or synthetic.
2. The rope is lowered into the water where mussel spats settle on it.
3. Harvesting is carried out when the mussels reach a shell length of 70–80 mm.
4. The rope full of mussels is lifted into the boat.
5. The mussels are removed from the rope.
6. The shells are removed and the flesh packed into plastic bags to be taken to the market for sale.

The table (right) shows that Johor is the main producer of mussels in Malaysia, where total production increased by 53 per cent from 1163 metric tons in 1996 to 1779 metric tons in 1997.

Source: Annual Fisheries Statistics 1997

MUSSEL CULTURE 1997

STATE	MUSSEL CULTURE FARMS	MUSSEL CULTURE AREA (sq m)	NUMBER OF CULTURISTS
Perlis	0	0	0
Kedah	5	760	3
Pulau Pinang	3	1010	3
Perak	2	4000	16
Selangor	7	1100	6
Negeri Sembilan	21	3730	21
Melaka	29	4590	19
Johor	317	50 000	77
Pahang	0	0	0
Terengganu	0	0	0
Kelantan	0	0	0
Sarawak	0	0	0
Sabah	87	1850	87
Total	**471**	**67 040**	**232**

Health risks

In Malaysia, there have been periodic outbreaks of gastro-intestinal diseases caused by shellfish that have been contaminated by bacteria and viruses. Cockles and mussels can also be contaminated by high levels of pesticides or heavy metals, but the effect of these contaminants, although more serious, often takes a long time to manifest itself.

Bivalves are easily contaminated by bacteria and viruses because of the way they feed. Mussels and cockles both feed by sending a current of water through their gills by beating the cilia on their gills. Food particles, including sediment, detritus, plankton, bacteria and even faecal particles are trapped by the beating cilia, along with a mucous secretion, and directed towards the mouth.

Cockles and mussels contaminated with bacteria or viruses can be cleansed by a purifying process which involves passing clean sea water through the bivalves. Bacteria are washed off the bivalves' gill surface and faeces and then passed through an ultraviolet light source which destroys the bacteria. After suitable filtration, the water is recirculated through the bivalves. This purification process is not effective for the treatment of bivalves contaminated with pesticides or heavy metals because the contaminants are incorporated into the bivalve's body tissues and are not easily removed.

Red tide

Outbreaks of 'red tide' have periodically been reported in the coastal waters off Sabah and Sarawak and, to a lesser extent, in the Strait of Melaka. Red tides are algal blooms. These occur when very favourable growth conditions for the algae exist. In Malaysia, the major red tide species is the plankton *Pyrodinium bahamese var compressum* (see 'Plankton').

These organisms contain neurotoxins which accumulate in the tissues of bivalves. As the toxins are heat resistant, cooking does not reduce their toxicity. Eating bivalves contaminated with such neurotoxins causes illness and can even result in death. Bivalves contaminated with red tide organisms are not easily purified and the best strategy is simply to ban harvesting for a time.

On 8 March 2000, *The Star* reported an outbreak of 'red tide' in Sabah. The Department of Fisheries Malaysia banned the export of cockles from the state because of the outbreak.

The depuration process removes bacteria or viruses from contaminated cockles or mussels.

Export ban on Sabah cockles due to 'red tide'

Jellyfish

Jellyfish are an important fisheries resource in Malaysia where they are considered a delicacy. The seas harbour more than 100 species, ranging in size from a small ball to an umbrella. They are most commonly found in inshore waters and, in response to changing light levels, have the ability to move vertically through the water column. About 90 per cent of the annual jellyfish landings—some 11 000 tons—are made in Sarawak. The state also exports the greatest amount of processed jellyfish, valued at RM15 million per annum.

The *Cyanea* sp. (top), found off Pulau Pemanggil, Terengganu, is host to the young of fish such as jacks, which stay within its tentacles although these tentacles can be lethal to other organisms. The *Schyphomedusa* sp. (bottom), does not have such dangerous tentacles.

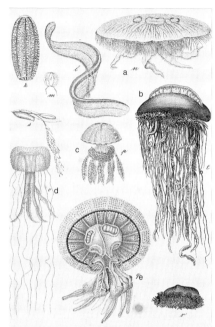

This chromolithograph from *Naturgeschichte* by Dr G. H. von Schubert (c. 1886), includes several species of jellyfish found in Malaysia: (a) *Medusa aurita*, (b) *Physalia arethusa*, (c) *Cephea papuensis*, (d) *Pelagia panopyra* and (e) *Rhizostoma aldrovanti*.

Characteristics

Jellyfish possess two body forms in their life cycle: the polyp form, which grows attached to rocks in the sea, and the free-swimming medusa form, which is called a jellyfish. The medusa resembles a bell or an umbrella with the convex side upward and the mouth in the centre of the concave under surface. The tentacles hang down from the margin of the bell.

A jellyfish is a simple creature consisting of only two layers of cells. The outer layer (epidermis) covers the external body surface while the inner layer (gastrodermis) lines the intestines. Between the epidermis and the gastrodermis is a thick mass of elastic, jelly-like substance (the mesoglea), which gives the creature its name. The simple stomach cavity (coelentron) acts as a gullet, stomach and intestine connected to a single opening that acts both as a mouth and an anus. The common white jellyfish's mouth has been modified to form eight oral arms, which are used to transport food captured by the tentacles.

Being both carnivorous and specialist feeders, jellyfish follow migrations of small prawns, other crustaceans and tiny fish. The appearance of jellyfish coincides with the prawn season, especially in Sarawak, and with schools of tiny fish in coastal areas. The larger species are capable of capturing and devouring large crustaceans and fish. After capturing their prey using their tentacles, jellyfish inject poison into them through tiny needles. The prey are paralysed and are then pulled back by the tentacles into the mouth.

A jellyfish moves by contracting the muscle fibre at the base of the umbrella. This forces water out of the mouth. The expulsion of water creates a pulsating movement. However, this movement is only sufficient to move the animal up and down at the surface level of the water. Most movements are at the mercy of the currents.

Diversity and ecology

Jellyfish are members of the phylum Cnidaria, which has three classes: the Hydrozoa (hydras), Schyphozoa (jellyfish) and Anthozoa (sea anemones and corals). The wide range of jellyfish living in Malaysian seas includes the edible commercial species, the white jellyfish (*Phacellophora* sp.), known locally as *ubur putih*, the red jellyfish (*Rhizostoma pulmo*), called *ubur merah*, and the deadly box jellyfish (*Chironex fleckeri*).

Although jellyfish are found throughout the Malaysian seas, they are more common in coastal waters and river mouths because these locations provide plenty of food. Rocks and islands in coastal areas also provide shelter and attachment surfaces for the polyps. As jellyfish are sensitive to light, they move vertically to the surface during the morning and late afternoon sun, and down into deeper waters at the height of the midday sun. Fishermen

Life cycle of a jellyfish

Male jellyfish release sperm into the water which enter the females through the mouth where the eggs are fertilized. In the first stage of the life cycle, larvae (planula) are released. Later, the larvae attach themselves to a surface and become polyps. When polyps divide, they become strobila, the next stage in their development. They then grow into young jellyfish (ephyra), and finally into adult jellyfish (medusa).

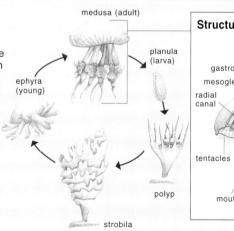

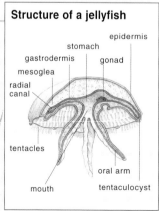

Structure of a jellyfish

make use of this behaviour pattern to collect the animals. As part of the food chain, jellyfish play an extremely important role in the ecosystems of coastal and estuarine areas. Jellyfish are carnivorous predators and they themselves also constitute an important food source for turtles as well as fish, such as spadefish and sunfish. Some of the *Rhizostoma* species provide protection for young fish, with certain species of Carangids going in and out of the jellyfish tentacles freely since they are immune to the stings.

Jellyfish are an important economic commodity. Processed jellyfish is a popular delicacy that usually appears as a cold dish on the menus of Chinese restaurants. They are one of the most valuable food commodities from Malaysian seas. Since edible jellyfish are believed to have some medicinal value, they are also traditionally used for the treatment of high blood pressure and bronchitis.

A jellyfish of *Rhizostoma* species.

On the negative side, jellyfish often sting swimmers and beach-combers, and although some stings merely cause skin irritation others are poisonous and some are even deadly. *Chironex fleckeri* (known locally as *ampie-ampie*), one of the deadliest of the box jellyfish species, has stings that cause intense pain and skin destruction as well as muscle spasm which can result in heart and respiratory failure. When present in large numbers, jellyfish can be a nuisance to fishermen, clogging trawl and drift nets. Jellyfish also cause problems for aquaculture. Young jellyfish which enter fish rearing cages cannot escape when they grow larger. They also kill fish fries and sometimes even adult fish.

Cannonball jellyfish (*Stomolophus* sp.) clog trawl nets and reduce the catch of fish. Although they are not processed for food in Malaysia, they are edible and have the potential for commercial processing.

Jellyfish fisheries

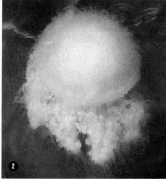

1. A boat returns to shore with its catch of white jellyfish, which were caught using a hand scoop (inset).

2. The white jellyfish (*Phacellophora* sp.).

3. The tentacles of the red jellyfish are removed before they are processed.

Landings

Over 90 per cent of the jellyfish in Malaysia are landed in Sarawak. In Peninsular Malaysia, most of the jellyfish are caught in the seas off Selangor and Johor.

The two main local species exploited commercially are the white jellyfish (*Phacellophora* sp.) and the red jellyfish (*Rhizostoma* sp.). The white jellyfish is larger (36–70 centimetres in diameter) and can weigh up to 15 kilograms. The smaller red jellyfish ranges from 18 to 45 centimetres in diameter, and can weigh up to 2 kilograms.

There are two main seasons in the year for catching commercial jellyfish: January–April and August–December. However, the red jellyfish is available throughout the year. When the sea is calm, jellyfish come up to the surface. When the sea is rough, they sink deeper under the water to prevent their fragile tentacles from being damaged and broken.

During the jellyfish season, thousands of individuals move up to the surface daily, drifting towards the coastal and estuarine areas with the incoming tides. At this time, hundreds of small motor boats converge on the schools of jellyfish. Using scoop nets, fishermen collect the jellyfish and load them into their boats.

There are a number of other methods of catching jellyfish used by fishermen. These include drift nets, bag nets, barrier nets and trawl nets. On a good day, each boat can can take on board between 100 and 400 jellyfish.

Processing jellyfish

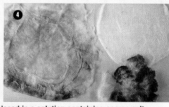

1. After being washed and cleaned, jellyfish are placed in a solution containing coarse salt, potassium alum and sodium bicarbonate (soda) in the ratio of 90 : 12 : 2, for both dehydration and preservation.

2. After 2–3 days, a smaller quantity of the salt mixture is added and the jellyfish kept for another 4–7 days. The jellyfish are then transferred to a solution containing pure fine salt for 5–7 days for further dehydration.

3. In the final stage, the jellyfish are placed on wooden boards for draining away excess water and placed in the shade to dry. This takes 3–4 days.

4. The final products: the texture of red jellyfish, which takes 14 days to process, is finer, making it more expensive than white jellyfish, which takes 21 days to process. Only the oral arms of the red jellyfish (bottom right) are processed, and these can fetch the same price as the body of the white jellyfish.

TRENDS IN TOTAL LANDINGS

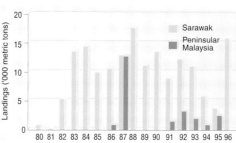

Sarawak
Peninsular Malaysia

Landings ('000 metric tons)

Source: Department of Fisheries Malaysia.

Because of the increased demand for processed jellyfish, the total landings in Malaysia rose to 53 811 metric tons in 1997. Most of the landings (49 665 metric tons), came from Sarawak. Landings in Peninsular Malaysia are much smaller due to coastal development, which has jeopardized the food supply and optimum environment for jellyfish. Statistics are not available for landings in Sabah.

Sustaining yields

Malaysian fisheries are characterized by small-scale harvests of multiple species, using a variety of fishing gear. Fishing has traditionally been concentrated in inshore areas, but since the mid-1980s the government has been trying to develop offshore areas. The fishing industry is being carefully managed by the Department of Fisheries to sustain yields that are now valued at around RM2.7 billion per annum. Complications arise, however, because controlling measures applying to only one species cannot be applied to the Malaysian multi-species fisheries.

Fish are abundant in marine parks, such as off Labuan (a federal territory) where fishing is prohibited. Such prohibition helps to sustain fisheries yields in Malaysia, where the increasing demand for live coral fish in restaurants has led to overfishing.

Fishing the traditional way, using small fishing boats, helps to sustain yields as it avoids the overfishing that is often associated with large, well-equipped modern boats.

Because of intense fishing pressure, catches now increasingly comprise smaller sized fish, such as the *ikan selar kuning* (yellow-striped trevally).

Maximum sustainable yield

Maximum sustainable yield is the largest catch that can be continuously taken from a stock under existing environmental conditions. When no fishing occurs, the fish stock level is affected by losses from natural mortality and gains from reproduction and growth. If fishing does occur, and the catch level plus natural mortality are equal to the gains, the stock levels will remain unchanged. The catch from this optimal level (which is difficult to manage) of fishing is known as maximum sustainable yield.

A catch that is larger than the maximum sustainable yield will, in the long run, decrease the fish stock and will not be sustainable, resulting in overfishing and a decrease in total catch. With the prevailing environmental conditions and at the current level of fishing effort, the maximum sustainable yield for inshore fisheries in Malaysia is around 900 000 tons per year. An additional 400 000 tons per year of offshore fisheries resources is exploitable provided fishing activities expand beyond traditional fishing grounds into new areas in the Exclusive Economic Zone.

Fisheries management

National policies and international agreements work towards promoting optimal harvesting practices. Fish should not be caught at too small a size, nor should they be caught before they have had a chance to reproduce at least once. In the face of uncertainties, such as the effects of environmental pollution, current fisheries management in Malaysia adopts a precautionary approach. One form of control is through strict licensing of fishing boats and gear. This first-level control limits entry into fisheries. Licensing is more stringent for fully exploited inshore fisheries. The Fisheries Regulations, made under the Fisheries Act (Maritime) 1985, provide the legal tool for limiting the types of fishing gear.

Other technical measures include zonation and closure of fishing grounds, mesh size and engine size. In Malaysia, the 1997 marine production figure

shows that about 90 per cent of production came from the more productive inshore areas, especially along the west coast of Peninsular Malaysia, partly due to well-managed mangroves. At the same time, the inshore waters suffer the highest fishing pressure, so fishing zones are allocated to commercial trawls and fish purse seines, as well as traditional methods.

The trawl net cod end (back of the net) mesh size is currently regulated at 25 millimetres. Consideration is being made for increasing this mesh size to allow more undersized fish to escape.

Excluder devices are fitted to trawl nets to allow sea turtles and other by-catch to escape. Drift nets with mesh of more than 25 centimetres are banned because these entangle sea turtles.

Certain types of fishing gear, such as the mechanized push net, beam trawl and pair trawl, are also banned. So is the use of explosives and poisonous chemicals. However, some measures are

Fishing zones in Malaysia

FISHING ZONE AND DISTANCE FROM SHORE (NAUTICAL MILES)	FISHING GEAR ALLOWED	GROSS REGISTERED TONNAGE (GRT) OF VESSEL ALLOWED
A 0–5	Traditional gear (e.g. hooks and lines, portable traps, lift nets, barrier nets)	up to 40
B 5–12	Commercial gear (trawl nets and purse seines)	up to 40
C 12–30	Commercial gear (trawl nets and purse seines)	over 40
C2 over 30	Commercial gear (trawl nets and purse seines)	over 70

In Malaysia, different fishing zones are drawn up for various categories of fishing vessel and gear. Such a measure helps traditional inshore fishermen protect their livelihoods. There are no restrictions on the use of traditional gear should fishermen venture beyond their allocated fishing zone. Similarly, commercial gear licensed to fishermen in Zone B can be used to fish in Zone C as well. Fishing boats licensed for Zones A and B must fish within state waters. Vessels licensed to fish in Zone C can be used to fish out of state waters, but must land their catches at their registered port of operation.

Marine landings in Malaysia

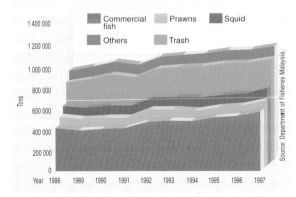

Marine landings in Malaysia show an upward trend due to the increase in landings of offshore fisheries from the Exclusive Economic Zone.

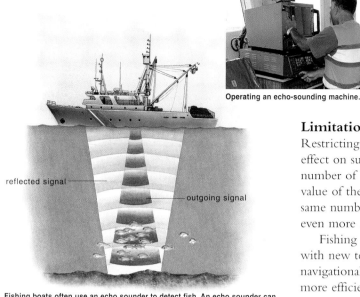

Operating an echo-sounding machine.

reflected signal

outgoing signal

Fishing boats often use an echo sounder to detect fish. An echo sounder can also determine the water depth by measuring the time interval required for a sonic wave to travel from a ship to the sea bed and back.

Developments in fisheries through changes in the type and number of fishing gear used and also by increasing efficiency of gear further complicate the picture.

Limitations and future development

Restricting the number of fishing boats has little effect on sustaining yields. At a time when the total number of boats has decreased, the high landed value of the catch encourages fishermen using the same number of fishing vessels and gear to fish even more intensely.

Fishing vessels are increasingly being equipped with new technology, such as echo sounders and navigational and positioning equipment, to become more efficient in detecting the presence of fish. The size of fishing boats and nets is also being increased. This results in higher catches.

The day may come when even fully exploited and sustained fisheries will not be able to support the demand from a growing population. It has been suggested that one solution will be to enter into joint fishing ventures with other countries in waters beyond the Malaysian EEZ. The other is, of course, to continue to develop the aquaculture industry using sustainable practices.

Turtle excluder devices

The fitting of a turtle excluder device (TED) is encouraged to reduce the incidental catch of sea turtles. A TED is a grilled hatch fitted at the front of shrimp nets. Small sized bycatch—tiny fish and prawns—can swim through the grille and escape. The weight of a turtle pushes the hatch open and thus allows it to escape. In this way, only the target of the catch is caught.

not easy to implement because of the multi-species and multi-gear nature of Malaysian fisheries.

To conserve and rehabilitate marine life, marine parks and reserves have been established in Malaysian coastal waters. In a marine park, there is permanent closure of an area of 2 nautical miles around the coral reefs which serve as breeding and nursery grounds for marine life.

Complications

Experiences in other similar fisheries have shown that it is not possible to manage a fishery by applying measures to only one species in a multi-species situation. This is because fish are related in complex ways to one another as well as to other species and to the environment.

Young fish grow faster than adult fish. If no fishing occurs, a population of old, slow-growing fish will be left behind. It is therefore prudent to remove some mature fish at a controlled level so as to maximize the yield from that population, and also to promote natural regeneration of the population which should replenish stocks.

If only one species of fish that is being harvested is present, the decline in the catch will be clear. If many species co-exist, no decline in the total may be observed because the species left behind may compensate for the loss of the species that have been fished out.

There would, however, be an accompanying change in the species composition. For example, in the Gulf of Thailand, severe overfishing has removed many predatory fishes and led to an increase in squid landings. In Malaysian trawl landings, there is an increase in the trash component, consisting of undersized commercial fish species not marketable as food, over the commercial size species. This shows that the fishery is shifting to smaller sizes of catch because of intense fishing pressure. One species that has virtually disappeared from the commercial fish landings in Malaysia is the false trevally (*Lactarius lactarius*), known locally as *ikan shrumbu*.

Artificial reefs

Artificial reefs are one type of fish-attracting device which aims to enhance the biological productivity of fisheries resources, to rehabilitate and conserve marine habitats, and to help generate recovery and increase stocks of fish. They comprise groups of discarded tyres, concrete pipes, rocks or other materials sunk at suitable places in the sea to generate growth of corals and other organisms on their surfaces. They also include wrecks of fishing vessels. Fish have been found to colonize any artificial reef within four months of construction.

In all, 58 artificial reefs have been constructed along the coast of Peninsular Malaysia. About 70 per cent of these are located off the east coast, because the west coast waters have the disadvantage of a soft, muddy bottom and cloudy waters which discourage coral growth.

Fish congregate around an artificial reef created by a car wreck off Mersing, in the southern state of Johor.

Concrete reef balls are put in the sea to create artificial reefs to attract fish.

An artificial reef can also be formed from artificial structures, such as this concrete culvert.

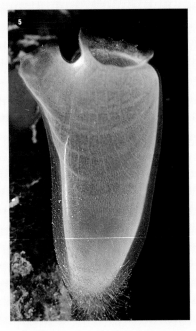

1. In Malaysia, the seas are a major lure for tourists, who can visit many beautiful beaches, islands and marine parks. Here, on Pulau Redang, Terengganu, is a typical tropical beach.

2. The coral reefs, with their colourful soft corals, are a major attraction to tourists, many of whom go snorkelling and scuba diving to view the corals and other marine life.

3. Windsurfing is a popular sport among tourists to Malaysia.

4. A PETRONAS petroleum refinery.

5. In Malaysia, studies have been carried out carried out on crude extracts of sea squirts, including *Rhopalaea* sp. When tested on five species of mosquitoes, they were found to be toxic to the mosquito larvae.

6. Petroleum is the main non-fisheries resource in Malaysian seas. Here an oil drill is being fixed on an offshore oil platform off the coast of Terengganu.

NON-FISHERIES RESOURCES

Malaysia's seas provide a wealth of non-fisheries resources, the three major ones being oil and gas fields, tourism centres and the development of pharmaceuticals from marine organisms. Of these, oil and gas production is currently the most valuable.

The large oil and gas deposits—the carbon-rich legacy of once-living organisms—are located in the shallow Malaysian seas of the Sunda Shelf and are relatively easy to tap. Through its national petroleum corporation, Petroliam Nasional Berhad (PETRONAS), Malaysia has adopted the practice of production sharing to exploit its resources, by contracting international oil and gas companies to participate in the exploration, development and production of its petroleum resources.

Many sponges, such as these (*Asteropus sarassinorum*), are likely to have pharmaceutical value. They await research and development.

Tourism is also a valuable non-fisheries resource in Malaysia, contributing almost RM10 billion ringgit annually to the economy. Many tourists, especially those from temperate countries, come in search of the sun and the sea. Since over half of the Malaysian tropical coastline comprises sandy beaches, these form the main focus of the country's tourism. In addition, many of the coasts are endowed with fringing coral reefs, such as those around the east coast islands of Redang, Perhentian and Tioman. These reefs and the oceanic reef off Sipadan, eastern Sabah, are a major draw for diving and snorkelling. Although mangroves may not appear as visually attractive as coral reefs, they have great potential for ecotourism. They are home to many species of birds and animals and attract migratory birds from all over the world. Recognizing the need for conservation and the potential for tourism, the government has turned some mangroves into parks, such as the Kuala Selangor Nature Park. It is now widely accepted that marine tourism development needs to be carefully planned and controlled in order to avoid damage to the environment.

Many pharmaceutical products are derived from marine organisms. At present, seaweeds, which are plentiful along Malaysian shores, contribute substantially to such products. Malaysia has one of the highest marine biodiversities in the world. It is thought that many chemical compounds are yet to be identified and isolated from the great diversity of the country's marine plants and animals. Extracts from a species of sea cucumber (*Stichopus variegatus*), known locally as the golden sea cucumber, have recently been commercialized for use in painkillers as well as in toothpaste and skin creams. Traditional medicines make great use of marine organisms, and as the commercial development of marine-originated pharmaceuticals is still a young industry in Malaysia there are, no doubt, many other uses and applications to be discovered over the coming years.

Oil and gas

The petroleum industry is one of Malaysia's newest sources of maritime wealth. The first offshore oilfield, Baram, was discovered in Sarawak in 1963. Since then, other finds—oilfields off Sabah and Terengganu and gas off Sarawak and Terengganu—have made Malaysia Asia's third largest oil producer. It is the richest non-fisheries resource and contributes significantly to the nation's GDP and industrialization. The shallow waters off Malaysia make exploitation relatively easy.

The offshore platform must be raised high enough above the waves to withstand even the worst weather conditions. From a single platform, a number of wells may be drilled in a configuration that will drain the field most economically.

Parts of a drilling rig

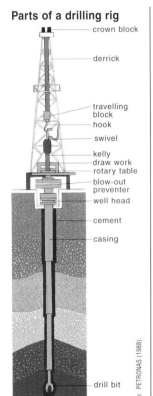

- crown block
- derrick
- travelling block
- hook
- swivel
- kelly
- draw work
- rotary table
- blow-out preventer
- well head
- cement
- casing
- drill bit

Source: PETRONAS (1988).

Reserves

Over millions of years, the organic remains of microscopic plants and animals buried in the sea bed have been built up into thick layers of sediment. The lower layers eventually hardened into rock, due to the pressure from the weight above them. Within these sedimentary rocks, the organic remains (carbon) are subjected to extreme heat and pressure, and transformed by chemical reactions into petroleum—oil and natural gas.

Oil and gas collect in the many pores or openings in the rocks. The rocks which are capable of containing petroleum are known as reservoir rocks. Many of these, however, often only contain water. The permeable sedimentary rocks allow the oil and gas in them to move from pore to pore. Unless trapped underground by geological structures, the petroleum may rise to the surface and escape. As petroleum is formed mainly in the sea, oil and gas are usually found together with water. Gas, being lightest, lies at the top of the reservoir, above oil, or above water if there is no oil.

Finding and testing reserves

Activities involved in both the exploration and exploitation of petroleum are known as upstream activities. These include acquisition of rights, exploration, appraisal, development and production.

As in many countries, the government of Malaysia owns all the petroleum resources in the country. Therefore, permission must first be obtained from the government before exploration

can begin. Such permission is given usually in the form of a lease, concession or contract. Malaysia, through its national petroleum corporation, Petroliam Nasional Berhad (PETRONAS), adopts the practice of production sharing in managing its upstream sector by contracting international oil and gas companies to participate in the exploration, development and production of petroleum.

The first step in exploration is to undertake initial prospecting to select strategic locations for test drilling. This is necessary as drilling is expensive, and justifiable only if a certain probability of success is first established. Initial prospecting techniques range from surface observations to seismic surveys. If the survey results appear promising, the location for a test well, called a 'wildcat', is then chosen.

Rarely is oil or gas struck in the first well drilled. If the well yields a deposit of petroleum, it is called a discovery well, and the discovery is appraised. Appraisal wells are then drilled to estimate how much oil or gas lies in the reservoir, as well as the size of the reservoir. If it is established that there are sufficient petroleum deposits, the development of an oil or gas field can begin.

Seismic surveys

A seismic survey at sea is carried out by creating shock waves with a compressed air gun. The shock waves travel down and the time taken for the waves to bounce back to the surface from the rock underneath is measured. These vibrations are picked up at the surface by receivers towed behind a survey vessel. The measurements, recorded on an instrument called a seismograph, reveal the presence of oil-bearing rocks.

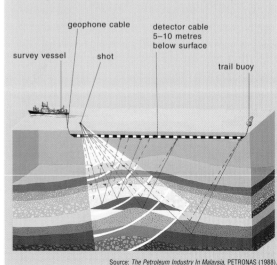

- geophone cable
- detector cable 5–10 metres below surface
- survey vessel
- shot
- trail buoy

Source: *The Petroleum Industry in Malaysia*, PETRONAS (1988).

Petroleum traps

The upward movement of oil and gas is often blocked by a layer of impermeable rock. These petroleum traps are created by intensive geological movements. The most common formations are the anticlinal, fault and stratigraphic traps where about 80–90 per cent of the world's known petroleum reserves are found.

- gas
- oil
- water

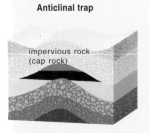

Anticlinal trap

impervious rock (cap rock)

Fault trap

impervious rock (cap rock)

Stratigraphic trap

impervious rock (cap rock)

Source: *The Petroleum Industry in Malaysia*, PETRONAS (1988).

Oil and gas producing areas

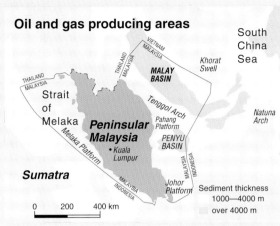

Petroleum products include (from left to right) lubricating oil, liquefied petroleum gas for cooking, and chemicals.

In Malaysia, petroleum is mostly found offshore. Of the total exploration acreage of 515 600 square kilometres, 332 300 square kilometres lie in shallow water, 98 600 square kilometres in deep water, and only 84 700 square kilometres on land.

Malaysia has eight sedimentary basins, three of which are now commercially producing petroleum. They are the Malay, Sarawak and Sabah basins. Most of the traps in these basins are anticlinal and associated with faults. The most common reservoir rock here is sandstone. However, the biggest gas accumulations are found in limestone reservoirs in the Sarawak Basin, especially in Central Luconia province. With total reserves amounting to 3.4 billion barrels of oil and 84.4 trillion standard cubic feet of gas as at 1 January 2000, Malaysia is ranked as the world's 27th largest oil reserve and 12th largest gas reserve. Malaysia is now producing 630,000 barrels of oil and about 5 billion standard cubic feet of gas per day.

Drilling wells

The development phase involves the drilling of wells over the reservoir, as well as putting in place the facilities needed to produce the oil or gas. The basic equipment used is the drilling rig. During extraction, drilling mud is constantly pumped down the drill string. This mud cools and lubricates the bit, carries the rock cuttings up to the surface, plasters and seals the walls of the hole and, with its weight, helps to prevent a blow-out should oil, gas, or water be encountered under high pressure.

After a well has been drilled to the required depth, a casing (steel pipe) is used to line the well to prevent it from collapsing. The casing is cemented in place to make it stationary, and to prevent the migration of fluids between permeable zones in the surrounding rock. Tubing pipes are then inserted in the casing to bring the oil or gas up to the surface.

After this, a piece of equipment called a 'Christmas tree' is fitted onto the well head and the drilling rig removed. The 'Christmas tree', a series of valves, controls the well pressure and the flow of petroleum. Once it is in place, holes are made in the casing so that oil or gas in the surrounding layer can enter the well and be brought to the surface.

Production

Permanent platforms are installed for the production of crude oil and gas. These are huge, fixed structures resting on steel legs driven into the sea bed, and serve as the offshore operations centre for the oil or gas field. Malaysia has many such platforms.

When oil comes out from the ground, it contains gas, water and impurities. The oil has to be treated to separate it from the gas, and to allow water and impurities to settle and be drained off. After treatment, the oil is ready for export, or processed for domestic use at a local refinery into petroleum products, such as liquefied petroleum gas, petrol for motor vehicles, aviation fuel, kerosene, diesel fuel, fuel oil and bitumen. The gas produced will either be transformed into liquefied natural gas for export or processed into sales gas for the domestic market, and gas feedstock or raw materials for the local petrochemical manufacturing industry.

The future

Current estimates put the life of Malaysia's oil and gas reserves at 35 years. Recently, good progress has been made in the exploration of deep-water areas.

Bringing energy to the consumer

Crude oil is transported by tankers to export markets.

Liquefied petroleum gas for sale to consumers.

This gas processing plant is at Kerteh, Terengganu.

Petroleum products are retailed nationwide.

115

Island and coastal tourism

Malaysia, with its long coastline, many islands and tropical climate, has a superb natural resource which has been increasingly tapped for its tourism potential. For the long-term sustainability of the industry and the environment, it is important that serious conservation and sustainable development efforts are encouraged. Current efforts are directed at saving the mainland beaches, islands and coral reefs by managing them sustainably and by educating tourists, tour operators and developers.

The Marang Resort and Safari on the coast of Terengganu accommodates visitors in chalets designed along the lines of the traditional Malay house.

Destinations

Island and coastal tourism in Malaysia can be divided into three main types: marine parks, beaches and mangrove swamps. As well as offering a variety of water sports activities, the first also boasts a wealth of sea life, most notably corals which are a great draw for diving and snorkelling. The beaches and Malaysia's appealing sunny climate have fostered the growth of resorts of various type and scale, in particular many along the Peninsula's coastline. Mangrove swamps are a less common destination but offer great bird watching and wildlife holidays.

Tourism's negative impacts

Although tourism development can bring many benefits to a region and the economy it can also bring problems. Sometimes new resorts and developments can be so large as to completely change the nature of the area; building styles may be at odds with local architecture and natural vegetation may be lost. Vital habitats such as mangroves (breeding and nursery grounds for many

Popular marine destinations and activities

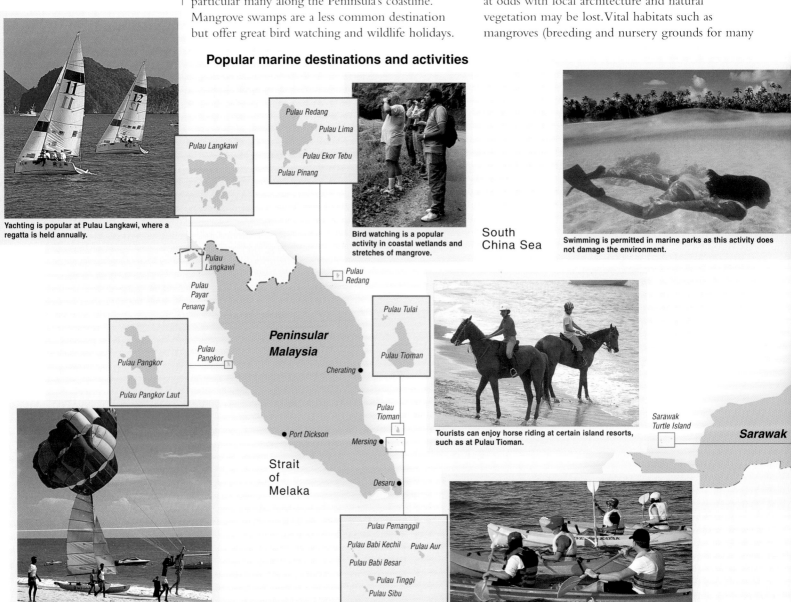

Yachting is popular at Pulau Langkawi, where a regatta is held annually.

Bird watching is a popular activity in coastal wetlands and stretches of mangrove.

South China Sea

Swimming is permitted in marine parks as this activity does not damage the environment.

Pulau Redang
Pulau Lima
Pulau Langkawi
Pulau Ekor Tebu
Pulau Pinang

Pulau Langkawi
Pulau Payar
Penang

Pulau Pangkor
Pulau Pangkor Laut

Pulau Pangkor

Peninsular Malaysia

Pulau Redang

Pulau Tulai

Pulau Tioman

Cherating

Pulau Tioman

Port Dickson

Mersing

Desaru

Sarawak Turtle Island

Sarawak

Strait of Melaka

Pulau Pemanggil
Pulau Babi Kechil   Pulau Aur
Pulau Babi Besar
Pulau Tinggi
Pulau Sibu

Tourists can enjoy horse riding at certain island resorts, such as at Pulau Tioman.

Parasailing is an unusual sea sport, seen on the beaches of Penang and Pulau Pangkor.

Canoeing is one of the many water sports on offer at Malaysia's beaches and coastal resorts.

marine species) may be chopped down to make room for such developments, and the pressures of large numbers of visitors can have harmful results, such as damage to corals and problems with rubbish disposal and pollution. Local traditions and ways of life may be compromised as the economy changes to one of servicing the needs of visitors.

Managing change

To be completely successful, apart from purely economic considerations, it is important to plan developments to be sustainable. The carrying capacity of the area needs to be established to prevent it from being adversely affected by developments and the increased pressures they will bring.

A number of positive measures have and continue to be taken in Malaysia to encourage sustainable and responsible development and to mitigate against the negative impact of the growth in tourism. Coral reefs, for example, are vital to the tourism industry on Malaysian islands. Forty islands have, therefore, been gazetted as marine parks (see 'Marine parks and reserves'). Unfortunately, despite this, the reefs are affected not only by mainland pollution, but by illegal collection of corals, which goes on despite the prospect of harsh penalties (a fine of up to RM20,000 or two years' jail).

Educating tourists and developers to be environmentally aware is a key factor. Because of ignorance, many tourists break off pieces of coral, not realizing that the most important parts of the coral are the very parts that are most sought after or most easily broken off. Coral growth is slow. The branches of the fastest growing corals from the *Acropora* species grow only 15 centimetres per year, while those of the slowest growing corals—*Porites* species—grow only 9 millimetres per year. Many tourists are ignorant of the damage they cause to marine habitats by their numerous activities, such as walking with fins over the reef flat, indiscriminately dropping and dragging anchors over the reef and dumping rubbish into the sea. Guide training centres are being developed in various places, encouraging guides, among other tasks, to help educate tourists to visit coastal tourist destinations in as responsible a manner as possible.

Some of the more progressive hotel and resort developers and owners attempt to play their part in managing the region's environment sustainably. Some hotels, for instance, promote environmentally friendly practices, such as encouraging limited towel washing and using eco-friendly detergents. Traditionally styled, small-scale resort develop-ments, sympathetic to local surroundings, have become popular in recent years.

The Malaysia Tourism Promotion Board produces and distributes many brochures to inform tourists of the country's coastal attractions.

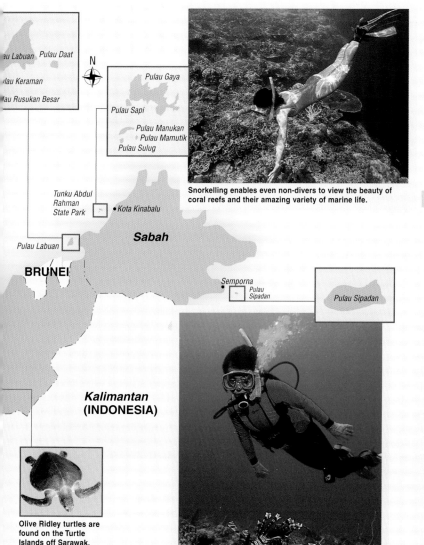

Snorkelling enables even non-divers to view the beauty of coral reefs and their amazing variety of marine life.

Olive Ridley turtles are found on the Turtle Islands off Sarawak.

Some islands with beautiful reefs, such as Pulau Sipadan, have become well-known scuba diving sites.

TOP TOURIST RECREATIONAL ACTIVITIES

Most tourists to Malaysia prefer to go to the sunny mainland beaches and islands where they can enjoy various sea sports.

DESTINATIONS	BIRD WATCHING	CANOEING	GOLF	HIKING	HORSE RIDING	PARASAILING	SAILING	SCUBA DIVING	SNORKELLING	WATER SCOOTERING	WINDSURFING
Cherating	✓	✓	✓	✓	✓	✓	✓			✓	✓
Desaru (Johor)	✓	✓	✓	✓	✓	✓	✓			✓	✓
Kuantan	✓	✓	✓	✓	✓	✓	✓			✓	✓
Labuan Marine Park	✓	✓		✓				✓	✓	✓	
Mersing Marine Park	✓	✓		✓				✓	✓	✓	
Penang	✓	✓	✓	✓	✓	✓	✓			✓	✓
Port Dickson	✓	✓	✓	✓	✓	✓	✓	✓	✓	✓	✓
Pulau Langkawi	✓	✓	✓	✓	✓	✓	✓			✓	✓
Pulau Pangkor	✓	✓	✓	✓	✓	✓	✓	✓	✓	✓	✓
Pulau Payar Marine Park	✓	✓		✓				✓	✓	✓	
Pulau Redang Marine Park	✓	✓		✓				✓	✓	✓	
Pulau Tioman Marine Park	✓	✓	✓	✓	✓	✓	✓	✓	✓	✓	✓
Sarawak Turtle Islands	✓							✓	✓		
Tunku Abdul Rahman State Park, Sabah	✓	✓		✓			✓		✓	✓	

Map labels:
au Labuan · Pulau Daat
lau Keraman
au Rusukan Besar
Pulau Gaya
Pulau Sapi
Pulau Manukan
Pulau Mamutik
Pulau Sulug
N
Tunku Abdul Rahman State Park
Kota Kinabalu
Sabah
Pulau Labuan
BRUNEI
Semporna
Pulau Sipadan
Pulau Sipadan
Kalimantan (INDONESIA)

Pharmaceuticals

For many centuries, marine organisms have been recognized as sources of chemical compounds with medicinal properties. Both sea cucumber and sea horse extract have long been used in Malay and Chinese traditional medicine. Since less than 1 per cent of the potentially useful compounds have been screened so far, there is considerable scope for development in this field in which Malaysian scientists are actively researching and uncovering new commercial applications.

Three local species of seaweed which contain pharmaceuticals:
1. *Acanthopora spicifera.*
2. *Sargassum oligocystum.*
3. *Halymenia* sp.

Extracts from sponges found in Malaysian seas, such as the one above (*Stylotella aurantium*), have been tested on human tumour cells with promising results.

Local research

Extracts from marine organisms have been used for medicinal purposes for centuries in many countries, including China, India, Europe and Malaysia. In Malay traditional medicine, an extract from the sea cucumber or *gamat*, is a known painkiller. Chinese medicine, also practised in Malaysia, uses dried seahorse extract for respiratory disorders such as asthma. However, only about a dozen or so marine-derived drugs are in use today worldwide because of problems with collection, isolation of compounds, clinical evaluation and funding.

A number of Malaysian scientists have been exploring the possibility of extracting new medicinal compounds from marine organisms. For instance, they have tested extracts from sponges on cultured cells in the laboratory to determine whether the sponge extract can kill human tumour cells. Of the 51 samples of marine sponges (Class Demospongiae) tested from Pulau Tiga, Maganting and Pulau Tabawan, 20 were found to be toxic to the cells. Crude extracts from 10 samples of marine sponges were also tested on bacteria (*Bacillus subtilis* and *Escherichia coli*). All these samples showed antibacterial activity.

Crude extracts from the sea squirts or tunicates *Polycarpa aurata* and *Didemnum molle* were found to be moderately toxic, and work on isolating and understanding these compounds continues. Specific studies have also been carried out on another set of crude extracts from six species of sea squirts (*Didemnum* sp., *Aplidium* sp., *Rhopalaea* sp., *Atriolum* sp., *Eudistoma* sp., *Clavelina* sp.). These have proved to be toxic to mosquito larvae and may prove to have applications in pesticide production.

In Malaysia, seaweeds have been studied extensively because of their abundance and ease of collection in shallow waters. Chemical extracts from seaweeds, particularly the red and brown species, have been found to be antibacterial. At least three kinds of antifungal agents have been found in a common species of sea cucumber, *Holothuria atra*.

The goodness of *gamat*

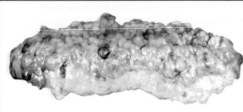

Dr Hassan Yaakob (top left) with his catch of golden sea cucumber (left).

Extracts from a species of sea cucumber (*Stichopus variegatus*), known locally as the golden sea cucumber or *gamat*, have been used as a medicine for over 300 years by the Malays in the northern part of Peninsular Malaysia. However, the use of the gamat has become noticeably popular over the last two decades.

In 1990, this spurred a team of scientists from Universiti Malaya to begin conducting studies to determine the exact benefits and level of efficacy of gamat extracts. Tests included boiling the gamat extract for some time to degrade the protein into peptides (molecular amino acids) which contain healing properties. The tests indicated the many painkilling, anti-inflammatory and anti-itching properties of the sea cucumber. For example, it was found that the extract is a potent healing agent for stomach ulcers as well as a painkiller. When incorporated into toothpaste, it is reported to improve blood flow and health of gums. In cream form, it can be used to treat pimples, nappy rash, athlete's foot, wounds, insect bites, itching, abrasions and minor burns.

Convinced of the benefits of gamat extract, the team at Universiti Malaya is now farming the gamat commercially and marketing a number of products. Gamat has been incorporated into a variety of products, such as gel facial wash, body lotion and moisturiser, because the scientists discovered that the gamat's body contains elastin fibres and collagen properties.

Because commercial harvesting of the gamat has drastically reduced the population of sea cucumbers, particularly at Pulau Langkawi and Pulau Pangkor where they were once abundant, the team is now breeding the gamat at Pangkor.

TOP: A research team at Universiti Malaya conducting laboratory tests on the *gamat*.

LEFT: Some products, including skin creams and cleansers, containing *gamat* extract.

Tests on extracts from sea squirts, such as the species above (*Didemnum molle*) living on a purple sponge, showed they were toxic to mosquito larvae.

In order to survive the environmental conditions unique to their habitats, many marine organisms secrete chemical compounds which can, incidentally, have properties beneficial to mankind.

Although studies so far have concentrated on larger organisms, micro-organisms are also likely to contain such useful compounds. Screening of marine organisms has revealed that sponges, corals, tunicates, algae and others produce compounds exhibiting antibiotic, antitumoural, anti-inflammatory or antiviral properties.

To prevent threats to biodiversity and sustainability, scientists are also synthesizing analogues, that is, developing artificial versions of these compounds. Analogues are slightly modified forms of the natural compounds.

MARINE ORGANISM (SPECIES)	TYPICAL COMPOUNDS PRESENT (OR EXTRACT)	PHARMACEUTICAL PROPERTIES OF COMPOUNDS/ USES AND POTENTIAL USES
Sponges (e.g. *Acanthella carteri*, *Asteropus sarassinorum*)	Nitrogenous compounds	Antibiotic, antiviral, toxic to human carcinoma (cancer) cells.
Red seaweeds (e.g. *Gracilaria* sp., *Catanella* sp., *Acanthopora* sp., *Halymenia* sp.,)	Agar	Antibacterial. Used as a mild laxative and microbial culture medium.
	Carrageenan	Antiviral, anticoagulant. Prevents ulcers and cholesterol absorption.
Brown seaweeds (e.g. *Sargassum* sp., *Turbinaria* sp., *Chaetomorpha* sp., *Amphiroa* sp., *Phyaephyceae* sp.)	Alginic acid, laminarin sulphate, alginates	Anticoagulant. Used in bandages.
Sea cucumber (*Holothuria atra*)	Holothurin	Antifungal.
Golden sea cucumber (*Stichopus variegatus*)	Extracts only, compound not isolated	Anti-inflammatory, anti-itching, painkilling. Used in toothpaste, skin creams, skincare products.
Prawns (e.g. *Penaeus monodon*, *Metapenaeus affinis*, *Parapenaeopsis sculptilis*)	Chitin, chitosan	Stabilizing and emulsifying. A binding agent for isolating enzymes. Antifungal.
Jellyfish (*Carybdea rastoni*)	Biotoxins (from extracts only)	Cytotoxic (i.e. kills all cells). Potential use not yet identified.
Sea squirts or **tunicates** (*Didemnum* sp., *Aplidium* sp., *Rhopalaea* sp., *Atriolum* sp., *Eudistoma* sp., *Clavelina* sp.)	Extracts only, compound not isolated	Larvatoxicity (toxic to mosquito larvae), haemolytic (used for diagnostic purposes, such as blood testing).
Estuarine catfish (*Plotosus canius*)	Biotoxins, plotoxin and plotolysin	Neurotoxic (toxic to nerves) and haemolytic. Potential use as a painkiller in controlled doses .

Sponge (*Stylotella aurantium*)   Calcified seaweed (*Halimeda tuna*)   Sea cucumber (*Holothuria* sp.)   Red seaweed (*Halymenia* sp.)   Tiger prawn (*Penaeus monodon*)

Chitin and chitosan, which are substances extracted from prawn shells, are used as emulsifiers in foods, cosmetics and pharmaceuticals. They are also known to have fungicidal properties and can be used in producing pesticides.

The development of marine pharmaceuticals in Malaysia faces a number of constraints. These include the long period of the research and development phase and high costs. As a result, little local research has advanced beyond initial stages.

Legal protection

In Malaysia, the commercialization of marine biotechnology is protected under laws concerning intellectual property rights which enable an inventor to exclude imitators from the market for a specified period of time. However, with rapid developments in the biotechnology field and increasing globalization, laws and global agreements will need to be formulated and strengthened to further safeguard rights in the future.

Research and development

Although recent advances in genetic engineering and the technology of chemical separation have facilitated the investigation and development of new marine chemicals and pharmaceuticals, few have come on to the market. Progress is limited by difficulties associated with the collection and isolation of the pharmacologically active constituents, their clinical evaluation and processing, as well as the long period of time involved (about 10 years) in development and the associated high financial commitment. A potential marine pharmaceutical product must go through several stages of research and testing before it can be marketed.

Stages
1. Screening is done to find out which marine organisms are most likely to have pharmacologically active substances. Initially, this involves observing the behaviour and interactions of the organisms in their natural environment.

2. Identifying the organic compound which is responsible for the behaviour of interest. The researcher extracts various classes of compounds from the organism and tests them for pharmacological activity.

3. Isolating the active substance or substances. Compound isolation and identification are difficult because most of these substances have large, complex structures.

4. Synthesizing the compounds. Artificial means must be developed for the synthesis of these compounds.

5. Obtaining approval from the relevant authority. The substance must be tested on animals initially. If significant benefits are found and no adverse side effects are observed, the drugs are then tested on humans.

6. Developing economically effective manufacturing methods. This includes developing synthetic compounds.

7. Assessing market potential and marketing the product.

Researchers at Pulau Tabanan, Sabah, weighing, photographing and preserving sponge samples in ethanol before transporting them to the laboratory.

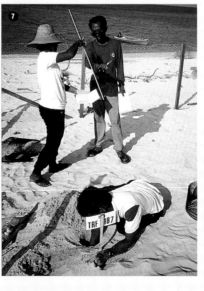

1. A WWF Malaysia (World Wide Fund for Nature Malaysia) officer teaching a group of children about the seas during one of the organization's many educational projects.

2. Planting mangrove seedlings in the Matang mangroves, Perak. Replanting is necessary for conservation as mangrove trees are felled for making charcoal.

3. Breakwaters, such as at Chendering, Terengganu, are built to protect a harbour. However, they often interfere with the natural transport of sediments by longshore drift, causing deposition of sediments inside the harbour. Thus, man-made efforts at sustaining the seas do not always succeed.

4. Concrete frames are put into the sea to act as artificial reefs to attract fish.

5. Juvenile giant clams (*Tridacna squamosa*), which have been artificially bred on land in a Malaysian project aimed at saving giant clams, are released into the sea.

6. Many brochures are available to educate the public on the importance of saving sea turtles. These are distributed especially to tourists who come to watch the turtles lay their eggs on Terengganu beaches.

7. Volunteers at work at a turtle hatchery on Pulau Redang.

8. Baby green turtles (*Chelonia mydas*), which were bred in a hatchery on Pulau Redang, make their way to the sea.

SUSTAINING FOR FUTURE GENERATIONS

The seas serve many purposes: transport, food, recreation, even sewers. Because many Malaysians live, if not by the sea, close to it, much pressure is put on the coast. It is clearly important to value the coast and utilize it and the seas on a sustainable basis, not just for present but for future generations as well.

Generally, the seas have been considered public property, with many exploiting them, but few taking responsibility for sustaining them as national and international resources. The United Nations Convention on the Law of the Sea, to which Malaysia is a party, is an attempt to promote a more enlightened approach and ensure that countries live harmoniously with their neighbours and that disputes over marine resources be peacefully settled. Although such international agreements are welcome, enforcement remains an extremely difficult task.

One important aspect of sustaining marine ecosystems is control of pollution, much of which is land based. Two of Malaysia's early industries, rubber and tin, polluted Malaysian rivers and estuaries to such an extent that some species of animals and plants were affected. In more recent years, palm oil waste products, fertilizer and presticide runoff and sewage have become major pollutants. The long-tailed shad or *terubuk* (*Hilsa toli*) was once a common fish but has decreased in numbers greatly on the west coast of Peninsular Malaysia because of pollution. Over the years, much effort has been made to reduce the loads of organic matter in rivers and estuaries; but these efforts will only have truly succeeded

This booklet provides guidelines for tour operators on how to protect Malaysian marine parks.

when the *terubuk* returns in large numbers. Oil spills, which also pollute the seas, are best prevented by enforcement of laws. Nevertheless, as accidents do happen, the country has a national contingency plan to combat oil spills.

Malaysia has had a few notable successes among its sustainable development projects. Mangrove management in the Matang mangroves in Perak is arguably the best in the world. Other positive local conservation efforts include turtle hatcheries and the artificial breeding of giant clams. Unfortunately, however, efforts to save the leatherback turtle (*Dermochelys coriacea*) look as though they will fail for this species, which is projected to become extinct within the decade. The establishment of marine parks can be an effective way of protecting the seas. Malaysia has, since the early 1980s, designated eight marine parks and six fisheries protected areas. Uncontrolled and uncoordinated tourism development on adjacent coasts has, however, reduced the impact of conservation efforts in these parks. Integrated Coastal Management (ICM) is one recently fashionable approach to managing development for the good of all affected communities and the environment. To date, four ICM plans have been drawn up, for Johor, Penang, Sabah and Sarawak. Hopefully, they will be applied and bring long-term benefits and sustainability to the marine ecosystem. The importance of education and public awareness in getting mass support for the sustainable approach is championed by organizations such as the WWF Malaysia and in the country's universities.

The Law of the Sea

Seafaring nations have long argued over control of the sea and the definitions and boundaries of coastal waters. Beyond a narrow strip, a few miles wide adjacent to the coast, the high seas were regarded as open to all nations. Throughout history, and especially with the growth of international trade, disputes over control of the resources and routes the seas offered increased. It was not until 1982, with the United Nations Convention on the Law of the Sea (UNCLOS), that this global issue was comprehensively addressed and an important multilateral ocean treaty negotiated under the auspices of the United Nations.

Ships of all parties to the UNCLOS enjoy freedom of navigation, including passage through the Strait of Melaka. The Danish vessel *Clifford Maersk*, the world's largest container vessel, is seen here berthed at Port Klang.

Malaysia ratified the Law of the Sea in 1996.

Historical view

Throughout history, as states and empires have waxed and waned, sea boundaries have changed as much as those on land. Safe passage through straits, access to fish and other resources, routes to far-off products and markets and, recently, petroleum and mineral resources, all mean that coastal nations hold strong views over ownership and exploitation rights. Even today, these rights are a constant source of conflict, as can be seen in arguments over such aspects as fishing quotas, ownership of uninhabited islands, including the Spratlys, and control over pollution and acts of piracy.

United Nations Convention on the Law of the Sea

This important treaty covers all aspects of ocean space and its uses, including navigation, fishing, overflight rights, resource exploitation, exploration, conservation and marine pollution. It was the most complex and comprehensive treaty in the history of modern international relations and took over a decade to negotiate. Today, 125 nations, including Malaysia, have ratified it.

Malaysia was a signatory to the UNCLOS treaty in 1982 but ratification only took place in 1996. Ratification further reinforced Malaysia's maritime obligations. The UNCLOS reduced the size of the high seas, which are regarded as open to all states, and expanded the national jurisdiction of coastal states. It also reaffirmed the right of coastal states over the resources in the Exclusive Economic Zone (EEZ). This is important to Malaysia, which obtains petroleum and other resources from the sea and transports 90 per cent of its exports by sea. By providing the country with an extended 200-mile EEZ, and by securing Malaysian rights to exploit marine resources, the UNCLOS advances the interests of the nation as a coastal state.

Key features of the UNCLOS

Certain features stand out among the 321 provisions of the UNCLOS. Coastal states can exercise sovereignty over their territorial sea up to 12 nautical miles in breadth, but foreign vessels are allowed to exercise the right of innocent passage through the waters.

- Ships and aircraft of all parties are allowed transit passage through straits used for international navigation. Straits states, such as Malaysia and Singapore, are allowed to regulate navigational and other aspects of passage, including denying vessels carrying hazardous materials, such as plutonium and other radioactive materials, passage through their straits. Sovereign rights of coastal states extend to the continental shelf for exploration and exploitation. The shelf extends 200 miles from the coast, beyond which it comes under a different regime.

- Coastal states also have sovereign rights in a 200-nautical mile EEZ with respect to natural resources and certain economic activities, and also exercise jurisdiction over environmental protection and marine science research.

- The territorial sea, EEZ and continental shelf are determined in accordance with certain rules. Rocks which cannot sustain human habitation have no continental shelf or economic zone.

- States bordering enclosed or semi-enclosed seas are expected to cooperate in managing living resources and environmental activities. They are obliged to prevent and control marine pollution, and are liable for damage caused by violation of national legislation and international obligations to combat pollution.

- All states enjoy the freedom of navigation and the right to fly over the EEZ, as well as the right to lay submarine cables and pipelines. They also enjoy the traditional freedom of fishing and scientific research, as well as the construction of artificial islands. They are obliged to adopt or cooperate with other states in adopting measures to conserve living resources.

- Land-locked and geographically disadvantaged states have the opportunity to participate in exploiting part of the fisheries in the EEZ of adjoining countries on an equitable basis when coastal states are unable to harvest them all. However, highly migratory species of fish and marine mammals are protected.

- Whenever disputes arise concerning the interpretation or application of the convention, the states are obliged to settle by peaceful means.

Piracy

Acts of piracy are headline-grabbing events. Although the UNCLOS treaty defines piracy as happening on the high seas, the International Maritime Organization includes criminal activities within inshore territorial waters. This partly explains the apparent growth in piracy over recent years. It is, however, a real problem, particularly in the waters around Malaysia. While some involve large and valuable cargoes, there is also small-scale armed robbery. Kedah fishermen have, for example, become the targets of Thai 'pirates' who kidnap them and their boats for ransom.

A small and relatively inexpensive satellite-based device, Shiploc, has recently been developed which can be hidden on board. By activating it, the International Maritime Bureau in Kuala Lumpur can be notified. They can then order local law enforcement agencies to rescue the ship and crew.

Thai pirates targeting M'sian ships

By FARID JAMALUDIN

ALOR STAR: Thai pirates are kidnapping Kedah fishermen for fast and lucrative returns.

The syndicate will normally target lone Malaysian registered fishing vessels which venture too close to the Malaysian-Thai border.

Kedah police uncovered the activities of the syndicate following eight pirate attacks.

Sunthorn Norarat and Perlis CPO Syed Mokhtar Barshilian.

Nik Ismail said that according to their investigations, the syndicate used several islands near Satun in the Thai southern province as their base.

He said the number of pirate attacks could be higher as some of the cases were not reported to the authorities.

He said the Thai authori-

Vessel Tracking Management System (VTMS)

The Department of Fisheries Malaysia, makes use of a Vessel Tracking Management System (VTMS). This is a computer and satellite based system which tracks deep-sea fishing vessel fleets in the surrounding seas to check, for instance, on illegal fish landings. It also monitors vessel movements to ensure the navigational safety of ships in the Strait of Melaka—the world's second busiest shipping lane.

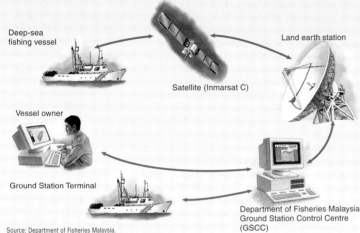

Source: Department of Fisheries Malaysia.

Location of radar stations and control centres

Adopting the provisions

To reaffirm commitment to the UNCLOS treaty and to benefit fully from it, Malaysia needs to adopt the convention and incorporate its provisions into national laws. Policy planners in Malaysia are currently focusing on seven areas:

Legislation. Malaysia is studying further what new legislation needs to be introduced to be consistent with the new obligations.

Regulation by activity. Malaysia has to regulate the activities of the different users of the sea to avoid conflicts, such as over shipping and fishing.

Publication and notification. Malaysia already has laws regarding dissemination of information, such as the publication of notices to mariners and charts showing traffic separation schemes in Malaysian waters to facilitate safe navigation.

Surveillance and enforcement. Policies and measures to ensure that provisions are enacted, such as allowing the right of innocent passage by foreign vessels, enforcing criminal jurisdiction on board foreign vessels in territorial seas, and dealing with piracy and illegal fishing, are to be improved. The introduction of the Vessel Tracking Management System (VTMS), in the late 1990s, is one strong measure in this area.

Administrative requirements. This section calls for evidence that provisions are being put into operation. For example, charts have to be produced to show the different maritime jurisdictions.

Cooperation with third parties. In recognition of the global nature of ocean management, certain provisions call for cooperation with third parties and international organizations. One example of this is that a Malaysian now sits on the Commission on Limits of Continental Shelves. Malaysia also needs to clarify the multilateral mechanisms for cooperation regarding safe navigation in the Strait of Melaka.

Scientific and technical aspects. Although Malaysia has some expertise in oceanic affairs, the nation needs a larger pool of trained manpower. Resources need to be allocated to build up the required expertise and technical knowledge.

The dispute over the Spratly Islands

The Spratly archipelago in the South China Sea consists of 96 small islands, coral reefs and atolls. There are overlapping claims to the Spratlys, considered important for strategic and economic reasons.

The Spratlys are claimed in part by Vietnam, the Philippines, Malaysia and Brunei, and in full by China and Taiwan. Malaysia maintains that her claims are based on international law, in particular the UNCLOS. So do the others.

Economically, the Spratlys have rich marine resources such as fish, oil and gas. The islands are also ideal spots for marine tourism as demonstrated by the resort on Malaysia's territory of Layang-Layang.

Conflict over the Spratlys is likely to be protracted. There are too many parties involved and, with the exception of Brunei, all have deployed their military forces to defend their claims.

When signing, ratifying or acceding

Pulau Layang-Layang, a popular tourist resort in the South China Sea, belongs to Malaysia.

to the 1982 UNCLOS, states can resort to the UNCLOS for settling their maritime disputes. They can choose from one or more of the following: the International tribunal for the UNCLOS at Hamburg, the International Court of Justice at the Hague, an arbitral tribunal or a special tribunal. However, it is no easy task to get the many claimants over the Spratlys to agree on which one.

At best, the conflict over the Spratly Islands can only be managed in the hope of avoiding a military confrontation between the claimants. One of the mechanisms for managing this conflict is to develop strong confidence-building measures throughout the region which rely on peaceful settlement of disputes. One such measure is to create joint development programmes, which can provide economic gains for all the parties concerned.

Effluents

Effluent discharges into the sea normally originate from industries, domestic and municipal sources, as well as from agricultural activities such as pig farming. The discharges are both organic and inorganic and include toxic chemicals, such as heavy metals, pesticides and oxygen-consuming materials. The increase in levels of these pollutants in Malaysian seas is one repercussion of the massive development which occurred in the country during the 1980s and 1990s. A number of measures have been taken locally to control these discharges.

This dark strip off the west coast of Selangor, in Peninsular Malaysia, is caused by effluents being discharged from a nearby factory.

Organic matter

There are various types of effluents, with some causing more concern than others. Although there has been a lot of debate regarding the harmful effects of heavy metals, synthetic organic compounds and polyaromatic hydrocarbons on various organisms, including humans, the most significant effects in developing countries like Malaysia are still those related to the increase in oxygen-consuming compounds (including organic matter) and nutrients.

Excessive discharge of organic matter, such as raw sewage and other oxygen-consuming compounds, has resulted in massive fish kills, especially in protected coastal areas where flushing is limited. In these areas, the organic matter and other oxygen-consuming compounds are initially broken down by bacteria. This process uses up dissolved oxygen in the water and by-products of the process include carbon dioxide and inorganic nutrients. As the oxygen level in the water is depleted, the more mobile animals living in the area start to leave while those which are sedentary or have limited mobility, such as molluscs, eventually die.

When the area reaches anoxic (no oxygen) conditions, sulphur bacteria starts acting on the organic matter, using sulphur instead of oxygen in the decomposition process. The immediate by-product is hydrogen sulphide, the gas which smells of rotten eggs, that pervades enclosed coastal areas receiving a high input of organic matter.

Associated with the discharge of raw sewage is the increase in bacteria—particularly *Escherichia coli*—in the water system, as well as in fish and shellfish tissues. High bacteria counts in the tissues of cockles from a few culture areas in Malaysia have affected sales of this food source. Microbial contamination of local shellfish has been linked to several hepatitis outbreaks in the country.

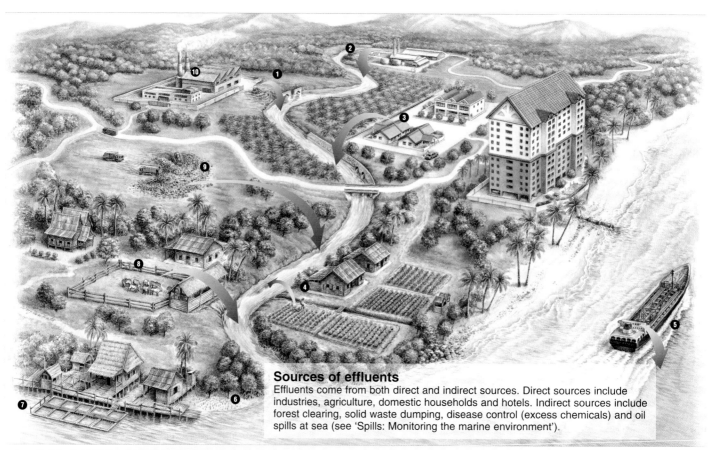

Sources of effluents

Effluents come from both direct and indirect sources. Direct sources include industries, agriculture, domestic households and hotels. Indirect sources include forest clearing, solid waste dumping, disease control (excess chemicals) and oil spills at sea (see 'Spills: Monitoring the marine environment').

1. Some factories discharge industrial waste directly into rivers, contaminating them.

2. Buried industrial waste can cause dangerous seepage.

3. Some chemical household cleaners are non-biodegradable, and may flow straight into the sea. Untreated domestic sewage also flows into the sea in some places.

4. Some persistent pesticides do not decompose and after being sprayed they are washed by the rain into rivers and down to the sea. Excess fertilizers are also washed down.

5. When an oil tanker discharges its ballast water, it is adding organic matter to the sea. It may also be transferring aquatic organisms from one place to another, causing biological pollution.

6. Mangrove forests act as a buffer for land-based erosion. Therefore, loss of mangroves can cause soil erosion and lead to polluted sediments being washed into the sea.

7. Effluents from aquaculture ponds contain high amounts of organic matter. They may also contain residues of chemicals, such as antibiotics.

8. Effluent discharges from intensive farming of livestock (especially pig rearing) are high in organic matter.

9. Dumped rubbish is rich in organic matter and may contain toxic wastes which can run off.

10. Palm oil mills produce harmful effluent that can run off into the sea.

Inorganic nutrients

Effluents can also consist of inorganic nutrients, including nitrate, phosphate and silicate. These can come directly from excess fertilizers used in agriculture and from the management of golf courses, as well as from excessive use of laundry detergents. Indirect sources include remineralization processes during the bacterial decomposition of organic matter and other oxygen-consuming compounds. The increase in the nutrient content of the water is termed eutrophication.

Initially, eutrophication has a positive effect because it encourages the growth of algae which supply the rest of the food chain. When it is prolonged, however, the area becomes too rich in living and non-living organic matter and, in turn, oxygen levels become depleted and organisms die.

Synthetic compounds

Although the contamination of synthetic organic compounds in Malaysian coastal waters may not seem serious, this may be due to ignorance of the situation rather than reality. In its 1990 report on the state of the marine environment, GESAMP (Group of Experts on the Scientific Aspects of Marine Environmental Protection) indicated that, although there is sufficient information on a few of these compounds, there are at least 500–1,000 others included in some of the discharges.

Some of these are dioxins, chlorophenols, PCBs (polychlorinated biphenyls) and DDT (dichloro-diphenyl-trichloroethane). The organo-chlorine pesticides and PCBs are of special concern because of their persistence in the environment, their storage in the fatty tissues of animals, and their ability to become concentrated in parts of the food chain.

In Malaysia, the use of DDT in malaria eradication programmes has been banned since 1988. However, traces of the group of chemicals making up DDT are present in the environment, indicating that it is still being used illegally.

Another chemical pollutant that exists in Malaysian coastal areas, but of which little is known, is TBT or tributyl tin. Initially, this chemical was used as a biocide—a chemical that kills any living organism but is mainly used to remove micro-organisms. Since the mid-1960s, it has also been used as an ingredient in anti-fouling paints. Studies on the west coast of Peninsular Malaysia have shown that exposure to TBT can cause imposex (a change in sex) in marine snails.

Many of these synthetic substances have been shown to cause major human health problems. The pollution problem in Malaysia due to effluent discharge is far from being solved. Existing legislation is adequate but enforcement is lacking, mainly because of a manpower shortage. Some states are approaching the problem through integrated coastal zone management (see 'Integrated coastal management'), with emphasis on environmental awareness and public participation programmes.

Local efforts to control effluents

Local newspapers highlight the problem of pollution from effluents and the efforts being taken to reduce such pollution.

Malaysians are becoming increasingly aware of how effluents can damage the environment, thanks to the efforts of both government and non-governmental organizations as well as corporations. Consequently, more and more industries are trying to reduce pollution caused by their methods of production or by their waste products. *The Star*, a local newspaper, has reported the following efforts at controlling effluents.

WASTE TREATMENT PLANT

Malaysia has an intergrated hazardous waste management centre at Bukit Nanas in Negri Sembilan. Operated by a consortium called Kualiti Alam, the plant has been operational since 1997. It can handle 107 types of hazardous waste listed in the Environment Quality Act, but not explosives, hospital (infectious) and radioactive waste. There are four major facilities within the plant. One is the physical-chemical treatment plant where inorganic wastes, such as acid, are treated before being stabilized into inert forms to prevent the leakage of toxic substances into the ground.

At the stabilization and solidification plant, inorganic waste is mixed with cement or lime to form solid or semi-solid materials which are then packed into drums or bags and buried in the landfill. Organic waste, such as lubricating oil, solvents and contaminated drums, are burnt in the incinerating plant. All treated waste is then deposited in solid or semi-solid form in the landfill which is lined with impermeable layers of rock.

Bags of stabilized waste lie partially buried in the landfill at the Bukit Nanas waste treatment plant in Negri Sembilan. In the background is the incinerator.

Cleaner batik production

Batik printing can result in discharges of small amounts of waste water polluted with dyes, fixers or wax. This can end up in rivers and seas. However, there are ways to minimize this pollution. In a cleaner technology demonstration project organized in early 1999 by Sirim (Standards and Industrial Research Institute of Malaysia) and Danced (Danish Environmental Development, a Danish government initiative that funds environmental development projects in developing countries), the Penang Batik Factory demonstrated how it could reduce waste water generation. The factory replaced its old, leaking, wooden dyeing troughs with fibreglass tanks. The leakage incidents where dramatically reduced. The order in the dyeing and rinsing areas was also rearranged to reduce spillage, and the factory changed to less toxic reactive dyes and recycled water.

FAR LEFT: The batik factory formerly used wooden troughs to dye and rinse the dyed fabric, and these leaked easily.

NEAR LEFT: To minimize leakage, fibreglass tanks have replaced the old wooden dyeing troughs.

Less waste, more sauce

Another local factory which benefited from the Sirim–Danced Cleaner Technology project is Khong Guan sauce and food manufacturers in Penang. Sauce production involves organic material as its raw material—a mixture of wheat and soya bean. Both soy sauce and its raw material need large quantities of oxygen to decompose. Therefore, if they get into the sea, they deprive fish and other marine organisms of oxygen. Because spillage from the hydraulic presses caused the factory to lose much soy sauce, it received a filter press from the Sirim–Danced project to replace the old hydraulic presses. With the new press, spillage is almost non-existent.

The new filter press in the soy sauce factory receives raw materials directly from the fermentation tanks, then presses, filters and transfers all the sauce into a receiving tank with minimum spillage. Less water is required for cleaning the floor, resulting in less waste water being discharged.

Spills: Monitoring the marine environment

In Malaysia, most major oil spills occur in the Strait of Melaka because it is one the busiest shipping routes in the world. Smaller spills occur in the more open South China Sea. Since oil spills often have disastrous consequences, including the destruction of marine life and the pollution of tourist beaches, monitoring the marine environment is vital. The Department of Environment Malaysia (DOE) therefore carries out regular surveillance of the seas and has a national contingeny plan to combat spills. It also enforces laws regarding spills.

Oil slicks from the collision of the oil tanker MT *Nagasaki Spirit* and the MV *Ocean Blessing* in 1992 polluted the mangroves along the coast of Pulau Langkawi.

Illegal desludging from ships pollutes beaches.

Statistics reveal that oil and grease constitute the main pollutants in Malaysian seas.

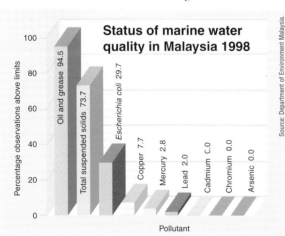

Surveillance

A special unit within the DOE monitors oil spills at sea, conducting regular aerial and sea surveillance. The Airborne Surveillance Programme jointly conducted by the DOE and the Police Air Wing, using helicopters and other aircraft, is employed to detect illegal oil and oily waste discharges in Malaysian seas. In addition, the Royal Malaysian Air Force assists the DOE with such surveillance.

Oil spill combat equipment is also placed at high-risk areas, such as ports and oil installation sites, to facilitate action.

National contingency plan

To ensure the effectiveness of Malaysia's oil spill monitoring and control programmes, a national contingency plan to combat oil spills was developed in 1976. It aims, first, to provide an immediate and coordinated response system in combating spills. Secondly, it strives to enhance the effectiveness of the response with existing equipment, manpower and training resources. It also aims to minimize potential impacts of the spills on the environment.

The plan is updated on a regular basis and promotes the setting up of good communication links and facilitates the making of well-informed decisions in emergencies. A committee set up under the plan coordinates the activities of the various agencies involved in spill control operations and accelerates the necessary actions. Chaired by the Director-General of the DOE, the committee consists of 16 government and private agencies, with each member being allocated a specific task and role as prescribed under the national contingency plan.

When a major spill occurs, or when a spill spreads into the waters of neighbouring countries, the coordination for foreign assistance will be made by the national oil

Sources of spills

DOE officers inspecting a ship. The bags of sludge need to be brought to a licensed disposal site on land. If they are illegally thrown into the sea, the bags will break and the sludge will pollute the sea and beaches.

Oil spills at sea occur mainly when ships collide or when vessels carry out desludging and illegal discharging. Desludging is the cleaning and removal of oil residues from tankers during repairs or when cargo is changed. Illegal discharging is the accidental or intentional discharge of oil from vessels, oil platforms and oil installation terminals. Of these, illegal discharging is the most common source of spills as fishing vessels are also involved. Less common sources include overfilling or explosions at a depot.

REPORTED CASES OF OIL SPILLS IN MALAYSIAN WATERS 1998

SOURCE OF SPILL	CAUSE	NUMBER OF CASES
Oil well blow-out	Mechanical failure	1
	Human error	0
Pipeline	Rupture	0
Vessel	Collision	0
	Grounding	0
	Explosion and/or fire	0
	Illegal discharging	12
	Desludging	1
Terminal and depot	Overfilling	0
	Burst hose	0
	Explosion and/or fire	0
	Leaking valves and flanges	1
	Tank washing and deballasting	0
Unknown	Unknown	1
	Total number of cases	**16**

Source: Department of Environment Malaysia.

spill control committee. Several regional oil spill contingency arrangements have been developed. These include the Sulawesi Sea Oil Spill Network Response Plan, the Standard Operating Procedure for Joint Oil Spill Combat for the Straits of Melaka and Singapore, the Standard Operating Procedure for Malaysia and Brunei Darussalam, and the ASEAN-Oil Spill Response Action Plan.

Apart from having regional oil spill contingency plans, Malaysia is a member of a number of international conventions relating to spills, which further enhances the country's spill response capability and coordination. These include the International Convention on Oil Pollution Preparedness, Response and Cooperation 1990, the International Oil Pollution Compensation Fund 1971 and the International Convention for the Prevention of Pollution from Ships 1973/78.

Status of marine water quality in Malaysia 1998

Source: Department of Environment Malaysia.

Percentage observations above limits

Oil and grease 94.5
Total suspended solids 73.7
Escherichia coli 29.7
Copper 7.7
Mercury 2.8
Lead 2.0
Cadmium C.0
Chromium 0.0
Arsenic 0.0

Pollutant

Consequences of spills

The long Malaysian coastline is endowed with valuable marine resources and ecosytems. One unique feature is the presence of mangrove forests. Covering a total distance of 640 kilometres, these mangroves form important fish spawning grounds. The exploitation of these areas for economic development should be balanced with initiatives to preserve and protect the marine environment from marine pollution, especially arising from oil spills.

Marine organisms, including corals and sea birds, are affected by spills at sea. Spills also affect tourism as they pollute the coastal waters with oil slicks and the beaches with tar balls, and can leave lasting negative impressions which discourage tourists. Thus, the DOE conducts frequent awareness programmes to educate the shipping community on the consequences of spills. It holds dialogues with relevant parties to ensure compliance of laws and regulations. Its officers regularly attend courses and exercises to improve their preparedness.

Legislation

The Environmental Quality Act 1974 and its regulations are the main instruments for the control of pollution both on land and at sea in Malaysia. Sections 27 and 29 of this Act provide for a maximum fine of up to RM500,000 or five years' imprisonment for violations, including spills. Other legislation includes the Exclusive Economic Zone Act 1984, which imposes a maximum fine of up to RM1 million for violations.

There are, therefore, stringent laws and regulations dealing with oil spills. The DOE is stepping up enforcement of such laws to ensure the conservation of the marine environment.

Monitoring the quality of marine water

Besides monitoring oil spills, the DOE also conducts routine monitoring of marine water quality along the Malaysian coastline. Its objective is to provide the mechanism for ensuring effective implementation of marine pollution control and regulations for the protection and enhancement of the marine environment and resources.

The DOE has been monitoring the quality of marine water in Peninsular Malaysia since 1978 and that of Sabah and Sarawak since 1985. In recent years, the quality of marine and coastal waters along the Strait of Melaka has been deteriorating, as shown by the presence of suspended solids, oil, grease and the bacteria *E. coli* in the water, while the waters of the South China Sea remain cleaner by comparison.

A staff member of the DOE taking a sample of sea water to determine its quality. This is routine monitoring of Malaysian coastal waters.

Some major incidents

A number of major spills have occurred in the seas around Malaysia. For example, in September 1992, an oil tanker, MT *Nagasaki Spirit*, collided with a container vessel, MV *Ocean Blessing*, in the Strait of Melaka, spilling 13 000 metric tons of crude oil and threatening the coastal areas of the west coast of Peninsular Malaysia and the east coast of Sumatra. The clean-up operation on Pulau Langkawi arising from the spill involved over 200 people and yielded 1380 metric tons of contaminated debris. Another major incident involved the oil tanker MT *Evoikos*. On 15 October 1997, it collided with another tanker, the *Orapin Global*, in the Singapore Strait. More than 25 000 metric tons of marine fuel oil were spilled. Oil booms were placed in the Strait to prevent the oil from polluting the beaches. Oil was also spilled when the cruise liner SS *Sun Vista*, carrying holidaymakers, sank in the Strait of Melaka in May 1999.

❶

❷

3

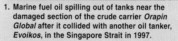

1. Marine fuel oil spilling out of tanks near the damaged section of the crude carrier *Orapin Global* after it collided with another oil tanker, *Evoikos*, in the Singapore Strait in 1997.

2. Spraying a chemical to disperse the oil which spilled from the damaged MT *Nagasaki Spirit*.

3. Putting out the fire from the collision between the MT *Nagasaki Spirit* and the MV *Ocean Blessing*.

Clean-up operations

If an oil spill is minor, it is often left alone since the oil will be dispersed by waves or evaporate because of high temperatures. However, a major spill has to be dealt with differently. One common method is containment and recovery, using equipment such as booms, skimmers and fast tanks. Another method is dispersant spraying—spraying the oil with an approved chemical to break it up into small droplets that can be dispersed easily by the natural actions of the sea and sunlight. This prevents oil from reaching the beach.

A skimmer is a machine that skims oil from the surface of the sea and transfers it into tanks.

A dispersant sprayer is used to spray oil slicks with chemicals to disperse them.

Local authority staff clean up a pollluted beach in Melaka by collecting tar balls.

Oil booms are placed in the sea off Johor to contain a spill. The booms in the foreground are black with oil.

Marine parks and reserves

A marine park is an area of the sea zoned as a sanctuary for the protection of its marine ecosystems. In Malaysia, there are five marine parks administered by the Department of Fisheries and three in Sabah administered by Sabah Parks. The main objective of such parks is to conserve and protect the corals, fish and other marine life. Conservation, especially of the coral reefs, is important to the economy because some of the commercial fish caught in the coastal waters originate from or make use of the reefs. The parks are also a major source of tourism revenue.

The Pulau Redang Marine Park Centre (top), established in 1990, is located at Pulau Pinang. The main office building is well equipped with various facilities, such as an exhibition hall, a laboratory and an aquarium. There are also camping sites, barbecue pits and restrooms for visitors, as well as a jetty. The Pulau Payar Marine Park Centre (below) offers the same facilities.

Establishment

Between 1983 and 1985, the Department of Fisheries Malaysia identified suitable areas that could be designated as federal marine parks. In 1983, the waters 8 kilometres from Pulau Redang off Terengganu were established as Fisheries Prohibited Areas (FPAs). In 1985, the waters 3 kilometres off 22 islands in Kedah, Terengganu, Pahang and Johor were also declared FPAs. In the same year, the Fisheries Act 1963 was repealed by the Fisheries Act 1985 and provision for marine parks was contained in the new act. The Pulau Payar Marine Park was then established in 1989. Between 1983 and 1994, although most areas were not yet legally declared as marine parks, they were administered as FPAs.

Finally in 1994, waters 2 nautical miles off a total of 38 islands in Peninsular Malaysia and the Federal Territory of Labuan were established as federal marine parks. These included the already established Pulau Payar Marine Park and existing FPAs. In 1998, the waters off two more islands were also gazetted as federal marine parks. The 40 islands are grouped into five marine parks (see map) for better administration and management. Besides these 40 islands, there are eleven islands in Sabah grouped into three state marine parks (see map). There is also now three FPAs in Sarawak, two in Melaka and one in Negeri Sembilan.

A diver gets a chance to see a green turtle at close range.

Benefits

Although the most important ecosystem in a marine park is the coral reef, the mangroves, mud flats and seagrass beds are also important. Their protection and conservation is necessary because, like the reefs, they contribute to the fisheries resources in coastal waters. They are breeding and nursery areas for fish, prawns and other marine life. Although the reduction in Malaysian fisheries resources is mainly due to the destruction of these habitats, overfishing and destructive methods of fishing also contribute to the diminishing numbers. Thus, the establishment of marine parks provides many benefits:

- Fisheries resources are managed through the conservation of biodiversity in the park.
- Scientists are given encouragement and opportunity to carry out research on biodiversity, for pharmaceutical and other purposes.
- Marine resources, especially the coral reefs which are the main attractions for visitors, are conserved and protected, as are marine animals such as sea turtles which are overexploited and face extinction.
- There are increased opportunities for education and awareness for students and the general public.
- Recreational opportunities for tourism are improved.

Park facilities

Each marine park has an administration and management centre which serves as a base for enforcement. At the centre, visitors can obtain information on the park in the form of posters, charts, slides or videos. The centre is also used as a focal point for marine environmental education, not only for the young but also for the public in general. It serves as a base for researchers, too. At the Pulau Redang and Pulau Tioman centres, there are laboratories with basic facilities and equipment for scientists. Lodging facilities for rangers and scientists are available in three of the centres—Pulau Payar, Pulau Redang and Pulau Tioman.

Management

A National Advisory Council for Marine Parks and Reserves was established under the Fisheries Act 1985. This council is chaired by the Secretary-General of the Ministry of Agriculture. In addition to federal and state government officers, its members comprise representatives from various sectors, such as non-governmental organizations, local universities and commercial firms.

One function of the council is to determine the guidelines for the implementation of regulations at national level, with respect to protection, conservation, utilization, control, management and progress of the marine parks and reserves. Another is to coordinate the development of any area of a marine park or reserve with the federal government and corporations. It also gives technical advice to state governments on any development project on any island situated in a marine park or reserve.

Location of marine parks in Malaysia

N

Pulau Payar Marine Park

Peninsular Malaysia

Pulau Pangkor

Strait of Melaka

Pulau Redang Marine Park

South China Sea

Pulau Tioman Marine Park

Mersing

Mersing Marine Park

Pulau Tunku Abdul Rahman Park

Pulau Tiga Park

Turtle Islands Park

Kota Kinabalu

Labuan Marine Park

Sabah

Sandakan

BRUNEI

Semporna

Sarawak

Kalimantan (INDONESIA)

0   160 km

Marine Parks Of Malaysia

- Pulau Payar Marine Park in Kedah, with 4 islands
- Pulau Redang Marine Park in Terengganu, with 11 islands
- Pulau Tioman Marine Park in Pahang, with 9 islands
- Mersing Marine Park in Johor, with 13 islands
- Labuan Marine Park in the Federal Territory of Labuan, with 3 islands
- Pulau Tiga Park, with 3 islands
- Pulau Tunku Abdul Rahman Park, with 5 islands
- Turtle Islands Park with 3 islands

Conservation of corals and other marine life

Marine parks are essential for the conservation of corals and other marine life. Because of the high diversity of marine life on Malaysian coral reefs, they are of great ecological importance. Recent chemical prospecting of the seas to determine the pharmaceutical value of reef organisms has revealed some chemicals of medicinal value (see 'Pharmaceuticals'). Traditionally, the reefs have been the fishing grounds of local fishermen as they are feeding and breeding grounds for many commercial fishes. They are also a major attraction for tourists.

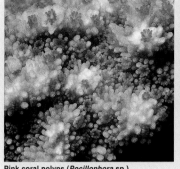
Pink coral polyps (*Pocillophora* sp.)

Clown fish (*Amphiprion bicintus*)

Red oyster (*Spondylus sp.*)

Shrimps (*Rhynchocinetes* sp.)

Porcellanid crab (*Neopetrolisthes maculata*)

Nudibranch (*Chromodoris lochi*)

Coral trout (*Cephalopholis miniata*)

Sea urchin (*Echinothrix calamaris*)

Because of the peculiar situation in Malaysia, where land matters come under the jurisdiction of the state government while the seas come under the federal government, ensuring that development on the islands does not jeopardize the marine ecosystem is an important issue. To ensure that development projects on land are environmentally friendly, the council advises each state which has a marine park to form its own committee to advise the state government on matters affecting the marine environment.

The Department of Fisheries, a federal agency, manages and administers all the federal marine parks in Malaysia based on the broad policy guidelines set out by the council. Monitoring and enforcement within the park is done by the park rangers with the help of the enforcement unit of the Department of Fisheries. Besides maintenance, administration and enforcement, the park rangers also carry out education and awareness work. Research in the parks is mostly carried out by the research arm of the Department of Fisheries, with the help of the park rangers. Scientists from local and foreign universities as well as non-governmental organizations are also encouraged and allowed to carry out research in the parks.

Funding

A Marine Park Trust Fund was set up in 1987 by the government with an initial grant of RM35 million for the establishment and administration of marine parks. Initially, most of the fund was used to acquire assets such as boats and vehicles and to build

Activities in marine parks

Permitted activities

Activities which do not harm the coral reefs and the environment are allowed and encouraged in marine parks. These expose the participants to the beauty and wonder of the underwater environment, increasing their knowledge and awareness of the importance of conserving it. Some of these activities include:
- Swimming
- Observation and appreciation of marine life
- Underwater photography
- Snorkelling
- Scuba diving
- Fish feeding
- Non-motorized boating, e.g. sailing, kayaking
- Nature walks and hill treks on the island
- Bird watching on the island

Prohibited activities

Activities which are destructive to the coral reefs and other important marine ecosystems are prohibited under the Fisheries Act 1985. Some of these include:
- Collecting living seashells, corals and other organisms
- Collecting sand, dead coral and dead shells
- Fishing and killing fish
- Speargun fishing
- Sling fishing
- Water skiing, jet skiing and speedboat racing
- Littering or polluting
- Vandalizing any structure or object in the park
- Anchoring of boats over reefs
- Constructing any building or other structure on the water (except with permission)

up the infrastructure. However, since the mid-1990s, the fund has mostly been used for operations and maintenance.

The regulations of this trust fund allow the Department of Fisheries to collect donations from private firms and the public. Funds can also be raised through the sale of books, posters and other souvenirs. Since the beginning of 1999, some marine parks have started collecting a 'conservation charge' from tourists who visit the parks and take part in the various marine activities on offer. The money collected helps in the conservation programmes.

Brochures on marine parks are available to educate tourists on the need for conservation.

The Matang mangroves

The Matang mangroves in Perak are among the best managed in the world. In 1998, Matang won the Green Award, given by the Ministry of Primary Industries Malaysia, for the best managed forest in Peninsular Malaysia. The management success is reflected in the extent of quality timber producing forests as well as a strong conservation programme. Matang not only supports a flourishing fishing industry but efforts have also been made to promote education and ecotourism.

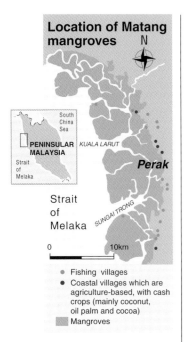

Location of Matang mangroves

- Fishing villages
- Coastal villages which are agriculture-based, with cash crops (mainly coconut, oil palm and cocoa)
- Mangroves

TOTAL ANNUAL VALUE OF FORESTRY AND FISHERIES PRODUCTS IN MATANG

ACTIVITY	ANNUAL VALUE (RM)
Forestry	
Charcoal production	20,027,000
Firewood production	50,000
Pole production	2,177,000
Total value	**22,254,000**
Fisheries	
Marine fish landing	120,356,000
Cockle culture	8,403,000
Cage culture	1,365,000
Total value	**130,124,000**

Location

Located on the west coast of Peninsular Malaysia in the state of Perak, the Matang mangroves stretch from Kuala Gula in the north to Panchor in the south, a distance of 52 kilometres. The forest ecosystem is essentially a delta drained by rivers, such as the Kalumpang, Selinsing and Sangga Besar.

The total forest area of 40 151 hectares is divided into three ranges comprising 19 reserves and 108 compartments. About 82 per cent are managed as productive forests, primarily of *Rhizophora*, which account for more than 90 per cent of the forest. The remaining 18 per cent are managed as functional forests for conservation, coastal protection, ecotourism, research and education. People continue to live in the area in a number of fishing villages which dot the coast.

Forest management

The Matang mangroves have been sustainably managed for wood production since their reservation in 1902. Management of the forests is based on 10-year working plans aimed at providing quality timber for the production of charcoal, firewood and poles, on a sustained yield basis.

Forestry practices carried out in the mangroves include stand thinning, final felling and enrichment planting. Stand thinning (reducing the number of trees in an area or 'stand') to enhance tree growth and natural regeneration has been practised since the 1930s. The process involves using a stick of prescribed length to regulate the intended interval between trees. Using a commercial tree of good quality as the centre, only trees occurring within the radius drawn by the stick can be felled. The initial distribution of trees in the stand will, of course, have a great effect on the process, which itself results in a harvest of wood for charcoal and firewood.

Systematic clear felling on a 30-year rotation is the harvesting system practised in the forests. Trees are felled and cut into lengths called billets before they are transported out of the forest using wheelbarrows. Two years after final felling, enrichment planting is carried out.

Enrichment planting

An important component of the working plans which have contributed significantly to the sustainable management of the Matang mangroves is the emphasis on intensive enrichment planting following clear felling. The rationale of reforestation is primarily to ensure a sustained supply of quality wood for the production of charcoal, firewood and poles. Other objectives include the maintenance of a healthy ecosystem. Reforestation programmes have become a routine annual silvicultural activity within the whole reserve.

Dense thickets of *Acrostichum* ferns require site clearing before tree planting can occur.

Clear felling is the harvesting system adopted. Note the presence of seedling regeneration.

Mangrove billets are transported out of the forest using a wheelbarrow pushed along a plank trail.

ABOVE: A mature stand primarily of *Rhizophora* trees.

LEFT: Nursery-raised *Rhizophora* seedlings are sometimes used in planting instead of direct planting using propagules.

Rhizophora apiculata and *Rhizophora mucronata* are the two commercial tree species most widely planted. As the planting operation, which coincides with the fruiting season, is simple it can be carried out by untrained workers. It essentially involves inserting propagules (seedlings) into the mud along predetermined lines and at fixed spacings. Except in areas covered by dense thickets of *Acrostichum* ferns, site preparation prior to planting is not necessary as planting is done two years after final felling when most of the logging debris has decomposed.

Production forests

Productivity of mangrove plantations depends on age, site conditions, rotation stage and form of utilization. Matang has demonstrated that, through intensive reforestation efforts, it is possible to attain highly productive plantations. In the early 1900s, when management for wood production began, forests in Matang were pristine with a rich representation of mangrove tree species. With clear felling as the harvesting system, followed by

Mangrove wood is heated in a kiln to produce charcoal which is used locally as a cooking fuel and is also exported, mainly to Japan.

Forest conservation

In addition to the intensively managed production forests of mainly *Rhizophora*, non-productive forests are also found at Matang. They are mainly dryland forests and *Avicennia* forests which occur along shores at the sea front. Located on the landward side, dryland forests denote the final stage of mangrove succession and represent a transition into inland forests.

Most of the non-productive forests in Matang are currently managed as functional forests. They include virgin reserves, archaeological reserves, bird sanctuaries, ecotourism forests and educational and research forests.

These functional forests support a rich diversity of flora and fauna. More than 30 tree species belonging to 24 genera have been found within the dryland forests. The two bird sanctuaries—at Pulau Kelumpang and Pulau Trong Utara—are important feeding, breeding and stopover sites for both resident and migratory shorebirds. A total of 155 bird species belonging to 40 families have been recorded. Bird watching is thus a very suitable activity which fits in with the management philosophy of the area.

Ecotourism is viable because Matang is situated within easy access of the north–south highway, near the town of Taiping in Perak. Matang is being developed as an ecotourism park in five phases. A museum is being built, including an aquarium, audiovisual room, library, restaurant and souvenir shop. Boardwalks have been built, too.

The last phase involves building a jetty and a resting shed along the banks of the Sungai Reba where the boardwalk ends. Visitors can book their field destination of choice from this jetty. They can choose to go on a number of guided tours or activities, such as to a bird sanctuary, an aquaculture farm, or a fishing village, or they can watch forestry activities like harvesting and planting.

1. *Avicennia* forests occur along the sea front.
2. Great egrets (*Egretta alba*), gather at Kuala Gula, Perak.
3. A boardwalk through the Matang mangroves.

enrichment planting, the species-rich and structurally variable forest ecosystem has been modified to plantations of predominantly *Rhizophora* species.

Socioeconomic benefits

Through proper management, both the productive and non-productive forests at Matang are able to sustain not only forestry activities but also a flourishing fishing industry. The forest ecosystem, with its associated habitats—mud flats and waterways—supports a wealth of fishing activities. These include the catching of mud crabs (*Scylla serrata*), culture of cockles (*Anadara granosa*) and cage culture of sea bass (*Lates calcarifer*). The total annual value from forestry and fisheries is estimated at about RM22 million and RM130 million respectively. Efforts are also being made to promote ecotourism and education. One of the most popular ecotourism opportunities at Matang is bird watching.

The villagers at Kuala Sepetang, a major fishing village at Matang, are dependent on the resources of the mangroves for their livelihood.

Integrated Coastal Management

Integrated Coastal Management (ICM) has been defined by the World Bank as a 'process of governance consisting of the legal and institutional framework necessary to ensure that development and management plans for coastal areas are integrated with environmental and social goals and with the participation of those affected'. Although relatively new in Malaysia, the concept is gaining acceptance as a viable alternative to traditional methods of coastal zone management, and one that needs to become an integral part of state and national economic plans.

Workshops on the development of physical planning guidelines are one of the activities carried out in a pilot ICM project.

Main stages in an ICM national development plan.

History of coastal management in Malaysia

Like many developing nations in Southeast Asia, Malaysia has, in the last two decades, experienced increased pollution in coastal waters, loss of critical habitats and decrease in fisheries resources because of rapid economic development and an increasing population. Such pressure on the coastal environment is expected to increase. If this happens, the fragile coastal ecosystems which have long generated valuable goods and services may become seriously affected and many coastal activities unsustainable.

It is increasingly evident that the conventional sectoral approach to coastal development and management has not managed to achieve wise and sustainable use of coastal and marine resources. The lack of integrated land-use and sea-use planning has often resulted in the need for expensive mitigating measures to arrest environmental degradation. Such situations and, in some cases, costs could have been avoided if the interface relationship between the land and the sea had been more closely considered.

Coastal resources assessment

It is against this background that various coastal resources management initiatives were introduced to Southeast Asia 15 years ago. The ICM concept is based on the extensive coastal zone management practices in the United States. In 1985, Southeast Asia launched its first Coastal Resources Management (CRM) project through the support of the United States Agency for International Development (USAID).

With growing concern over oil spills in the 1970s, a number of resource assessment initiatives were undertaken and contributed to a better understanding of the role coastal ecosystems play in Malaysia's growing economy. One of the early initiatives was carried out by a team of scientists from Universiti Sains Malaysia, who produced a comprehensive document on the coastal resources of western Sabah and an investigation on the impact of an oil spill. This led to a similar approach being adopted in the assessment of coastal resources on the east coast of Peninsular Malaysia, made by the staff of the same university in 1980.

Efforts on coastal resources assessment continued into the 1980s, including a coastal resource assessment of the coast of Sarawak and a fisheries resources assessment in the South China Sea and the Strait of Melaka. In 1986, the first ICM pilot project in Malaysia began in southern Johor, followed in the late 1990s by similar projects in Penang, Sarawak and Sabah. This is a step in the right direction as a main objective of an ICM is to include an integrated planning and management framework as a key part of state and national economic development plans.

Effluents (organic wastes) from palm oil mills are among the pollutants threatening Malaysian coastal waters.

Deforestation or the cutting down of trees often results in soil erosion, with sediments being discharged into the sea.

The need for Integrated Coastal Management (ICM) in Malaysia

Rapid development in Malaysia over the past two decades has caused some major coastal problems. Resource exploitation, such as coastal forest conversion, habitat destruction and overdevelopment of offshore islands for tourism, has led to environmental degradation. Many mangroves on the west coast of Peninsular Malaysia have been converted for other land uses, such as aquaculture, resulting in the loss of rich spawning and feeding grounds for fish and prawns. Conservation of marine and coastal ecosystems, such as mangroves, is thus an issue.

Tourism has also affected the seas adversely. Although marine parks have been established, the Malaysian system whereby the seas come under federal jurisdiction while the land remains under the state has resulted in the overdevelopment of certain islands. This creates problems, including the discharge of effluents into the sea.

It is thus important to integrate the planning and management of coastal resources (land use) with that of marine resources (sea use) because activities on land closely impact on the sea. ICM provides strategies to ensure that rapid development on land does not affect the seas adversely. Because of the legal and institutional framework in Malaysia, there is often insufficient monitoring of development activities and inadequate law enforcement. ICM coordinates and integrates the relevant policies, legislation and institutional arrangements—promoting a holistic approach—making monitoring and action more effective.

Integrated Coastal Management (ICM) initiatives in Malaysia

The South Johor ICM project

In the state of Johor, a long-term effort in the development of a comprehensive ICM programme was initiated in 1986. As part of a larger regional coastal resources management effort throughout the Association of Southeast Asian nations (ASEAN), and with financial support from the United States Agency for International Development (USAID), Malaysia identified South Johor—Pontian, Johor Bahru and Kota Tinggi—as a pilot site for a Coastal Resources Management Programme.

The primary objectives of the project were to raise public awareness of the importance of coastal resources and to adopt an integrated approach to addressing environmental issues and multiple resource-use conflicts.

South Johor was selected because it had been undergoing rapid economic development in line with the government's policy of industrialization. In addition, marine resources are its main source of income, food and employment for coastal communities, and environmental problems are prevalent along its coastal zone. South Johor also shares with Singapore the Strait of Johor which is affected by development in both countries.

Parties involved

More than 33 state and federal agencies, five universities, two non-governmental organizations and other private bodies, involving some 76 people, participated in the four-year project. One major aim was to provide the Johor state government with a data base on coastal resources, guidelines for sustainable development and a tool for the

evaluation of coastal development options. It was coordinated by the Department of Fisheries Malaysia at the federal level and the state planning unit at the state level. The focal point at the federal level was later changed to the Department of Environment (DOE).

The project developed management action plans to address the major issues related to environmental degradation and resource exploitation. It recommended the establishment of a comprehensive planning and management system for South Johor, covering a coastal policy to harmonize sectoral development in line with sustainable development goals, strengthen inter-agency coordination and promote policy, system and functional integration. The main institutional arrangement in the plan was the establishment of an inter-agency planning committee within major regional planning and development agencies and the provision of trained manpower.

Implementation

Although the ICM plan for South Johor was completed in 1992, no report was submitted by the national focal point to the state government until 1995. Despite this significant delay, the Johor state government has taken a keen interest in the recommendations and action plans proposed. It called a two-day seminar where key team leaders of the project presented the summary reports of the plan. In 1996, the state government formally established an ICM unit under the state planning unit to execute some of the plan's recommendations for South Johor.

Location of pilot site

1. The sustainability of recreation at beach resorts, such as the one shown at Desaru in Johor, depends on the ability to maintain clean water quality.

2. Development of the Johor port must take into consideration the impact of hazardous substances inside and outside the port area.

Other ICM initiatives in Malaysia

The ICM initiatives in South Johor, as well as the regional project as a whole, has had positive impacts on government policies and strategies in addressing coastal management issues. Ten years after the initiation of the South Johor project, the Malaysian government included coastal management in its seventh economic development plan.

With technical and financial assistance from the Danish government through the Danish Co-operation for Environment and Development (DANCED), three other ICM initiatives have been undertaken in Penang, Sarawak and Sabah. The DANCED efforts focus on resolving issues arising from coastal urbanization. A national coastal policy has also been initiated by the Economic Planning Unit of the Prime Minister's Department.

The Penang ICM pilot project, which came under the State Economic Planning Unit, started in September 1996 and ended in April 2000. It aimed to set up a system for integrated management and policies for the coastal zone in Penang; to prepare an initial proposal for an

integrated coastal zone management plan; to promote public awareness and public participation; and to strengthen the regulatory framework concerning development control in the coastal zone.

Five task forces were set up to carry out the analytical work related to the preparation of the ICM plan. Members comprised mainly government staff. With the support of local and foreign technical assistance, they were responsible for defining, analysing, selecting and acting upon specific tasks. Major activities and events included training courses, seminars, workshops and field activities.

1. Students from schools in the Sungai Juru area in Penang sail down the river to learn more about saving rivers during an environmental camp to create awareness.

2. Students at an environmental camp at Sungai Juru compare notes on their observations.

3. Participants at a seminar obtaining more information on the need for rehabilitating the Sungai Juru river.

4. Environmental awareness talks held for residents of the Sungai Juru locality.

5. The cover of a report outlining the findings of the Penang component of the ICM project. One of the findings contained in the report stresses the importance of public education and awareness of the neccessity for conservation of the mangroves.

Research and education

Although Malaysia is a maritime nation, marine science is a relatively new field in the country. A number of marine scientists from institutions such as the universities, Fisheries Research Institute, Royal Malaysian Navy, Malaysian Institute for Maritime Affairs, Department of Environment, as well as oil companies, are engaged in research on an individual basis, but no national body exists to coordinate marine science research. Marine science education also remains in its infancy although, increasingly, efforts are being made to educate Malaysians on the importance of their marine heritage.

A diver making notes on the barrel coral.

This marine research station, which belongs to the Centre for Marine and Coastal Studies of Universiti Sains Malaysia, is located on the northwest coast of Penang where the waters are relatively clean.

A mangrove tree tower provides access for measuring carbon dioxide changes in the air—useful data for studies on climate change.

Marine research in Malaysia

As a maritime nation, and a signatory to such international treaties as the United Nations Convention on the Law of the Sea, Malaysia is committed to obtaining basic knowledge pertaining to the seas. This involves both pure research (the scientific process of the quest for new knowledge) and technology (the application of scientific knowledge). For example, Malaysia's important cockle industry requires both scientific and technological input. Growing cockles requires technology, but finding out why natural cockle beds develop, where they grow, and how they are able to maintain themselves, involves pure research.

Investment in marine science research is very costly. Measuring instruments are expensive to purchase, use and maintain. Skilled scientists and technicians are required to operate and maintain them, and to interpret and use the data obtained from them. The marine environment is also harsh on instruments, and rapid corrosion and fouling invariably occur (see 'Barnacles').

For inshore research, relatively cheap boats can be used, but for offshore work, expensive ocean-going vessels fitted with the necessary equipment are required. In Malaysia, offshore work is presently conducted by the Royal Malaysian Navy, which has a number of hydrological vessels, and Universiti Putra Malaysia and Universiti Malaysia Sabah, which both have a single ocean-going vessel. Much of the research done by the Royal Malaysian Navy is classified. Marine research at the other institutions is largely limited to inshore work.

Knowledge of the seas

Most marine science research in Malaysia is applied, that is, it is related to such areas as fisheries and to monitoring pollution. In contrast, there is relatively little basic research into, and therefore knowledge of, the physical processes at work in the Malaysian seas. Yet, it is important to know how water moves and mixes in order to understand other marine processes, because water carries with it sediments and chemicals as well as living things, such as plankton, fish eggs and larvae.

It is also necessary to have basic oceanographic knowledge and an understanding of the numerical models used in predicting physical coastal processes, particularly in environmental impact assessments. Access to water current data is also important as in the event of a catastrophe such as an oil spill it can help marine scientists predict the path of the spill so that appropriate action can be organized. Although oil spill paths are largely determined by wind patterns because oil floats on the surface of the water, currents are an important consideration in areas where they are strong.

Compared with their knowledge of the physical processes of Malaysian seas, local marine scientists have a greater knowledge and understanding of the biological and chemical processes. A knowledge of biological processes is necessary to protect the very important Malaysian fishing industry, and a knowledge of the chemistry of the seas is needed for monitoring chemical and biochemical pollutants. In both instances, studies tend to be data

Universiti Putra Malaysia (UPM) has a hydrological research vessel, *Unipertama V*, which carries out offshore work.

A researcher at work in a laboratory at the Fisheries Research Institute at Batu Maung in Penang.

Researchers from Universiti Malaya take fish and prawn samples in a mangrove area.

based rather than process based. The Fisheries Research Institute has a resource branch which conducts research on all aspects relating to fisheries resources to provide the necessary information and technical support for the development and management of fisheries.

One area in which Malaysia is a world leader is research into mangrove ecosystems. A handful of mangrove scientists at Universiti Malaya, Universiti Sains Malaysia and the Forest Research Institute Malaysia have, over the past twenty years or so, quietly but diligently worked their way to the forefront of mangrove research. Malaysia also has some of the best managed mangroves in the world. The Matang mangroves, for example, have become an international showpiece for sustainable mangrove management. They have also earned local mangrove foresters an international reputation for effective processes and management of mangrove ecosystems.

A number of regional and international cooperative programmes have assisted marine science research in Malaysia. For example, the ASEAN–Australian Co-operative Programme on Marine Science has helped many Malaysian universities and other institutions to improve local understanding of Malaysian marine ecosystems.

There is also a significant amount of funds in the IRPA (Intensification of Research in Priority Areas), which is a government programme. This grant is administered by the Ministry of Science, Technology and the Environment. Generous amounts can be obtained for research on various aspects of the seas, with most research being initiated by individuals or groups of scientists. There are, however, some areas where an understanding of the seas is still limited and remains so despite the availability of research fundings. Manpower and training are also required.

Marine science education

School level

At the school level, marine science education is often the combined efforts of government and non-governmental organizations, such as World Wide Fund for Nature Malaysia (WWFM), the Malaysian Nature Society (MNS) and Friends of the Earth. One example is the Marine Education Kit (right), a teaching resource for use in both primary and secondary schools. It is a joint production of the WWFM, the Department of Fisheries Malaysia, and the Curriculum Development Centre of the Ministry of Education.

The kit comprises four units: Oceans and Seas, Mangroves, Seashores and Coral Reefs. Attractively packaged in a folder, each unit consists of teacher's notes, factsheets, worksheets, lists of indoor and outdoor activities, plus a poster. Unit One also comes with a Mangrove Snakes and Ladders gameboard (right). Each unit highlights the functions of each habitat, the threats facing it, and the urgent need for marine conservation. Regional workshops are held as well, to train teachers to use this kit.

A mobile education unit programme is being carried out by the WWFM. The coordinators travel in a van to various schools.

To teach school children about nature, WWFM also runs a mobile education unit funded by Bata. The unit visits both primary and secondary schools throughout Peninsular Malaysia to provide an interesting hour-long programme consisting of a slide show, songs and an educational quiz session.

Tertiary level

At the tertiary level, Universiti Sains Malaysia, Universiti Malaya, Universiti Putra Malaysia and Universiti Malaysia Sabah offer courses in different aspects of marine science. For example, at Universiti Sains Malaysia in Penang, the Centre for Marine and Coastal Studies (CEMACS) offers courses on coastal ecosystems (with particular emphasis on mangroves, estuaries and corals), mariculture and pollution. The Sungai Merbok Mangrove Estuary in Kedah has been

selected to provide a focus for these interdisciplinary studies. CEMACS has a main office with laboratories on the main Universiti Sains Malaysia campus in Penang and a research station near Muka Head on the northwest coast of Penang.

Public level

WWFM is carrying out a project called 'Malaysian Youth and the Environment', the main aim of which is to enhance awareness of conservation among the young. One objective of the project is to identify, plan and develop youth programmes and activities, as well as to train trainers for long-term programmes. It will assist the Ministry of Youth and Sports to run some Rakan Muda Cinta Alam (Youth and Environment) programmes in various ecosystems. The project often links up with field projects run by WWFM.

The Department of Fisheries has also identified and gazetted 40 islands as five marine parks in efforts to preserve the coral reefs and to provide opportunities to educate the public (see 'Marine parks and reserves'.)

Marine science education is thus being carried out at all levels, and with the continued and increased support of local corporations as well as non-governmental organizations, it should succeed in reaching a wider audience and achieving its objectives.

Children participating in a WWFM youth activity on Pulau Redang under the supervision of a WWFM marine officer.

A group of school children are brought to the beach to learn more about the seas and how to save them.

Glossary

A

Adaptation: Any change in the structure or functioning of an organism that makes it better suited to its environment.

Aerobic: Characterized by the presence of free oxygen.

Alga (*pl.* **Algae**): Group of simple organisms that contain chlorophyll and live in aquatic habitats and in moist situations on land.

Anaerobic: Characterized by the absence of free oxygen.

Annelid: Segmented worm with a soft, cyclindrical body.

Aphotic zone: Underwater area more than 200 metres deep where light cannot penetrate.

Aquaculture: Rearing of fish, prawns and molluscs in fresh, sea or brackish water.

Artificial reef: Fish-attracting device comprising groups of suitable artificial materials such as tyres and concrete blocks.

Atmosphere: Layer of gases surrounding the Earth.

B

Backwash: Return of a wave down the slope of a beach towards the sea.

Barrier island: Long, narrow, low-lying island of sediments parallel to the shore and separated from the mainland by a lagoon.

Bay: Part of a coastline where the land curves inwards.

Biodegradable: Material that can break down or decompose naturally without any special scientific treatment, and can therefore be thrown away without causing pollution.

Biodiversity (biological diversity): Variety of life on earth. Can refer to species diversity, habitat or ecosystem diversity (the number of kinds of habitats in an area) or genetic diversity within a given species.

Biogeochemical cycle: Cycling of a chemical element through the biosphere; its pathways, storage locations and chemical forms in the atmosphere, oceans, sediments and lithosphere.

Biomass: Amount of material, or organic material contained in living organisms, both as live (e.g. tree) and dead (e.g. fallen leaf) material.

Bivalve: Mollusc, such as an oyster, which has two outer shells hinged together.

Breaker: Wave that breaks upon reaching a beach.

Breakwater: Low structure built in the sea to intercept waves and protect a harbour.

C

Carbon cycle: Cyclic movement of carbon in different chemical forms from the environment to organisms and then back to the environment.

Carnivore: Animal that feeds almost exclusively on other animals.

Carrying capacity: Maximum population of a particular species that a given habitat can support over a given period of time.

Cephalopod: Class of molluscs, mostly without shells, such as squid, cuttlefish and octopuses.

Chlorophyll: Green pigment in plants responsible for absorbing the light energy required for photosynthesis.

Class: Category used in the classification of organisms that consists of similar or closely related orders. Similar classes are grouped into a phylum, e.g. there are six classes of molluscs in the phylum Mollusca.

Coastal zone: Relatively warm, nutrient-rich, shallow part of the ocean that extends from the high-tide mark on land to the edge of the continental shelf.

Continental shelf: Relatively shallow ocean area between the shoreline and the continental slope that extends to a 200-metre depth surrounding a continent.

Coral reef: Formation produced by massive colonies of tiny coral animals, called polyps, which secrete a stony substance (calcium carbonate) around themselves for protection.

Crustacean: Animal, such as a prawn or crab, with a hard shell and several pairs of legs, which usually lives in water.

Current: Movement of water in the sea or ocean.

D

Demersal: Living or occurring on the bottom of a sea, e.g. demersal fish.

Denitrification: Conversion of fixed nitrogen from dead organisms on land or in the sea back into molecular nitrogen in the atmosphere.

Density: Relation of the mass or weight of a substance or object to its volume.

Deposition: Process in which layers of a substance are formed on a surface over time.

Detritus: Dead organic matter, such as fallen leaves, twigs and other plant and animal wastes, that exists in any ecosystem.

E

Echinoderms: Phylum of marine invertebrates that includes starfish, sea cucumbers and sea urchins, with an exoskeleton of calcereous plates embedded in the skin.

Ecosystem: Organized group of organisms living at a particular place and time, interacting with one another and with their environment. It can be considered a self-contained sustainable ecological unit.

Effluent: Material flowing outward from a factory or area, e.g. the discharge of waste water from factories.

El Niño Southern Oscillation (ENSO): Weather phenomenon caused by sea–air interaction over the Pacific Ocean. Characterized by development of warm waters in the eastern Pacific, a weakening of trade winds and of equatorial ocean currents. Occurs once in every 3–8 years, bringing drought to countries in the eastern Pacific but heavy rains to the Americas bordering the eastern Pacific.

Environmental impact: Effects on the natural environment caused by human actions.

Estuary: Interface area where a river meets the sea, and where many biological, chemical and physical phenomena occur.

Eutrophication: Process by which pollution from such sources as sewage effluent causes a body of water to become overrich in organic and mineral nutrients so that algae grow rapidly and deplete the oxygen supply.

Exclusive Economic Zone (EEZ): Zone in the sea (200 nautical miles from the shore) where the coastal state has sovereign rights to natural resources and certain economic activities. Areas over which jurisdiction over environmental protection and research applies.

Extinction: The death of all individuals of a particular species.

F

Family: Category used in the classification of organisms that consists of one or several similar or closely related genera. Similar families are grouped into an order.

Fishery: Fish species being exploited, or a limited marine area containing commercially valuable fish.

Food chain: The transfer of energy and material through a series of organisms as each eats or decomposes the preceding one; see *Food web*.

Food web: Complex network of many interconnected food chains and feeding relationships.

Fossil fuel: Forms of stored solar energy (crude oil, natural gas, coal) created from incomplete biological decomposition of dead organic matter.

Fossils: Skeletons, bones, shells, body parts, etc. that provide evidence of organisms that lived long ago.

Fringing reef: Long line of coral reefs close to the coastline.

G

Gastropod: Mollusc with a one-piece shell coiled in a spiral.

Genus (*pl.* **genera**): Category used in the classification of organisms that consists of a number of similar or closely related species. Similar genera are grouped into families.

Groyne: Low structure built on a beach, often at right angles to it, in order to check erosion.

Gyre: Slow, circular movement of ocean current.

H

Habitat: Specific environment where an individual organism, species or population exists.

Herbivore: Organism that feeds on plants.

Holocene transgression: Sea level rise which reached its maximum around 5,000 years ago, in the Holocene period.

Hydrological cycle: Movement of water from the oceans to the atmosphere and back to the oceans by way of runoff from streams, evaporation and groundwater flow.

I

Integrated Coastal Management (ICM): Concept and process of integrating the planning and management of the coastal zone to achieve sustainable use of both coastal and marine resources.

Intertidal zone: Area of beach covered by water during high tide.

Invertebrate: Animal without a backbone.

L

Lagoon: Area of calm sea water separated from the ocean by reefs or sand banks.

Larvae: Free-living immature forms that occur in the life cycle of many organisms.

Leaching: Process in which materials in or on the soil gradually dissolve and are carried by water seeping through the soil.

Longshore drift: Movement generated when waves are driven obliquely against the coast and sediments are washed up on the beach in a forward sweeping curve.

M

Mariculture: Cultivation of fish or other marine organisms in sea water or brackish water.

Marine environment: Ocean environment that supports a distinctive array of seaweeds, plankton, fish, shellfish and other marine organisms depending on the temperature, water depth, nature of the bottom and the concentrations of nutrients and sediments.

Maximum sustainable yield: Largest catch that can be continuously taken from a renewable stock under existing environmental conditions without depleting the resource.

Micronutrients: Chemical elements required in very small amounts by some living things.

Mollusc: Invertebrate with a soft, unsegmented body and often a shell, e.g. snail, mussel and squid.

N

Nitrogen cycle: Biogeochemical cycle that moves vital nitrogen components through the atmosphere, land and sea. All living things need nitrogen.

Nutrients: Chemicals such as phosphorus and nitrogen which, when released into water sources, may cause pollution events such as eutrophication.

O

Omnivore: Animal that feeds almost equally on plant material and other animals.

Order: Category used in the classification of organisms that consists of one or several similar or closely related families. Similar orders form a class.

Organism: An individual living system, such as an animal, plant or microorganism, that is capable of reproduction and growth.

P

Pelagic: Living or occurring near the surface of a sea, e.g. pelagic fish.

Phosphorus cycle: Cyclic movement of phosphorous in different chemical forms from the environment to organisms and then back to the environment.

Photic zone: Undersea area of about 200 metres depth to which light penetrates and provides energy for marine plants to photosynthesize.

Photosynthesis: Production of food by plants, using sunlight as the energy source.

Phylum (*pl.* **phyla**): Category (sometimes called 'division') used in the classification of organisms that consists of one or several similar or closely related classes, e.g. the phylum Mollusca contains six classes of molluscs.

Phytoplankton: Photo-synthesizing plankton, consisting chiefly of microscopic algae, which form the basis of food for all other forms of aquatic life.

Plankton: Tiny or microscopic animals (zooplankton) and plants (phytoplankton) found freely suspended in the seas and carried by currents.

Polychaete: Marine annelid worm with a distinct head and paired fleshy appendages that bear bristles and are used in swimming.

Predator: Organism that captures and feeds on parts or all of an organism of another species.

S

Salinity: Amount of dissolved mineral salts contained in sea water.

Species: Category used in the classification of organisms that consists of a group of similar individuals that can usually breed among themselves. Species is the smallest group commonly used, e.g. there are over 100,000 species of molluscs in the phylum Mollusca.

Spit: Long, narrow, flat piece of land that extends out into the sea from the beach.

Sulphur cycle: Movement of sulphur in different chemical forms from the environment to organisms and back to the environment.

Sundaland: Prehistoric geographical region comprising land areas of Peninsular Malaysia, Borneo, Sumatra, Java, all the smaller islands and shallow seas around them, as well as the subsea area known as the Sunda Shelf.

Sustainable development: The practice of development which does not cause irreparable damage to the environment and its inhabitants and tries to ensure that future generations will inherit their share of natural resources.

Swell: Regular rising motion of a wave.

T

Thermocline: Zone of rapid temperature decrease between warm surface water and colder deep water in the ocean.

Toxic: Harmful, deadly or poisonous.

Trophic level: The position that an organism occupies in a food chain.

U

Upwash: Final movement of a wave up a beach.

Upwelling: Movement of colder, nutrient-rich water from the bottom of the ocean to the surface.

V

Vertebrate: Animal with a backbone.

W

Weathering: Breaking down of rocks as a result of physical, chemical and biological changes.

Z

Zooplankton: Small aquatic invertebrates that live in sunlit waters and feed on algae and other invertebrate animals.

Zooxanthellae: Algae living within the tissues of hard corals which provide the corals with food and colour.

Bibliography

Aikanathan, S. and Wong, E. (1994), *Marine Park Island Management and Conceptual Plan for Peninsular Malaysia*, Kuala Lumpur: Department of Fisheries Malaysia.

Allen, Gerald (1996), *Marine Life of the Indo-Pacific Region*, Singapore: Periplus Editions.

Annual Fisheries Statistics (1970–97), Kuala Lumpur: Department of Fisheries, Ministry of Agriculture Malaysia.

Assessment of Biological Diversity in Malaysia (1997), Kuala Lumpur: Ministry of Science, Technology and the Environment Malaysia.

Aw, Michael (1994), *Tropical Reef Fishes*, Pennant Hills, NSW: Ocean Geographic Media.

____ (1997), *Tropical Reef Life*, Carlingford, NSW: Ocean Environment.

Botkin, Daniel B. and Keller, Edward A. (2000), *Environmental Science: Earth as a Living Planet*, 3rd edn, New York: John Wiley.

Chin, P. K. (1998), *Marine Food Fishes and Fisheries of Sabah*, Kota Kinabalu: Natural History Publications.

Chua, T. E. (1998), 'Lessons Learned from Practicing Integrated Coastal Management in Southeast Asia', *Ambio*, 27(8): 599–610.

The Columbia Encyclopedia, 6th edn, (2000), New York: Columbia University Press.

Elder, D. and Pernetta, J. (eds.), (1991) *Oceans: A World Conservation Atlas*, London: Mitchell Beazley.

George, D. T. and George, J. T. (1979), *Marine Life: An Illustrated Encyclopedia of Invertebrates in the Sea*, London: Harrap.

Gremli, Margaret S. (1995), *Marine Life in the South China Sea*, Singapore: APA Publications.

Haas, W. de and Knorr, F. (1982), *The Illustrated Guide to Marine Life*, London: Harold Starke.

Hamblin, W. K. and Christiansen, E. H. (1998), *Earth's Dynamic Systems*, 8th edn, New Jersey: Prentice Hall.

Hardy, A. C. (1954), *The Open Sea, Its Natural History: The World of Plankton*, London: Collins.

Hartog, D. (c. 1970), *The Seagrasses of the World*, Amsterdam: North-Holland Publishing Company.

Hering, P. J.; Campbell, A. K.; Whitfield, M.; and Maddock, L. (eds.) (1990), *Light and Life in The Sea*, Cambridge: Cambridge University Press.

Ho Soon Lin (1992), *Coral Reefs of Malaysia*, Kuala Lumpur: Tropical Press.

Hotta, K. and Dutton, I. (eds.) (1995), *Coastal Management in the Asia-Pacific Region: Issues and Approaches*, Tokyo: Japan International Marine Science and Technology Federation.

Howard, R. K. and Edgar, G. J. (1994), 'Seagrass Meadows', in L. S. Hammond and R. N. Synnot (eds.), *Marine Biology*, Cheshire: Longman.

Information Malaysia 2000 Yearbook, Kuala Lumpur: Berita Publishing.

Japar Sidik, B.; Yusoff, F. M.; Mohd Zaki, M. S.; and Petr, T. (eds.) (1997), *Fisheries and the Environment: Beyond 2000*, Serdang: Universiti Putra Malaysia.

Jefferson, T. A.; Leatherwood, S.; and Webber, M. A. (1993), *FAO Species Identification Guide: Marine Mammals of the World*, Rome: FAO.

Kamaludin, H. (1989), 'Palynology of the Lowland Seberang Prai and Kuala Kurau, Peninsular Malaysia', *Geological Society Malaysia Bulletin*, 23: 199–215.

Karim, W. J. (1981), *Ma' Betise Concepts of Living Things*, London: Athlone.

Ketchum, B. H. (1983), *Estuaries and Enclosed Seas: Ecosystems of the World*, Vol. 26, Amsterdam: Elsevier Scientific.

Kiew, R. (ed.) (1991), *The State of Nature Conservation in Malaysia*, Kuala Lumpur: Malayan Nature Society.

Levinton, Jeffrey S. (1995), *Marine Biology: Function, Biodiversity, Ecology*, New York: Oxford University Press.

Lim Boo Liat (1991), *Poisonous Snakes of Peninsular Malaysia*, 3rd edn, Kuala Lumpur: Malayan Nature Society.

Lim Boo Liat and Indraneil Das (1999), *Turtles of Borneo and Peninsular Malaysia*, Kota Kinabalu: Natural History Press.

Malaysia: Environmental Quality Report (1998), Kuala Lumpur: Department of Environment, Ministry of Science, Technology and the Environment Malaysia.

Mann, K. H. (1991), *Dynamics of Marine Ecosystems: Biological-Physical Interactions in the Oceans*, Boston: Blackwell Scientific.

Mastaller, Michael (1997), *Mangroves: The Forgotten Forest between Land and Sea*, Kuala Lumpur: Tropical Press.

Miller, G. Tyler, Jr (1997), *Environmental Science: Working with the Earth*, 6th edn, California: Wadsworth.

Mohamed Mohsin and Mohd Azmi Ambak (1996), *Marine Fishes and Fisheries of Malaysia and Neighbouring Countries*, Serdang: Universiti Pertanian Malaysia Press.

Mohd Ibrahim Hj. Mohamed (1991), 'National Management of Malaysian Fisheries', *Marine Policy*, 15(1): 2–15.

Nebel, Bernard J. and Wright, Richard T. (1998), *Environmental Science: The Way the World Works*, 6th edn, New Jersey: Prentice Hall.

Ng, Peter K. L. and Sivasothy, N. (1999), 'A Guide to the Mangroves II: Animal Diversity', Singapore: Singapore Science Centre.

Payne, J. and Francis, C. M. (1985), *A Field Guide to the Mammals of Borneo*, Kota Kinabalu: Sabah Society and WWF Malaysia.

Petroleum Exploration Potential in Malaysia (1998), Kuala Lumpur: PETRONAS.

The Petroleum Industry in Malaysia (1988), Kuala Lumpur: PETRONAS.

Phang, S. M. (1994), 'New Records of Malaysian Marine Algae', *Hydrobiologia*, 285: 123–30.

____ (1998), 'The Seaweed Resources of Malaysia', in A. A. Critchley and M. Ohno (eds.), *Seaweed Resources of the World*, Japan: JICA Publications.

Pirie, R. G. (1996), *Oceanography: Contemporary Readings in Ocean Sciences*, Oxford: Oxford University Press.

Riley, J. P. and Chester, R. (1971), *Introduction to Marine Chemistry*, London: Academic Press.

Ruppert, E. E. and Barnes, R. D. (1993), *Invertebrate Zoology*, Philadelphia: Saunders College Publishing.

Sasekumar, A. (1974), 'Distribution of Macrofauna on a Malayan Shore', *Journal of Animal Ecology*, 43: 51–69.

Sim Yong Wah, Capt. (1993), *Malaysia's Undersea Heritage*, Kuala Lumpur: Discovery Editions.

Sivalingam, P. M. (1977), 'Chemical Oceanography of the South China Sea', *Sains Malaysiana*, 6(a): 139–52.

Steele, J. H. (1974), *The Structure of Marine Ecosystems*, Cambridge: Harvard University Press.

Tjia, H. D. (1984), 'The Sunda Shelf: Southeast Asia', *Zeitschrift füer Geomorphologie*, 24(4): 405–27.

____ (1992), 'The Coastal Zone of Peninsular Malaysia', Bangi: Penerbit Universiti Kebangsaan Malaysia.

Tomlinson, P. (1986), *The Bounty of Mangroves*, Cambridge: Cambridge University Press.

Tucker Abbott, R. (1991), *Seashells of Southeast Asia*, Singapore: Graham Brash.

Veron, J. E. N. (1986), *Corals of Australia and the Indo-Pacific*, Sydney: Angus and Robertson.

Wood, C. R.; Wood, E. M.; and Allen, G. R. (1994), 'Fishes', in *Pulau Sipadan: Reef Life and Ecology*, Kuala Lumpur: WWFM.

Index

Picture Credits

Abdul Aziz Ibrahim, p. 23, wave breakers, upwash and backwash. **Almah Awaluddin**, p. 113, sponges; p. 119, pharmaceutical research. **Antiques of the Orient**, p. 8, sea anemones; p. 64, acorn barnacles; p. 108, jellyfish species. **Anuar bin Abdul Rahim**, pp. 42–3, marine biodiversity in coral reefs; p. 76, Eurasian curlew, Malaysian plover; p. 73, white-bellied sea eagle; p. 89, lesser adjutant stork. **Bank Bumiputra Malaysia Berhad**, p. 69, *wang hantaran*. **Bernama**, p. 9, sea horses. **Borneo Marine Research Unit, Universiti Sabah Malaysia**, p. 78, bottlenose dolphins; p. 79, research vessel, beaked whale skeleton. **Chai Kah Yune**, p. 14, plankton; p. 21, tide station; p. 45, dinoflagellate skeleton; p. 51, starfish movement, leopard sea cucumber; p. 52, coral polyp; p. 57, gastropods, bivalvia, scaphopoda, cephalopoda, mono-placophora, polyplacophora; p. 57 & p. 59, squid; p. 58, p. 69 & p. 101, fisherman with net; p. 59, cuttlefish, squid movement (all pictures); p. 63, feeding habits of worms; p. 64, acorn barnacle, barnacle encrustation; p. 68, adult banana prawn; p. 69, roshna, fiddler, pink and rainbow prawns; p. 69 & p. 75, giant tiger prawn; pp. 72–3, Malaysian sea snakes (all pictures); p. 89, mangrove food chain; p. 101, Indian mackeral, round scad, long-tailed tuna, yellow-striped trevally, fringescale sardinella; p. 106, blood cockle, green mussel; p. 110, fish. **Chan Eng Heng**, p. 75, turtle egg incubation (all pictures); p. 121, baby turtles. **Chan Hung Tuck**, p. 120, planting mangroves; p. 130, fern thickets, clear felling, mangrove billets, *Rhizophora* seedlings; pp. 130–1, mature *Rhizophora* trees; p. 131, *Avicennia* forests, fishing village. **Chee Phaik Ean**, p. 102, ikan bilis, mending nets; p. 103, unloading, drying, sorting and grading anchovies. **Chia Boon Kiang**, p. 40, beach sediments. **Chong Ving Ching**, p. 68, life cycle of banana prawn (all pictures); p. 134, University of Malaya researchers. **Choo Poh Sze**, p. 71, rabbit fish; p. 82, floating fish cages; p. 93, white pomfret; p. 101, trash fish

landings, long-tailed shad; p. 104, tiger prawns, net cages; p. 105, cultured oysters, grouper, sea bass, culturing prawns (all pictures); p. 107, depuration units; p. 119, prawns; p. 134, laboratory researcher. **Chu Min Foo**, p. 46, brown and red seaweed; p. 66, fiddler crab; p. 74, olive Ridley, hawksbill, leatherback and green turtles; p. 84, mantis shrimp, sand dollar, ghost crab, hermit crab, bivalve; pp. 84–5, high and low tide levels; p. 104, red tilapia. **Chua Thia Eng**, p. 133, beach resort Desaru, Johor port. **Department of Environment Malaysia**, p. 126, oil slicks, desludging, DOE officers; p. 127, MT *Nagasaki Spirit*, MV *Ocean Blessing*, oil skimming machine, dispersant sprayer, collection of tar balls, oil booms, sea water sample. **Department of Fisheries Malaysia**, p. 58, cephalopod species poster; p. 68, commercial prawns species poster; p. 98, how a trawler operates (all pictures); p. 100, demersal fish species poster; p. 101, making *keropok*; p. 103, catching and boiling anchovies; p. 107, culturing mussels (all pictures); p. 117, olive Ridley turtle; p. 120, turtle brochure; p. 129, tourism brochures. **Discovery Editions**, Daniel D'Orville, pp. 16–17, Pulau Sibuon; p. 17, floating village; Capt. Y. W. Sim, p. 1, Pulau Paya; p. 4, Pulau Harimau coast; pp. 8–9, lionfish; p. 9, pyjama nudibranch; pp. 12–13, Pulau Sulug; pp. 30–1, coastline, Pulau Rawa; p. 33, corals, Pulau Sipadan; p. 50, granular starfish; p. 50 & p. 91, red-lipped starfish; p. 53, acropora coral, brain coral, pink staghorn coral, green tree coral; p. 54, harp coral, detail of harp coral, red feather star, crimson sea fan; p. 55, Gauguin sea fan, red soft coral, white sea fan, soft tree coral; p. 57, nudibranch (*Phyttidia varicosa*); p. 61, fringing reef; p. 64, barnacles on shipwreck; p. 71, spotfin lion fish; p. 80, hermit crab, anemone fish, Christmas tree worms; pp. 80–1, sandy beach; p. 90, hanging garden, parrot fish, diadem basslet, porcupine fish, blue damsel fish, spotted garden eel; p. 91, fringing reef, nudibranch, sea urchin, pacific lobster; p. 92,

dried squid; pp. 94–5, fishing village; p. 108, *Cyanea* sp. and *Cchyphomedusa* sp.; pp. 112–13, coral reef; p. 119, sea squirts; p. 129, pink coral polyps, clown fish, red oyster, shrimps, sea urchin. **D'Orville, Daniel**, p. 128, diver and green turtle; p. 129, porcellanid crab, nudibranch, coral trout. **Editions Didier Millet Archives**, pp. 10–11, Chinese junks; p. 35, mollusc fossils; pp.88–9, mangroves (back tint); p. 96, fishing stakes; p. 138, fish amid staghorn coral; p. 139, mud crab. **Embassy of Jordan**, p. 14, Dead Sea. **Forestry Department**, p. 131, mangrove wood kiln. **Gambang, Albert Chuan**, p. 109, cannonball jellyfish, jellyfish fisheries (all pictures). **Geoff Denney Associates**, p. 23, coastal erosion. **German, Penny**, p. 84, sea lettuce, sea hibiscus. **Gong Wooi Khoon**, p. 61, mangroves; pp. 80–1, mangroves; p. 88, mangrove seedlings, stilt mangrove roots, breathing mangrove roots, buttress mangrove roots; p. 131, boardwalk across mangroves. **Hassan Yaacob**, p. 118, diver with golden sea cucumber, golden sea cucumber, laboratory staff, gamat products. **Hermann, Bernard**, p. 40, golden sand beach. **Hiew, Kevin**, p. 128, Pulau Redang Marine Park, Pulau Payar Marine Park Centre. **Ibrahim Saleh**, p. 111, echo-sounding machine, turtle in net, artificial reef from concrete culvert. **Ishak bin Hashim**, p. 20, causes of tides. **Jabatan Muzium dan Antikuiti Malaysia**, p. 60, cowries. **Jacobs, Joseph**, p. 112, Pulau Redang. **Japar Sidik Bujang**, p. 48, sea horse, sea cucumber, seagrass bed; p. 49, seagrass fruit, curled-base spoongrass, spoongrass, dugong grass, toothed seagrass, estuarine spoongrass; p. 49 & p. 75, tropical eelgrass. **Kamaludin bin Hassan**, p. 34, measuring level; p. 35, microscopic shellfish, Kuantan coast; p. 36, mechanical drill, hand auger, taking samples, fossilized seashell, core sample, technician, pollen grains and spores; p. 37, satellite image; p. 61, mud shore Kuala Selangor. **Khang, Peter**, p. 67, mud skipper. **Kong Guan Sauce and Food Manufacturing**, p. 125, sauce production. **Kushairi Rajuddin**,

p. 29, bleached corals. **Lee Sin Bee**, p. 41, breakwaters; p. 65, fishing boat; p. 69, prawn products; p. 96, fish bait device; p. 103, fish products; p. 111, echo sounder; p. 123, vessel tracking system. **Lim Li Ching**, p. 121, tourism and recreation brochure. **Lim, Suan I.**, p. 7, cockles; p. 106, cockles curry, market, hawker stall. **Magnum Photos**, Jean Gaumy, p. 99, sampans. **Malaysia Meteorological Service**, p. 27, satellite image. **Malaysian Industrial Development Authority**, p. 11, freight containers; p. 104, feeding fish. **Maritime Institute of Malaysia**, p. 122, Law of the Sea document. **Michael Aw–Ocean N Environment**, p. 3, reef squid; p. 8, porcupine fish; p. 13 & p. 47, sea grape seaweed; p. 43, segmented worm; p. 50, feather stars, linkia starfish; p. 51, brittle star, pencil sea urchin; p. 52, coral colony, coral spawning; p. 53, dome-shaped coral, *Tubastraea faulkneri, Cynaria lacrymalis*; p. 54, soft corals, underwater cave; p. 55, leather soft coral, sea pen (*Virgularia* sp.), sea pen (*Pteroeides* sp.), red sea whips, soft corals; p. 57, tubercular nudibranch; p. 58, male oval squid; p. 59, oval squid eggs, young oval squid, reef octopus; p. 62, fan worm, Christmas tree worms, flatworms—*Pseudoceros lindae* and *Pseudoceros ferrugineus*; pp. 62–3, feather duster worms; p. 63, fan worm, flatworm, annelid worm (all pictures), ribbon worm; p. 64, barnacles on coral reef; p. 70, parrot fish, grouper, butterfly fish; p. 71, clown triggerfish, longnose butterfly fish, regal angel fish, rockmover wrasse, bronze trumpet fish, scalefin basslet, seal puffer fish; pp. 80–1, coral reefs; p. 91, reef crab, crown-of-thorns starfish; p. 102, school of anchovies; p. 110, Labuan marine park; p. 111, artificial reef; p. 112, sea squirt; p. 123, Pulau Layang-Layang. **Ministry of Culture, Arts and Tourism**, p. 117, tourism brochures. **Nanyang Siang Pau**, Koh Yoke Moi, p. 29, drought. **National University of Singapore**, Michael Holmes, Peter K. L. Ng, Leo W. H. Tan and Serena Teo Lay Ming, p. 44, phytoplankton—*Skeletonema* sp.

and *Chaetoceras* sp., various plankton; p. 45, copepod, adult jellyfish, barnacle cypris, zooplankton, shrimp protozoa, phyllosoma (*Thenus* sp.), dinoflagellates—*Ceratium* sp. and *Protoperidinium* sp. **Noor Azhar Mohd Shazili**, p. 64, barnacles. **Noramly Muslim**, p. 76, brown noddies, brown booby sea birds. **Ong Jin Eong**, p. 16, swimming pool; p. 17, Secchi Disk, spectroradiometer; p. 25, acoustic Doppler-effect current profiler; p. 44, plankton net, phytoplankton cultures; p. 82, mangrove-fringed estuary, aqua-culture, Merbok estuary; p. 83, estuary fishing; p. 87, button shell; p. 88, mangrove fruit; p. 124, effluent; p. 134, marine research station, mangrove tree tower. **Ong Leng Gin, Gregory** p. 43 & p. 61, ternate false fusus; p. 56, nautilus shell; p. 60, fisherman, seashells (all pictures); p. 61, seashells (all pictures); p. 136, cowrie shell. **PETRONAS**, p. 112, petroleum refinery; p. 113, offshore platform; p. 114, offshore platform; p. 115, crude oil tanker, liquefied petroleum tanks, gas processing plant, petrol station. **Phang Siew Moi**, p. 16, p. 47 & p. 119, red seaweed; p. 46, microscopic seaweed species; p. 47, *Sargrassum binderi, Sargrassum siliquosum*, red seaweed (*Amphiroa*), green seaweed (*Cheetomorpha*), green seaweed (*Cattlerpa racemose*); p. 118, *Acanthopora spicifera, Sargassum oligocystum, Halymenia* sp.; p. 119, calcified seaweed. **Picture Library**, David Bowden, pp. 92–3, stilt village; p. 116, canoeing; Chan Beng Yip, p. 97, mending nets; p. 101, dried fish; S. K. Chong, p. 8 & p. 99, Malay fishing boat; p. 112, windsurfers; p. 116, yachting; Chung Hui Hwa, p. 99, Malay fishing boats; Daniel D'Orville, p. 117, snorkelling, scuba diving; Marlane Guelden, p. 132, palm oil factory; Kam Shee Meng, p. 137, fishing boat; Leong Yew Wah, p. 12, jetty; p. 20, jetty; p. 84, sandy beach; Stanley Loo, p. 110, fishing boats; Teresa Ong, p. 116, bird watching; Pang Piow Kan, p. 132, deforestation; Geoffrey Smith, p. 98, fish and prawn trawlers; Superstock Inc., p. 116, swimming; Arthur Teng, p. 59, dried squid; pp. 92–3, fishing boat; p. 99, decorative guards; p. 110, yellow-striped trevally; p. 116, Marang Resort and Safari; Ricky Teoh, p. 46, drying seaweed; p. 95, boat festival; Teoh Yiew Aun, p. 116, parasailing; Sumio Uchiyama, p. 116, horse riding; Peter Walton, p. 26, crashing wave; Wong Yew Onn, p. 9, fishing trawler.

Pos Malaysia, p. 52, brain coral stamp. **Radin Mohd Noh Saleh**, p. 11, Buddha head, Nandi head; p. 59, sotong pack; p. 68, shrimp paste; p. 75, turtle watching sign board; p. 89, carved mask, wood sculptor; p. 98, fishing village; p. 99, fisherman's lunch and tackle boxes; p. 100, embroidery motifs. **Rossi, Guido Alberto**, pp. 12–13, Pulau Perhentian Besar; p. 92, pearl farm. **Royal Malaysian Navy**, p. 21, tide station maintenance. **Sakri Ibrahim**, p. 94, fish trawlers, fisherman's house; p. 95, shipyard, processing anchovy sauce, mending nets, salted dried fish. **Sarawak Museum**, p. 11, early trade imports; p. 61, Orang Ulu baby carrier; p. 66, crab tattoo. **Sasekumar, A.**, p. 81, grapsid crab; p. 86, collecting razor shells; p. 87, pea crabs, small whelks, carpet clams, gastropods. **Star Publications (Malaysia) Berhad**, p. 12, Kelantan floodwaters in monsoon season; p. 21, Port Klang floodwaters; p. 22, giant waves Teluk Cempedak beach; p. 25, Datuk Azhar Mansor, yacht *Jalur Gemilang*; p. 26, monsoon floods east coast; p. 27, mending fish nets; p. 28, fishing in haze from forest fires; p. 29, Sarawak forest fires; p. 45, red tide alert; p. 71, garfish, flying fish article; p. 78, dugong carcass, dugong articles; p. 83, padi fields near estuaries, fishing trawlers; p. 92, drying sea cucumbers; pp. 92–3, carpet clams; p. 95, basket weaving; p. 100, fresh fish stall; p. 102, anchovy purse seiner; p. 106, cockle spats; p. 107, red tide; p. 111, reef balls; p. 120, artificial reefs; p. 122, *Clifford Maersk*, pirates article; p. 125, water woes, toxic-free world, waste treatment plant, batik troughs and tanks; p. 127, *Orapin Global*. **State Economic Planning Unit, Penang**, p. 132, dredging, erosion; p. 133, sustainable management of mangrove forests brochure. **Sun Media Corporation Sdn Bhd**, p. 78, dugong articles. **Sui Chen Choi**, p. 66, sand and mud crabs; p. 67, mud flat and mangrove crabs; pp. 80–1, Malaysian coastline; p. 87, soft bottom communities; p. 104, mud crab. **Sulabayau Industries**, p. 12, harvesting raw salt; p. 15, salt evaporating ponds, salt crystals for collection, inside salt factory, salt bags. **Syed Ahmad Jamal**, p. 71, Malaysian crafts (all pictures). **Tan Hong Yew**, p. 10, bronze drum, sailing ships; p. 18, nitrogen cycle; p. 19, carbon cycle; p. 21, tide marks; p. 28, changes in sea–air interaction; pp. 28–9, map of El Niño affected area; p. 32, fossils;

p. 37, cross-section of coastal plain, shoreline alignments; p. 38, coastline shapes; p. 39, coastline profile; pp. 40–1, depositional features map; pp. 82–3, features of an estuary, estuarine circulation; p. 86, sandy beach; pp. 96–7, Malaysian fishing nets. **Tan Shau Hwai, Aileen**, p. 56, tiger cowrie, giant clam (*Tridacna gigas*), divers with cultured clams, giant clam (*Tridacna squamosa*); p. 57, rock oysters, nudibranch; pp. 120–1, diver with clam baskets. **Teh Tiong Sa**, p. 18, Pulau Tengah beach; p. 20, jetty at Pulau Perhentian Besar; p. 23, erosion Melaka beach; p. 30, shattered granite, coral platform, sand barrier, pebble spit; p. 33, coral cliff, double-tiered wave-cut terrace; p. 34, raised beach; p. 35, drowned karst, beach ridges, abrasion terraces, beach rock, marine notch, stranded coral heads; p. 35, bunds, flooding in Rungup; p. 38, Penang beach; p. 39, Pantai Batu Buruk, Miri cliff coastline, Johor mangroves, rocky coastline, eroding coastline; p. 40, reclaimed land, settlement on barrier, crescent-shaped bar, baymouth barrier; p. 41, black sand beach, white beach, sand bar, tombolo, bayhead beach, groyne, structural jetty; p. 41 & p. 120, breakwater; p. 86, sand flat, mud flat. **Tommy Chang Image Productions**, p. 5, sea turtle; p. 10, Labuan shipyard; p. 56, cultured oysters; p. 72, sea snake; p. 74, green turtles mating. **Universiti Putra Malaysia**, Sea Turtle Research Unit, p. 120, turtle brochure; p. 134, *Unipertama V*. **Wong Swee Fatt**, p. 124, souces of effluents. **World Wide Fund for Nature Malaysia**, p. 131, giant egrets; p. 135, diver and barrel coral; p. 143, soft coral. Sarala Aikanathan, p. 121, turtle hatchery; Eleanor Chen, p. 120, Pulau Redang; p. 135, youth activities with WWF Malaysia, youngsters learning about

the sea; D. J. W. Lane, p. 23, erosion and falling trees; p. 75 & p. 109, jellyfish; Loh Wai Meng, p. 135, research and education kit, mangrove snakes and ladders game; Oon Swee Hock, p. 80, purple heron; Slim Sreedharan, p. 76, little green heron; Peter Teh, p. 135, mobile education unit; Edward Wong, p. 77, nesting grounds. **Yeap Kok Chien**, pp. 6–7, map of Malaysia and map features; p. 14, salt comparison chart; p. 22, wave types, wave breaks; p. 36, fossilization (all pictures); p. 41, longshore drift; p. 43 & p. 77, frigate bird and common tern; p. 47, carrageenan, agar, alginate acid, dried seaweed, desserts, mixed items, textiles, traditional remedies, *fatt choy*; p. 48, marine life; p. 51, cooked sea cucumber; p. 58, *bubu sotong arus*; p. 65, life cycle of acorn barnacle; p. 72, snake tails; p. 73, snake head; p. 75, head, shell and plastron features of turtles (all pictures); p. 76, beaks and feet of sea birds, white-bellied sea eagle; p. 78, Indo-Pacific humpback dolphin, short-finned pilot whale, p. 79, Fraser's dolphin, Irrawaddy dolphin, pantropical spotted dolphin, long-snouted spinner dolphin, finless porpoise, false killer whale, dugong, bottlenose dolphin; p. 91, reef flat; p. 108, jellyfish life cycle; p. 114, drilling rig, petroleum traps, seismic surveys; p. 115, petroleum products. **Zubir bin Haji Din**, p. 132, workshop participants; p. 133, student excursion, seminar, environmental camp, environmental awareness talks. **Zulfigar bin Haji Yasin**, p. 16, underwater light effects; p. 50, four-legged starfish, crown-of-thorns starfish; p. 51, sea cucumbers (all pictures); p. 53, *Favida* sp., mushroom coral; p. 75 & p. 119, sponge; p. 91, boulder, brain and cabbage corals; p. 118, sponge; p. 119, sea cucumber; p. 144, coral reef in Telok Kadar.